The Moral Interp
of Religion

The Moral Interpretation of Religion

Peter Byrne

Edinburgh University Press

© Peter Byrne, 1998

Edinburgh University Press
22 George Square, Edinburgh

Typeset in 11 on 13 pt Sabon
by Hewer Text Limited, Edinburgh,
and printed and bound in Great Britain

A CIP record for this book is
available from the British Library

ISBN 0 7486 0784 6

The right of Peter Byrne to be identified as
author of this work has been asserted in accordance
with the Copyright, Designs and Patent Act 1988.

Contents

Preface

The aim of this book is to explore the idea of a moral interpretation of religion in modern philosophy and examine its strengths and weaknesses as an approach to religion.

In Chapter 1 the general character of the moral interpretation is defined. Its historical antecedents are discussed. Some initial problems in stating it coherently are set out and solutions offered.

In Chapter 2 the argument focuses on the question of whether morality and religion can be linked in the traditional style, whereby morality is seen to require belief in a personal deity to be fully intelligible or immune to sceptical attack. Various attempts to argue from the form and content of morality to the existence of a personal creator are considered. All are found wanting. The strongest argument considered is judged to be that which appeals from the fact of evil in human life to the need for a God to serve as the guarantee that the world is morally ordered after all. This argument introduces the 'secular problem of evil' which becomes crucial in later chapters to assessing the worth of versions of the moral interpretation of religion. It is argued that any satisfactory versions of the moral interpretation must contain some solution to this problem.

Chapter 3 begins the study of Kant's version of the moral interpretation. In this chapter an account is offered of what Kant means by God as a 'postulate of practical reason'. The precise construal of religious language arising from Kant's postulation of God is documented, as is the mode of belief in God that the postulate produces.

Chapter 4 deals with the strength of the arguments Kant offers for his moral interpretation. This chapter aims to show that Kant does not prove that reason itself forces us to postulate the existence of God. On the other hand, the Kantian interpretation does offer a viable response to the secular problem of evil and does point to something important about the essence of religion.

In Chapter 5 attention switches to the interpretation of religion offered by Iris Murdoch in her philosophical writings. Her endeavour to interpret religion in moral terms introduces new resources to the moral interpretation of religion: a detailed phenomenology of the moral life and concepts and insights from Platonism. Despite the value of her contribution in developing the moral interpretation, it is argued that her account lacks the minimalist realist thrust in the interpretation of religion found in Kant. This criticism is linked to her failure to address the secular problem of evil.

Chapter 6 turns to the Wittgensteinian tradition in contemporary philosophy for a further articulation of the moral interpretation. Two writers are discussed: D. Z. Phillips and Stewart Sutherland. The notion of religion as an eternal perspective on life is brought out by discussing their writings. As with Murdoch, it is argued that, notwithstanding the insights which reflection on Wittgensteinian themes adds to the moral interpretation of religion, these authors miss the importance of the secular problem of evil which so concerned Kant. Consequently, their interpretation of religion as an eternal perspective on life falls short of the minimal realism required of any worthwhile interpretation of religion.

In Chapter 7 the character of the moral interpretation derived from Kant is reviewed and defended against some fundamental objections. Kant's rational proof of his revision of traditional theism having been rejected in Chapter 4, an attempt is made to ground the Kantian interpretation of religion on a version of William James's 'will to believe' argument.

Thus by the end of this study readers should have an understanding of: the key problems in morality and religion which the moral interpretation of religion addresses; the appropriate way to formulate a moral interpretation in the most cogent manner (that is, by drawing on the essence of Kant's account supplemented by the resources revealed in Chapters 5 and 6); the strength of the moral interpretation's claim upon our attention.

The idea for this study was born out of conversations with the editor of this series, Paul Helm. I am extremely grateful for the time and attention he has given to the project, particularly in reading through and commenting upon successive drafts. Parts of the book have been read in seminars and conferences in King's College and I am grateful to colleagues and students for their comments. Martin Stone has been of particular assistance in giving bibliographical advice.

References follow the style which is standard for this series. In citing from Kant's writings I have followed what has now become normal practice in English-speaking philosophy. Citations from the *Critique of Pure Reason* give the page numbers of the first edition ('A') and the second edition ('B') of the original text. For other books by Kant, the page number of the English translation used is followed in square brackets by the relevant volume and page number of the complete Prussian Academy edition of Kant's works in German.

1

Introduction

THE MORAL INTERPRETATION OF RELIGION

Throughout the history of reflection on theistic faith, there have been philosophers who have sought to show that morality provides one sure route to belief in God. The primary concern of this book is to explore a particularly important variation of this theme in modern philosophy. This variation holds that morality provides *the* anchor for belief in transcendent, sacred reality and, consequently, provides *the* means for interpreting belief in a religious ultimate.

This mode of philosophical gloss on religion will be styled 'the moral interpretation of religion' or the 'neo-Kantian interpretation of religion' or 'moral faith'. We do associate this approach to the task of reflection on religion with the writings of Kant in particular, but the label 'neo-Kantian' is not meant to imply either that the approach started and ended with him, or that all whom we label in this way share in Kant's particular account of morality or the details of his linkage of morality to religion. There are other sources of the moral or neo-Kantian interpretation of religion. He is merely its most famous practitioner. The moral interpretation is typical of many liberal stances towards religion in general and Christianity and Judaism in particular. By a 'liberal stance' we mean one that places the ethics of religion before its doctrines and historical myths.

Prior to Kant, many deistic authors gave expression to this liberal stance through their readiness more or less to identify the concept of God with the concept of an eternal moral law in nature. It is a commonplace that eighteenth-century thought was prone to make nature a substitute for the God of Christian theologies – seeing in nature the source and standard of right action. This could lead more radical elements in the Enlightenment to transform the notion of deity into something akin to a Stoic logos, immanent everywhere in the nature of things. It was because of this strong belief in the perfect immanence and perfect omnipresence of the divine as moral law that these thinkers frowned upon the miracle-working, historical God of traditional theology – not as the textbooks say, because the deists' God was too transcendent to have anything to do with the world.[1]

Wherever liberal religious thought has spread so has the general message that the ethics of religion is more important than its metaphysics or historical claims. Within the English-speaking philosophical tradition, there has been a recent revival of the movement of thought which was pioneered by the deists and articulated with infinitely greater thoroughness by Kant. Writers such as Iris Murdoch, Stewart Sutherland, Ronald Green, D. Z. Phillips have given contemporary currency to the thought that the moral interpretation of belief in God is primary. Outside of philosophy, the influential literary critic F. R. Leavis propagated similar ideas. One of his sources was undoubtedly the writings of Matthew Arnold, whose thoughts about religion having its seat in ethics and the imagination are in large measure derived from traditions in late eighteenth-century and early nineteenth-century German philosophy, traditions which take us back to the thought-world of Kant. Among the things which link these very diverse thinkers is a distrust, if not outright rejection, of history and metaphysics.

History and its place in the grounding of belief in God is important in debates about morality and religion in so far as traditional Christian notions of God gain at least part of their content from beliefs about the actions of God in history. The Christian God is essentially a God who reveals himself and becomes incarnate in history. The modern writers who will be the focus of the bulk of this book are heirs to a rejection of history and historical beliefs as the locus for making sense of God and God's relation to the world. Once more we must remind ourselves that the nature and grounds of this rejection were first articulated in full form in English deism. In writers such as Matthew Tindal and Thomas Chubb it is possible to find epistemological, ethical and metaphysical reasons for turning one's back on the God of history.

Historical criticism of the biblical narratives fuels scepticism about the certainty of any beliefs about divine action in history. Such scepticism can be further strengthened by the thought that any God whose nature and purposes could only be known through revelation in history would be a God who is knowable by only a portion of the human race. For revelation in history is, by definition, historically and geographically situated and therefore necessarily limited in its availability to humankind. Epistemological doubts about the God of revelation then lead naturally to moral ones: for it follows from the epistemological critique that the God of history is partial in the offer of relationship, mercy and salvation he makes to humanity. This offer is freely available to some human communities who are historically and geographically favoured. Complicated, back-door routes for relating other folk to God must be found. All this added to the metaphysical incredulity on the part of the deists arising out of their reflection on the manner in which a perfect transcendent reality could be related to the world. It seemed obvious to them that divine perfection would preclude the divine from being more closely related to one portion of the world and its history than another. The God of traditional Christian theology is of course secretly omnipresent; yet he is also specially present in some events and to some people. Whether this idea is coherent is one matter that deistic philosophers raised, but from the idea of divine perfection they could infer that God was perfectly present in all things and would have no need of special relationships to selected events and persons.[2]

Metaphysical speculation has been the cornerstone of attempts philosophically to interpret and clarify belief in God in Western philosophy. It has been assumed by innumerable thinkers down the centuries that if questions are asked about what exactly it is to believe in God, they must be answered at least in part by listing and defining attributes of a being who is located in a metaphysical realm. Defining the exact nature of this being is a matter of explicating the metaphysics of notions like cause, time, action and personhood. Those philosophers who reject the idea that metaphysical speculations are meaningful or capable of attaining any certainty will seek an alternative way of offering philosophical explication and clarification of what belief in God amounts to. Kant is one source of scepticism about metaphysics. His doctrine that concepts are empty unless grounded in supporting 'intuitions', that is forms of sense-experience, condemns speculation about the putative objects of the metaphysical realm to idle futility. Modern philosophy has confronted the verificationist claim that all metaphysical statements (that is, statements purporting to state facts which cannot in principle be verified by sense-experience) are without cognitive meaning. The outright positivist rejection of metaphysics has been one element in the contemporary philosophical movement we are exploring, but it is important to see that thinkers like Murdoch and Sutherland are not directly dependent on it. There are two reasons why we must divorce the notion that morality is *the* interpreter of religion from the verificationist rejection of metaphysics.

First we must note that verificationism rests on very shaky ground. It is not difficult to show that the verification principle is a fusion of two theses about knowledge and meaning which are both highly questionable. One thesis is that all meaningful propositions must be decideable or testable. The other thesis is that the sole means of testing a proposition is by reference to sense-experience or inferences therefrom. Forceful rebuttals of these theses are to be found in the philosophical literature which point to the conclusion that verificationism is itself a species of metaphysical dogmatism.[3]

The Kantian and neo-Kantian programme in the philosophy of religion would thus be ill advised to rely on the positivist route to the rejection of metaphysics. Moreover, we find a second reason why it cannot take the positivist route when we reflect that its very aims are incompatible with verificationism. If verificationism is true, then two courses are open to the philosophical interpreter of religious language: non-cognitivism and reductionism. Either religious claims are not propositional at all, having some kind of non-cognitive (non-fact-stating) function in human discourse, or these claims are cognitive only in being descriptive of entities or states in the empirical world. The non-cognitivist interpretation is exemplified in R. B. Braithwaite's well-known attempt to give religious statements a purely action-guiding or prescriptive meaning.[4] A reductionist interpretation can be gleaned from the pages of Feuerbach's *The Essence of Christianity*.[5] Feuerbach's account of the latent but 'true' meaning of claims about God tells us that statements such as 'God is love' can be transposed into statements about the human essence. 'God is love' is really a statement about the human attribute of love and its importance and value in the realisation of human perfection. When they are reinterpreted thus, religious claims are still propositional in content, and many of them are indeed true; but they are not claims about a transcendent reality. So this is not non-cognitivism but rather reductionism.

Non-cognitivist and reductionist reinterpretations of religious language abandon theistic realism, where that is to be understood as a thesis about the reference of key religious concepts. For the purposes of this study, realism is the doctrine that religious concepts endeavour, with at least some measure of success, to refer to realities which exist beyond the human mind and the physical cosmos. Such concepts can be taken seriously as having a transcendent reference, where the transcendent is understood as a reality not exhausted by existence in the human mind or in the spatio-temporal world. The neo-Kantian strands of thought under review here need not immediately be taken to offer a moral interpretation of religious belief as a means of denying such realism. How far they do or do not abandon realism as defined above will be one of the issues our enquiry will pursue in relation to the examples of the moral interpretation selected for discussion. This entails seeing if some notion of the transcendent, however thin in content or problematic as an object of reference, is retained in the philosophical movement under discussion.

I propose to enquire how far these neo-Kantian ways of getting from morality to religion function as forms of 'revisionary realism'. If they are instances of revisionary realism, they will acknowledge and support a realist thrust behind some talk of the divine, but the content of talk about the divine will be altered and surrounded by a large degree of agnosticism. Only a portion of the content traditionally associated with talk of the divine will be allowed to pass through the revisionary filter and the referential import of what is left may be deemed problematic. What will be lost is the idea of assured reference, grounded in history and/or metaphysics, to an entity which is the supreme person (having all the perfections of personhood) and the possessor of the metaphysical qualities associated with ultimate reality since Greek philosophy (for example, aseity, eternity and immutability). A problematic, revisionary realism is the price of abandoning history and metaphysics, but it is not on first view at all the same as opting for a non-cognitivist or reductionist interpretation of religious language.

The preliminary characterisation of moral interpretations of religious belief reached so far is enough to indicate why they are inherently controversial and questionable. Three initial difficulties with the moral interpretation of religion can be aired.

In the first place a critic might wonder how the neo-Kantian procedure for explicating and grounding talk about God can avoid obvious self-contradiction. For all these moral interpretations of religion have in common the claim that *the* way of giving sense and point to the concept of God is via reflection on the form and content of morality. Metaphysics does not provide the means of supplementing the concept of God. To reason thus, however, is to suggest that, contra Kant, morality cannot lead ineluctably to anything outside itself. If reflection on moral concepts leads to the necessity of making use of religious concepts (because, say, vital features of morality cannot otherwise be made sense of), the content of those religious concepts must be other than purely moral. If the content of religious concepts is purely moral, then morality has not led anywhere: no route from morality to religion has been established.

The above point can be expanded to reveal a second objection to the entire enterprise. In order for a Kantian-style project in the philosophy of religion to succeed, *something* must be borrowed from the concept of the divine rooted in history and/or metaphysics. Only with such a borrowing can independent sense be given to the notion of the divine so as to give something for morality to lead to. Yet the moral interpretation will reject the God of history and metaphysics as incredible and unintelligible. What is at issue in the departure from traditional philosophical interpretations of God may be called 'supernaturalism'.[6] Kant and others have rejected supernaturalism in order to give a reinterpretation of the divine. But critics of the project may wonder if such a reinterpretation is not 'self-defeating or simply impossible' because it must rely on what it rejects.[7] More crudely, this second preliminary objection states that the enterprise is one of mere sentimentality and nostalgia: a way of thinking is rejected as being incompatible with 'modern' conceptions of self and the world while means of retaining the symbols associated with that way of thinking are naïvely sought.

A third initial objection to the moral interpretation of religion will demand to know on what grounds other than verificationism the metaphysical conception of divinity can be rejected. Contemporary neo-Kantians can be no more than positivists in sheep's clothing. If one rejects the positivist exposé of metaphysics, what grounds, short of sheer dogmatism, could one have for refusing to allow philosophy to develop a full-blown metaphysical conception of God with some suitable epistemological grounding? If there are religious, theistic implications to be drawn from morality, why should they not be seen as contributing to a larger picture of the divine completed by philosophical theology?

The first two objections ask what kind of supernaturalist reference the moral interpretation of religion can lead to if it does not give us the notion of God traditionally conceived. By way of reply, the neo-Kantian thinker will note that there is a huge variety of conceptions of the transcendent within human religious thought. Only some of these conceptions give us the notion of a personal deity. This variety can give us a generic notion of the transcendent: it is generically the idea of that which is the goal of human striving, the source and supreme embodiment of value. It is that whose reality is not exhausted by its manifestations in the spatio-temporal world. The moral interpretation of religion, if it is to avoid non-cognitivism and reductionism, must lead to the moral grounding of a reference to something having these generic, minimal qualities. In this respect, morality will be held to lead to something outside of itself which as it were occupies religious space. At the same time, it must hold that the only means of giving such reference secure grounding and content is by concentrating on the role the generic notion of the transcendent plays in morality.

That the moral interpretation is not allied to the specific conception of the transcendent familiar in theistic religious traditions may be seen as an advantage, for it could be taken as showing that the moral interpretation is a plausible response to religious diversity. If some minimal, generic notion of the transcendent is supported by the moral interpretation, it could be seen as being common to many different faiths, and it might justify the thought that all are referentially successful despite their specific differences. These differences might then be put down to the need to cloak the generic, moral notion of the transcendent with the living symbols of particular cultures.

In the light of the above remarks, it can be seen how the neo-Kantian project does and does not depend on prior religious or theistic forms of thought. It does in so far as it needs its audience to have a generic, minimal notion of transcendence if it is to gain a hearing. It does not, however, rely on any specific, traditional picture of transcendent reality. There are two ways in which we might clarify the exact kind of supernaturalism the moral interpretation is committed to.

One way in which we can do this is by allying the moral interpretation with forms of apophatic theology found in many traditions. These hold that the divine cannot be spoken about literally and positively at all; it can only be spoken of negatively. Such a view faces an immediate objection: if there is no positive notion of the transcendent how can one make clear *what* is being said to be capable of only negative description? The reply is: the kind of thing of which we say that it cannot be positively described is located initially by a combination of negative and relational description. The transcendent or divine is that which: (negatively) enjoys a reality not exhausted by its spatio-temporal manifestations and which (relationally) is the goal of human striving and the source and sum of all value human beings can cognise. The moral interpretation joins with other, long-established ways of presenting talk about the divine in suggesting that descriptions of the transcendent beyond this minimal core are either metaphorical or have primary reference to the effects or manifestations of the divine in immanent realities. The former notion (metaphor) will of course allow the neo-Kantian to use and rely on traditional descriptions of the divine without endorsing them as literally true while yet ruling out any metaphysical science of the transcendent. The latter idea (the transcendent's having manifestations in immanent reality) will fit naturally with the development of the thesis that it is the implications of the minimal, generic notion of the transcendent for morality that give us the clearest, surest ways in which the transcendent can be described. Morality is thus seen as the paramount immanent reality which contains manifestations of the transcendent which we can describe.

The moral interpretation can further clarify the kind of supernaturalism it draws upon by using the distinction between 'piecemeal' (or 'crass') and 'refined' supernaturalism expounded by T. L. S. Sprigge.[8] Sprigge describes the piecemeal supernaturalist as one who believes in a supernatural reality which intervenes in and is active within human history. Such a reality is naturally conceived as personal, the proper object of petitionary prayer and the source of miracles. The refined supernaturalist rejects the notion that the supernatural is an agent with causal power affecting our world in detail or which may be invoked to intervene in it. He or she believes instead that there is an *overall* pattern to, or dimension of meaning in, human life pointing to something beyond humanity and material reality as the source of that pattern or meaning. On this conception, the supernatural enters into human living through the character it gives to the human search for meaning or the hopes human beings entertain about the final point of human striving. On this conception, the divine need not be thought of as personal at all. Both forms of supernaturalism have a quarrel with naturalist portrayals of reality, but only piecemeal supernaturalism seeks to account for specific events in history in non-natural terms. Refined supernaturalism merely disputes the pretension of naturalism to legislate on the overall meaning of reality and history. The deistic interpretation of the divine described above is an early example of refined supernaturalism. Like those furthering the neo-Kantian project, the deists saw the immanence of the divine in morality as the surest clue to the overall religious meaning to life.

We have tried to defend the moral interpretation of religion from the initial charge that its notion of the transcendent must be empty or incoherent. It turns out to be indebted to more traditional interpretations of the divine, but it is self-consciously selective in that indebtedness and so can rebut the charge that it is inconsistent in both relying on and rejecting theistic notions. Whether or not its endeavour to reformulate the concept of the divine in philosophy of religion is an exercise in mere sentimental nostalgia depends on our view of the strength of whatever case some version of the moral interpretation offers for its particular route to the revisionary realism we have described.

On what ground may the neo-Kantian stand in refusing to explore the idea of divinity through the metaphysics of traditional philosophical theology? It is essential to many versions of the moral interpretation of religion that they find in morality itself reasons why they must reject the God of traditional philosophical theology. It will add to the completeness of the moral interpretation if it can argue that our experience of good and evil both leads to some reference or other to the divine but rules out seeing a personal God behind morality. We shall take up this theme in the next section.

What further can the upholder of the moral interpretation point to by way of defending the need for a reworking of religious realism? Disputes about the interpretation of morality itself have been set aside for the moment and we have seen that the dogmatic positivist rejection of metaphysics will not suffice. The neo-Kantian might further appeal to the fact that many folk in our culture find the God of history and philosophical theology incredible, yet they may for all that retain a sense of the divine or be unpersuaded of an out-and-out naturalistic account of reality. Thus, it may be important to see if we can find in moral experience something that both justifies and gives content to a reference to the transcendent. Contemporary philosophical theologians working in the West are unlikely to think that this admitted fact about the prevalence of doubt about the traditional God is of any philosophical (as opposed to sociological) interest. For they will want to know if such doubt rests on any arguments and if it can rebut the arguments in favour of more traditional conceptions. In the absence of an argumentative case of this kind, then the verdict of sentimental nostalgia on neo-Kantianism looks in place.

If we turn to contemporary philosophical debate about the God of traditional theism, we find interminable and seemingly inconclusive debates on the coherence and rationality of belief in that God.[9] That inconclusiveness suggests the need for an alternative version of the religious outlook beyond belief in a personal God. Such reasoning can be strengthened if we hark back to the fact of religious diversity. The very existence of markedly different and incompatible accounts of the sacred and the seeming inability of one tradition to persuade the others of its correctness can be a reason for taking the neo-Kantian project seriously. For diversity suggests that agnosticism (minimal and problematic realism about the transcendent) may be the appropriate stance to adopt. It also suggests that we should look for forms of experience common to the traditions on which to base that agnostic account of the divine: if common forms of moral experience can be found, they will do the job very nicely.

So far we have seen reasons for taking the neo-Kantian interpretation of religion seriously which do not depend on positivist dogma. However, it must be admitted that scepticism in Kant concerning the possibility of a positive metaphysic of God is associated with theses about knowledge and experience which appear to be forerunners of verificationism:

> Knowledge, which as such is speculative, can have no other object than that supplied by experience; if we transcend the limits

imposed, the synthesis which seeks, independently of experience, new species of knowledge, lacks the substratum of intuition upon which it alone can be exercised.[10]

Such passages which tie knowledge to experience can be placed alongside many others declaring that our concepts and principles become null and void when taken beyond experience. It is on these grounds that, in the section of the *Critique of Pure Reason* headed 'Critique of All Theology Based upon Speculative Principles Of Reason', Kant repeatedly objects to any use of the principle that all effects have causes to infer the existence of a necessary being behind the world of contingent things. But it would be wrong to indict Kant for being dependent on a dogmatic empiricism in his rejection of knowledge of the God of metaphysics. In the first place the official teaching of the first *Critique* allows room for some meaning to remain when concepts are applied to the transcendent. That meaning is the merely logical meaning of the various categories or forms of judgement when considered in abstraction from their application to experience. So that, for example, a formal, but inevitably somewhat empty, sense could be given to the notion of an a-spatial, a-temporal God as a 'substance'. It would not be that of a spatially located object enduring through time, but would merely be that of something whose name could occupy a subject place in a declarative sentence. One could support Kant's claim that the notion of cause 'lacks meaning' when applied to the God of metaphysics in a similar way.

Causes in the physical world are productive and active agents or the triggers which provoke such agents into action. Our notion of causality is given its content by our knowledge of things behaving as productive and active agents and is bound up with our awareness of them as physical things in a physical world. Now, to conceive of a cause whose character is utterly unlike any physical thing in being a-spatial and a-temporal does something to the meaning of 'cause'. It reduces its content. God 'causing the world' can have no more substantive content than 'God stands to the world as ground to consequent' – in the relation one fact stands to another when the first materially implies the second. No content, Kant might argue, attaches to 'God creates the world' other than God is a sufficient condition for the world's existence. But this formal sense of 'cause' is quite unable to capture what must be naïvely intended by talk of divine causality, since, for example, it quite fails to bring any notion of the direction of causality. If God is merely the sufficient condition for the world's existence, then the latter is the necessary condition for God's creative act, just as the non-existence of the world would be a sufficient condition for the non-activity of God. As endless discussions in the literature on the meaning of 'cause' show, our notion of causation has the content it has because its sense includes more than the merely logical relations between propositions connected by material implication.[11] Kant is thereby supported in supposing that, when we reason from the character of cause and effect in this world to a transcendent cause, the fallacy of equivocation results and we use the notion of causality in talk of God in a quite altered sense.

Here I am suggesting the rationale in Kant's claim that we cannot employ the metaphysical notion of God in a constitutive sense, that is in a sense which yields knowledge of a determinate object. Something too radical happens to our basic forms of description for that to be a possibility. Here we might have grounds, derived from Kant, for being sceptical of the full intelligibility of talk about the God of metaphysical, philosophical theology. These grounds are independent of the normal ones recognised by proponents of such theology, namely a proof of some criterion of meaning which would rule out talk of the transcendent as meaningless or a proof that the notion of God employed in philosophical theology was incoherent (that is, self-contradictory or entailing a contradiction). The former is not open to Kant, for some problematic gesture to the possibility of transcendent realities is necessary to allow the concept of God to be used regulatively. The latter is also out, for Kant preaches a radical agnosticism about the precise character of things transcendent. One of the elements in that agnosticism is that there can be no proof that there is no God. The reality of God is not reached by the road of speculative proof but it remains an ideal 'without a flaw'.[12] To appreciate the agnostic, revisionary realism behind the neo-Kantian project we should keep in mind Kant's thought that talk about God does not yield constitutive claims, that it does not constitute God as an object of knowledge.

GOODNESS, EVIL AND THE INTERPRETATION OF RELIGION

We can distinguish two ways of arguing from morality to religion. The dominant way in the philosophy of religion uses premises about morality to infer the existence of the personal God with the traditional 'omni' attributes. What we have styled the neo-Kantian approach uses similar premises to support a problematic and exiguous reference to the transcendent, the reference then being cashed in terms of its implications for moral thought and experience.

We have seen that one reason why the moral interpretation of religion will not expand reference to the transcendent by calling upon the concept

of God belonging to traditional philosophical theology lies in independent
scepticism about the metaphysical and epistemological underpinnings of
such a concept of God. But it is important for the neo-Kantian approach to
the philosophy of religion to recognise that authors exemplifying it have
typically argued that our perception of good and evil itself rules out
expansion of transcendent reference in the direction of a personal God. In
other words, belief in God, old style, is morally corrupt and corrupting.

A way of summing up this difference in the manner in which philosophy
can connect morality and religion is as follows. The traditional view is that
morality depends on religion. The neo-Kantian view is that religion
depends on morality. The first of these theses relies on our being able
initially to give content to the notion of religion independent of the moral
context. This is accomplished by using the notion of God as a personal
being as further refined by metaphysics. The second thesis relies on our
being able to give independent content to the notion of the moral without
calling in aid belief in God. Rather morality's form and content is used to
decide what is acceptable in the idea of God – more properly, the idea of
the sacred and transcendent. So only a morally purified and problematic
reference to the divine is left.

Our perceptions of good and evil thus become a battleground in the
debate between these two approaches to the philosophical task of
explaining the conceptual links between morality and religion. The moral
interpretation of religion will see our perception of good as being distorted
by efforts to trace morality's foundations to a personal God in virtue of the
way such a link threatens the autonomy of morality. Traditional theists
will counter with the claim that morality is impossible without a foundation in a personal God.

The first charge to consider is that the attempt to ground morality in the
nature and actions of a personal God will inevitably entail that the theist
will base moral judgements, rules and principles on considerations which
violate the notion of a proper moral reason established by the form and
content of morality itself. For example, the consequence of founding
morality on the pre-given notion of a personal God appears to be that
what makes principles right and actions praiseworthy is that they are
commanded by God. But, for reasons more fully spelled out in the next
chapter, the wrongness of, for example, murder cannot be the wrongness
of an act type forbidden by some legislator, because that latter type of
wrongness is created solely by the act of proscription and is reversible.
What makes a given act murderous and wrong, it will be argued, must
depend on the intrinsic character of that act and its relationships to its
surrounding circumstances. So the grounds of the moral rule 'Do no

murder' cannot be found in divine will. A theory which says that rightness and goodness are constituted by divine commands must be mistaken.

Here we are in the territory mapped out by the Euthyphro dilemma. The dilemma offers alternatives to those who say that matters of right and wrong are founded upon the will of a God: either what is right is so simply because God commands it, or God commands what is right because it is independently right. To accept the first horn is to maintain that morality does depend on a personal deity, with the consequence that morality's autonomy is destroyed in the fashion noted above. To adopt the second horn is to recognise that morality is autonomous and thus can properly serve as an independent test of the admissibility of religious conceptions, including the conception of a personal God.[13]

The notion that there are distinctive forms of reason and ground operating in morality which must be respected by any account of its foundations is linked to the notion that moral agency is likewise distinctive. Referring morality back to a personal God can be held to destroy what is distinctive in such agency, as well as – or as part of – the destruction of the proper grounds of moral judgement. Thus, it will be alleged against the thesis that morality depends on religion that it must entail that moral agents subordinate their conscientious judgements about the right and the good to what divine commands tell them to do. They must give something other than properly moral motives prime place in ordering their actions. A religious foundation to ethics turns out to entail the relegation of conscience.[14]

Allied to these thoughts about the autonomy of morality and moral agency is the belief that admission of the dependency of morality on God will lead to the dethronement of moral considerations from their status as supremely important in judging conduct and encourage the thought that final human fulfilment can be achieved other than by virtuous conduct. This line of thought is clearly evident in Kant's efforts in Book IV of *Religion within the Boundaries of Mere Reason* to dismiss as 'pseudo-service' and 'superstitious illusion' the idea that one could be well-pleasing to God through acts of worship and devotion distinct from the acts of a good person.[15] The fundamental thought under attack here is that if the greatest human good lies in being favoured by God, there will be means to attaining it other than by morally motivated conduct.

In the next chapter we shall review arguments going in the opposite direction. Proponents of the thesis that morality depends on religion contend that, without an idea of God worked out largely independently of morality, moral knowledge and agency are impossible. They argue that, with regard to morality itself, notions of goodness and badness can have no purchase on reality unless grounded in a divine legislator. They contend that key features of moral agency, such as the fact that it frequently involves forms of self-sacrifice, are unintelligible or irrational without the backing of a theistic outlook, so that moral agency is in fact illuminated by the thought that moral acts are performed as part of the service of a personal God.

The philosophical question before us is not whether morality leads inevitably to religion but how it does.

Just as the precise relation between goodness and the idea of the divine is at issue in this study, so is the precise relation between evil and God. The familiar problem of evil has the following form. How can the beliefs about God to the effect that he exists as the creator of all and is omnipotent, omniscient and wholly good be reconciled with the fact that there is evil in the world? The possession of these three divine attributes entails, or at least implies, that there should be no evil in any world God creates, for it gives this God the power, the knowledge and the motive to prevent evil arising in it.

One way in which the problem of evil relates to the issues surveyed in this study is that it provides moral interpreters of religion with grounds for not fleshing out reference to the transcendent in terms of a personal God. The fact of evil provides some thinkers with grounds for at least being agnostic about the God of traditional theism.[16] However, the role of evil in the debates under review goes beyond that one possible line of argument. We can see this when we reflect on the fact that what is of primary importance in discussions of the problem of evil is the idea of this world embodying a moral order.

There is a variety of forms of evil distinguished in clarifying the problem of evil. But what stands out as the most difficult to reconcile with theism is unjust evil to sentient beings. It is the evil consisting in suffering, disability, handicap, shortened life to thousands upon thousands of creatures that is not in any apparent way deserved by them which calls into question the existence of a morally perfect, all-powerful creator. Such a creator would want and would be able to bring about a moral order in the world. If suffering or handicap or shortened life fell only on those who were evil and were visibly in proportion to their crimes, then the given world would equally visibly constitute a moral order and the moral goodness and power of God would not be in question.

The charge that evil shows conclusively that there is no all-good, all-powerful God, because his existence would entail that there should be no evil in the world, can easily be met. What the defining beliefs about God entail is that either there is no evil in the world or that any evil that exists should be such that God has a morally sufficient reason for bringing it about or permitting it. The problem of evil can then be pressed again: there are many evils around us for which there appears to us to be no morally sufficient reason. The job of theodicies is to indicate how a God with the defining attributes of power and goodness might plausibly have purposes which enable evils to be backed by morally sufficient reasons. Hence, we see that standard theodicies endeavour to show that, despite appearances, the world can be considered as embodying a moral order. Hick distinguishes between Augustinian and Irenean theodicies.[17] The former type endeavours to present the evils of the world as the just and necessary consequences of some primal human act of disobedience. So there is some, however strained, order of retributive justice in things. Irenean theodicies try to present the world as embodying a teleological moral order: sufferings and the like which are undeserved in the individual case are yet part of an order which is moral overall, since they are unavoidable facets of a world which is fit for moral and spiritual growth. Both kinds of theodicy can see future, post-mortem experience as completing the hidden moral order they postulate behind things. In the Augustinian theodicy post-mortem existence is one in which the retributive process is completed through the rewards of heaven and punishments of hell. In the Irenean theodicy post-mortem experience allows the process of moral and spiritual development, which mandates a world in which evil comes apparently haphazardly, to reach fruition.

So, at the heart of standard theodicies lies the contrast between a surface appearance that the world is without any moral order and a deeper view which says that underneath it is morally ordered through and through. From the right standpoint, says the theodicist, the forces that drive the orders of nature and history can be seen to be under the guidance of moral goals: the amoral natural order is a morally necessary part of a larger, divine or metaphysical order which is through and through moral. I want to draw out two implications of the centrality of the notion of moral order for traditional theism.

The first implication is paradoxical. Just as the problem of evil can be cited as a reason for not inferring a personal God from the character of morality, so it can be cited as a reason for making that inference.[18] Evil is one of the gravest objections to theism, but evil is frequently cited in moral arguments for God's existence. It is thus cited when the arguments turn around the fact that the world we live in is by appearance one embodying a purely natural and therefore amoral order, whereas moral values and/or moral conduct would make no sense unless the true order of reality is a moral order. We shall see in the next chapter that arguments can be offered for the conclusion that the metaphysical underpinning required for taking moral values and principles seriously is precisely the belief that the true order of reality is moral. We shall find arguments which purport to show that the policies involved in pursuing the good above all else would make no sense to reflective moral agents unless they believed that the true order of things was a moral order.

The paradox of evil (as constituted by violations of moral order in the world immediately around us) being both an argument against and for the traditional concept of God is heightened by the kind of arguments employed by those who argue that morality depends on God. The more they press the extent to which moral values and agency look out of place in the world conceived merely naturalistically, the more they open the gap between how the world appears to observation and how we might expect it to appear if it were the product of omnipotent goodness. So the evidence from evil against God's existence seems greater.

The second implication of the centrality of the notion of moral order is that, once we put it centre stage in discussions of evil, we see that there are other ways to ground belief in moral order than through traditional theism. For example, belief in the universal and strict operation of the law of *karma* plus belief in rebirth give non-theistic Eastern religious traditions an affirmation that the world's fundamental organisation is moral which is as equally firm as that provided by theism. We can press a variant of the theistic problem of evil against such non-theistic symbols entailing belief in moral order. We can pursue the gap which exists between, on the one hand, the perceived character of the world and the histories of human beings in it and, on the other, the assertion that it is through and through morally ordered. We can question the plausibility of the non-theistic claims about the allegedly deeper ordering of things which license the continued belief that there is such a deeper moral order in the universe, just as we can question the plausibility of claims about divine purposes in standard theodicies which indicate how a personal God might conceal a moral order behind the appearances.

The belief that the apparent order of reality conceals a moral order which is the true order of things seems to lie at the heart of many religious outlooks. Later in this study (in Chapter 4) we shall broach the question whether the presence of such a belief is not a necessary condition of anything's counting as a religion or a religious view of the world. Belief in moral order will naturally raise a question about the status of moral interpretations of religion. We have pointed out how important it is for these neo-Kantian approaches to religion to present themselves as forms of revisionary realism, on pain of otherwise collapsing into non-cognitivism or reductionism. But now we are able to press the moral interpretation of religion with the issue of precisely what it is being revisionary about. It is one thing to be revisionary about the concept of a personal God tied to a particular set of historical and metaphysical claims; it is another to be revisionary about belief in the underlying moral ordering of reality. Eastern religions contain clear examples of systems of thought which maintain belief in the reality of moral order while having no belief in a personal God. This chapter has aired reasons drawn from a variety of sources, including the character of morality itself, for not grounding belief in moral order by way of belief in a personal creator. But we have seen that it is *prima facie* difficult to use the problem of evil to ground rejection of theism while yet maintaining belief in moral order, for the problem of evil at its most fundamental level bears upon *any* religious affirmation of the underlying reality of moral order. This fact means that we shall have to interrogate closely authors such as Sutherland who use the problem of evil to advance revisionary realism. We must see to what extent their employment of the problem of evil entails abandoning belief in moral order altogether.

As this study proceeds we shall see emerging as a crucial question how far *any* cognitivist, non-reductionist interpretation of religion can proceed which does not endorse belief in the reality of moral order. If this part of the 'Legacy of Theism'[19] is jettisoned along with belief in the God of history and metaphysics, is anything worthwhile left which can be called 'religious'?

The above doubts about the available room for a revisionary realism based upon morality can be put another way. We argued above that revisionary realists can hold on to a generic, minimal notion of the transcendent while abandoning the God of history and metaphysics. This notion allows the transcendent to function as the focus of human striving, the source and sum of value, while having a reality somehow beyond the spatio-temporal. In later discussions, we shall have to bear in mind how far such a notion is of any religious value if it does not include the idea that the transcendent is that which is the source of an underlying moral order in reality.

NOTES

1. See Byrne *Natural Religion*, particularly chapter 3, for a fuller account of these matters.
2. For further illustration of the deists on God and history, see Byrne *Natural Religion*, chapters 3 and 4.
3. See, for example, Heimbeck *Theology and Meaning*, and the essays in Wisdom *Paradox and Discovery*.
4. Braithwaite 'An Empiricist's Account of the Nature of Religious Belief'.
5. First published in 1841, translated into English in 1845 by George Eliot (Mary Anne Evans).
6. After Michalson, *Fallen Freedom*, p. 2.
7. Michalson *Fallen Freedom*, p. 133.

8. Sprigge 'Refined and Crass Supernaturalism'.
9. For a good entry to such debates see Gale *On the Nature and Existence of God*.
10. Kant *Critique of Pure Reason*, A471/B499.
11. Material implication is that logical connective which corresponds to 'If . . ., then . . .' in ordinary language. In logic, a statement of material implication is true in all cases save where the antecedent (that is, the 'if' clause) is true and the consequent (that is, the 'then' clause) is false. There need be no connections of relevance for a material implication to be true. Thus 'If Elizabeth is queen of Britain, money does not grow on trees' is a true material implication.
12. Kant *Critique of Pure Reason*, A641/B669.
13. The problems generated by the Euthyphro dilemma surface again in the next chapter. For a survey of responses to it see Byrne *Foundations of Ethics*, p. 145ff.
14. As argued in Rachels 'God and Human Attitudes'.
15. Kant *Religion*, p. 186 [6/165].
16. Reasoning along these lines can be found in Sutherland *God, Jesus and Belief*, ch. 2.
17. See Hick *Evil and the God of Love*, p. 220.
18. See Sorley *Moral Values and the Idea of God*, pp. 451–2 for this paradox.
19. The subtitle of Sutherland *God, Jesus and Belief*.

2

Moral Arguments for God's Existence

MORALITY AND THEISM

In order for morality to provide any kind of basis for arguing to the existence of a personal God, it must be conceived as having genuine cognitive status. If moral perceptions are regarded as no more than the expressions of personal or societal preference, then they cannot constitute a distinctive item in our consciousness which might need theistic explanation. So to get the argument going we must assume that at least some of our moral beliefs constitute a body of critically defensible thought or knowledge about how we ought to act.

Although philosophers differ markedly in how they describe and explain the nature and structure of moral knowledge, some points can be made about the character of moral thought which all or most moral theories will accept.

We can note first that moral perception and belief manifest themselves on at least three levels: judgement, rule and principle. We take ourselves to know a range of judgements about specific acts, to the effect that they are right or wrong. We believe a range of moral rules to be valid which specify the moral character of types of act. We also hold to a number of moral principles which specify general goals of conduct or describe desirable traits of character. So moral thought is a rich mixture of perceptions and beliefs about the specific and of awareness of more general claims.

We have already pointed to a striking fact about the form of our awareness of moral judgement, rule and principle: we unhesitatingly use cognitive language of it. That is to say, we use language of truth, rationality and discovery to characterise such awareness. We diagnose lack of moral awareness using language implying cognitive failure. We will, for example, say that it is false to suppose that killing the innocent is permissible for reasons of state. We will describe a racist as thinking and acting out of prejudice. So, if we respect this aspect of morality's form, we have to say it has the metaphysics and epistemology appropriate to an attempt to engage with a realm of facts and considerations independent of human cognition of them.

Many philosophers are sceptical of the cognitive pretensions of moral discourse.[1] One of the major factors fuelling such scepticism is the combination of the alleged cognitive character of morality with another of its major formal features: moral 'facts' are normative in force. To say of an act that it is morally wrong is at the same time to accept that it is not to be done. If there are moral facts, they appear to be odd in having a force which binds the will to pursuit or avoidance. Another way of putting this point is in terms of 'qualities'. If moral perceptions and beliefs latch on to qualities in reality, these qualities cannot be at all like, or reducible to, natural qualities of reality.

However, if there is discovery, truth and rationality in moral thought, it appears to many that the epistemology and metaphysics which make sense of such notions in this context must be unlike those which we employ to make sense of discovery, truth and rationality in science. Out of this common perception arise influential modes of thought about the grounds of morality which agree that no naturalistic view of the world and human nature can support the cognitive pretensions of morality. Either one can be true to a naturalistic epistemology and metaphysics and explain away morality's alleged cognitive pretensions as illusory;[2] or one can argue that morality must call on theism to provide the required epistemology and metaphysics.

One broad category of arguments from morality to a personal God can now be distinguished: they fasten upon the general form of moral thought and deal in epistemological-cum-metaphysical reasons for saying that this form is best accounted for by invoking the God of traditional philosophical theism.

Moral beliefs differ but morality has a typical content as well as form. It deals with what is right and wrong, good and bad from a perspective independent of self-interest or expediency, with how one should act *qua* human being. A certain impartiality is embodied in moral reflection. So the binding force claimed for moral 'facts' is one that obtains regardless of what is expedient for the agent, or for some restricted social group.

The above point about morality's typical content provides the basis for further arguments for theism, but their true character can only be seen when we amplify our picture of morality further by bringing in reference to the virtues. In addition to containing knowledge of judgements, rules and principles, morality also promotes the virtues. Virtues are broad traits of character, habits of choice, which at once arise out of practice in acting upon judgement, rule and principle and also lie behind such practice. The just person is not one who is merely aware of the judgements, rules and principles with delineate justice. He or she is one who has a disposition to act in certain ways. This disposition is a compound of belief, emotion and perception. Belief is there in the ability to deploy judgements, rules and principles about what is and is not just. Emotion is present in so far as one who is just will feel, for example, distaste at the contemplation of unjust acts and states of affairs. Perception is present for unless someone is schooled in forms of insight, understanding and sympathy, he or she will not be able to see when the demands of justice arise. It can be argued that the virtues should have pride of place in any full account of the epistemology and psychology of morals, for ethics is essentially a practical science and art and other forms of moral cognition (such as an awareness of moral rules) can never, singly or collectively, be a substitute for the insight that consists in possession of the virtues.[3] The aim of the moral life should be the acquisition of the virtues.

If the acquisition of the virtues is given this place in the moral life, the point that morality binds regardless of self-interest and expediency gains an extra dimension. For morality is to be seen as the means whereby the human good is attained. The virtues are traits of character, habits of choice, underlying moral cognition and action. They have also been thought of as the highest human excellences. To conceive of the virtues as the highest excellences, to be pursued above other human achievements and traits, is another way of making the point that morality binds. Given the notion that the virtues are *the* human excellences, a strong tradition dating from Greek philosophy has taught that possession of them constitutes the good for human beings. Moral thought and action is unified by a teleology in which the virtues are the constitutive means of attaining a good, perfected life. Morality, via the virtues, constitutively leads to the human good.

The fact that morality binds regardless of self-interest and expediency gives room for an argument from the broad content of morality to God – one that says the only or best explanation of the motives required for this kind of impartiality comes from citing God as the source of moral obligation. If we are true to the Classical tradition's thinking about the virtues as the underpinning of morality and as the means of attaining the human good, then there is still more scope for the theistic apologist. For it can be argued that only within a divinely structured created order could it be guaranteed that living a life embued with the virtues brings the human good with it.

In the sections which follow we shall first look at sample arguments aiming to show that we need the idea of a personal God to make sense of the epistemology and metaphysics of morality. Then we shall look at sample arguments for the conclusion that only such a God could provide motives for obeying binding moral rules or guarantee a moral order in reality which enabled morality to be constitutive of pursuit of the human good. Any of these arguments, if sound, would establish the dependency of morality on religion, though the mode of dependence would differ from case to case.

Three types of critical issue will be found to arise in discussing these arguments. First, if we accept that some feature of moral thought and action is puzzling, we can ask if it is made any the less puzzling by referring it to a cause in a personal God. Second, we can seek to find means within morality itself to explain the features seized upon by the apologist. Third, we might argue that, granted some facet of morality is best explained religiously, there are alternative religious conceptions beyond those of personal theism that will do just as well.

DIVINE WILL, EPISTEMOLOGY AND METAPHYSICS

Suppose we fasten upon the apparent fact that morality is binding independent of personal desire or social consensus. A typical argument from that fact to theism is very well illustrated by A. E. Taylor's discussion in *Does God Exist?*[4] Taylor asks us to accept that in morality we find a set of laws binding all human beings at all times. These laws are valid independently of our own preferences and recognition of them. The rule 'Do no murder' would obviously illustrate this point. He then supplies the premise that a law cannot be valid unless there is an 'intelligence which recognises and upholds it'.[5] Now, our awareness of moral law is partial and incomplete. So we must look for another kind of intelligence which upholds and recognises the moral law, namely an eternal consciousness and will. In similar vein, Philip Devine examines various naturalistic alternatives to God as the source of the truth and bindingness of moral norms, such as: the demands of our society, the direction of history's alleged progress, our self-imposed preferences. All are judged to leave moral imperatives based on shifting, disputed grounds or to be open to the obvious critical retort 'But can't we ask if, for example, society's demands are right?' Only the decrees of a personal God will give moral norms the requisite stability, guarantee of consistency and ability to bind the will:

'The theistic account of the binding force of ethical norms is thus the most plausible of those available'.[6]

The underlying logic of such popular arguments is reminiscent of a premise of legal positivism: the bindingness of a norm depends on its being legislated.[7] It seems a sufficient reply to Taylor's and Devine's demand to find a 'source' of moral norms that we recognise many kinds of authoritative norms of which it would be odd to say they derive from a legislative source. Consider the norms of logic, for example:

> If someone affirms both 'p' and 'p implies q', he or she must affirm 'q'.
> It is wrong to assert both 'p' and 'not-p'.

Such norms share many similarities with moral ones. They are valid quite regardless of our wishes. We cannot choose with propriety to obey or not to obey them. They cannot be thought of as dependent on preference or social demands. They have a certain universality and timelessness. They bind the will. Yet none of these characteristics is derived from the fact that they are legislated by some sovereign body. If we can accept that such norms are intelligible without recourse to the idea that they are legislated, why cannot the norms of morality be accepted as intelligible in the same fashion?

Building on this reply, we might put the norms of logic and those of morality in one broader class: the norms of reason. We can then argue that if we allow some members of this class to function without appeal to a legislator, why can we not accept them all on the same terms? The implicit claim here is that, if the non-theistic moralist is given the notion of reason and its norms (and all that pertains thereto), then there is no good ground for saying that we must be sceptics about moral reason in the absence of theistic belief.

A number of strategies are open to the apologist by way of reply. For the moment I shall pursue only one for the sake of getting to a crux in many of these debates. Devine extends the argument summarised above by contending that all the norms of reason require explanation in terms of theistic metaphysics. The idea that there is a 'logical must' we are bound to obey and the idea that there is empirical truth we should discover and respect once discovered depend on the notion of God. Divine decree gives us the necessary transcendent and binding source of the norms of reason and truth.[8] In the absence of theism we can choose only between nihilism and relativism. Nihilism says that there is no truth transcending our interests to be discovered and in any event we ought not to care if there is or is not. Relativism tells us that truth, knowledge and reason, and the authority of all these, are a function of the cognitive frameworks we just happen to work within. Thereby we lose the idea of a source of truth and reason which transcends passing human interests and contingencies.

No full critique of Devine's many-faceted case can be attempted here, but we can raise one fruitful issue: how far does postulation of God solve any of these problems? For, it is not obvious that *if* we must look for a necessary transcendent and binding source of the notions of truth, reason and goodness, divine decrees will fit the bill. Taking the hint from the shortcomings of legal positivism, we can ask how any of these notions (truth, goodness, the authority of reason) could derive their sense from decrees. The notions of decree and will depend for their meaning on a context of choice. What is decreed or willed thus, could have been decreed or willed otherwise. If the truth and authority of *modus ponens* or of the norm forbidding murder depend on decree or will, they depend on something which could have been otherwise or which could now be altered. However, the thought that such truths could have been otherwise or could be altered seems barely intelligible. It is of course possible to conceive of a universe in which the proscription of murder did not apply. A world without persons would illustrate that. A world in which the only persons who existed were indestructible would be another. In such universes murder would be a physically impossible act, but this fact does not alter the status of the norm 'Where it is possible to kill other persons, do no murder'.

The above point takes us back to criticisms of divine command theories of morality introduced in the last chapter and to the problems surrounding the Euthyphro dilemma. The first horn of the dilemma asks how a divine decree could create moral requirements simply in and of itself. The second horn affirms that there must be some surrounding moral context for divine decrees to be morally significant. The dilemma thereby points to a problem in the legal positivist thinking that underlies appeal to divine legislation to explain the authority of moral norms. In evacuating the notion of valid law of any moral content, positivism can be accused of hiding the question of which laws exist *with authority* behind the question of which laws exist as promulgated and enforced. For law to exist with authority it is not enough that it derive from a legislative source which happens to be sovereign; it must have legitimacy as well. In the political sphere legitimacy is compounded of many things: the means by which the sovereign authority came to its power; the way in which its exercise of that power stands with regard to the customs of the community; and, most importantly, the extent to which its decrees are just. It seems indispensable to the notion of power creating law that it be legitimate and that its authority be dependent on the moral context and content of its decrees. God's law bears on right and wrong because his authority is supremely legitimate, which means that it stems from a morally structured relationship God has to us. God, if real, must be conceived as supreme in moral authority because he stands at the apex of the moral relationships that bind us together as persons. Moral relationships are ones constituted by the mutual recognition of moral norms. God is judged supremely good in the light of notions of goodness which have content independent of thinking about the divine nature. To say that is not to say that religion has nothing to contribute to an understanding of morality, for it may be that our notions of goodness can be refined or extended in the light of the idea that God is the apex of moral values. What we can conclude, however, is that the notion of divine decree is insufficient of itself to yield the idea of valid and binding moral norms.

All of the above is admitted in a fashion by Devine. He rejects the suggestion that God could have decreed right what we now believe to be evil. He responds by writing goodness and its principles into the divine nature, so that they are not subject to God's arbitrary will.[9] God's power to will this or that is not independent of his goodness. Rather God is an absolutely simple and necessary being. His goodness and power are one. The principles of right reason and of goodness are somehow aspects of God's own nature. Such moves are not untypical of responses to Euthyphro objections to divine command theories.[10] I note three consequences of such moves. One is that the element of decree or command now employed in the theistic explanation of ethics is thereby thinned. We have moved away from the notion of a being exercising choice among open options. Next, the sense in which God is a person is also thinned. Finally, the mysteriousness of the divine nature is altogether increased. We have a stress on divine simplicity, necessity, aseity plus a matching stress on the divine as personal. The combination of such ideas to refer to one and the same entity leads to obscurity. While some may be able to understand the resultant product, the notion that it helps explain what is otherwise unclear in morality stands in need of defence.

At this point we can face the theistic apologist with a dilemma. Either your conception of God makes out God to be a person or it does not. If God is a person then the notion that the divine will establishes moral principles is open to the objections aired above. God's willing and the basis of morality itself become arbitrary. Rather as one person among others, God must be thought of as being bound by moral principles in his actions. If 'God' is not the name of a person, then the model of acts of legislation creating rules will not fit whatever role the divine plays as the source of morality. Some other model for the grounding of morality in the divine will need to be developed. Here we can note Alston's suggestion that God might serve as the source of moral standards in the way in which a paradigm serves as the source of standards (for example, things are a metre long to the extent that they are like the standard metre in Paris).[11]

The best personalism can do by way of linking divine will and ethics is the route offered by Meynell and Swinburne.[12] Both these authors note that, since the divine will is responsible for the existence and character of creation, God determines which moral principles and rules will have application in the world. In respect of its applicability to our world morality depends on divine will. In developing this idea the appropriate analogy is between morality and a system of geometry. The general principles of the system are necessarily true. As such they are neither created nor uncreated. It is a contingent fact that any particular system of principles has application in the universe and such a fact reflects the character of divine will in creation. So, only in respect of their applicability to our world, not in respect of their truth or authority, can we say that moral principles derive from divine will.

It is possible to escape this limited conclusion by opting for the view that fundamental moral principles and rules are contingently true. One could contend that rules and principles such as 'Other things being equal, promises should be kept' and 'Respect the lives and interests of others' are contingent because they reflect the fact that following them generally creates greater consequential good than not. If we ground all moral notions on a consequentialism of this kind, then in creating the physical structure of a cosmos and human nature to go along with it, a creator God would also create the truth of the moral principles which should govern personal agents in this cosmos. This suggestion can accept the idea that if the divine will had been different, another morality would have been true, since moral principles, rules and judgements are no more than contingently true statements about the consequences for human happiness of general policies and particular acts.

But there are two problems with this approach. One is that, to avoid the difficulties over arbitrariness we have noted, there would need to be one moral principle which is not the result of divine legislation, namely the general statement that moral rightness is a function of the promotion of happiness. A root consequentialist principle of this kind would be the true ground of the truth of lesser principles and rules and its truth would not be a function of divine will. The second problem with this approach is that there is a nest of difficulties surrounding the idea that moral rules and principles are one and all contingent consequences of a consequentialist first principle. We cannot enter into all these difficulties now.[13] One pointer to them will be offered. Consider the moral principle that friends are not to use each other as means but must respect and attend to each other's interests and wishes. Such a principle spells out what is involved in the specific trust relationship manifested in friendship. It is hard to conceive that persons may be so situated as to stand in the relationship of friend to friend and yet not be guided by the principle of respect and attention, for the very nature of the relationship is constituted through such principles. The relationship's identity is given through seeing that it embodies a particular form of trust between persons. Many forms of human relationship embody forms of trust and thus are made possible only through the mutual if tacit recognition of principles of trust.[14] These principles are, therefore, not contingent.

Reference to ethics growing at least in part out of the moral constitution of human relationships takes us away from the notion that moral principles have their source in divine legislation. Instead, some at least arise out of the very structure of human life. This is not to say that such a reference is incompatible with or could not be illuminated by themes drawn from forms of theism. For example, the idea that interaction between divine and human is structured by a covenant relationship is at the heart of much Jewish and Christian theology. And the theologian may find ample opportunity to read the covenant notion with its theological overtones back into an understanding of the character of human trust relationships. Yet all this is far from producing knock-down arguments for the conclusion that morality depends on theistic religion.

If we return to Devine's arguments for the necessity of God as the source of morality, we see that what in essence he is after is a principled reply to nihilism and relativism. At one level, nihilism and relativism are to be defeated by providing a reference for moral concepts and an object of description for moral statements that are quite other than the interests of dominant groups or the patterns of personal or social preference. For Devine, a metaphysical object, in the form of a personal God and his decrees, is the appropriate one to meet these requirements. Only thus do we retain firm hold of the idea that there is a moral truth 'transcending human purposes and conventions'.[15] My argument has been that the nature of moral thought indicates that a personal God and his decrees are far from appropriate and I have hinted that other conceptions of the divine which might be more appropriate are obscure to the point where it is not clear that they help in meeting the challenges posed.

Theistic apologists wish to give morality a metaphysical grounding in realities which transcend the human world altogether. They will reject the possibility that a metaphysical reality immanent in the world serves the purpose.[16] But here we must question how far metaphysical speculations about the transcendent are sufficient to explain the realist character we see in moral discourse or to defeat the doubts of those who are sceptical about such realism. For what anti-realists will argue (be they nihilists, conventionalists or relativists) is that *the character of moral thought itself* is insufficient to justify the presumption that it attains truth, or reliable belief, or is anything more than a reflection of shifting interests and purposes. The idea that there is a transcendent anchor for morality will be of no use in this context unless it can be shown, from the character of moral thought itself, that we are *in touch with it*. This showing would, of course, be a matter of pointing to aspects of moral considerations which reveal them as being the object of genuine cognitive states and as having a depth and universality which belies a relativist interpretation of them. (My mention of the link between some fundamental moral norms and the structure of human relationships is an example of the kind of response needed.) At the very least, it would consist in demonstrating that the arguments of various non-realists and sceptics are not strong enough to dismiss as deluded the cognitive vocabulary we use in connection with morality.

The point of the above line of reply to the theistic apologist is to insist that, on any view of its overall meaning and reference, morality must be able to pull itself up with its own bootstraps when it responds to moral scepticism. This is as much as to say that we can leave as a topic for independent discussion which if any metaphysical interpretation of the grounds of morality is the best. The thought of 'bootstrapping' also carries with it an incipient scepticism about the value of such metaphysical discussion. If we can establish in response to the sceptic or anti-realist that there are no good grounds for dismissing the apparent cognitivity of morals, then we have a right to ask in what respects this cognitivity becomes clearer or more easily defensible by introducing a metaphysical grounding of it. We should not seek to explain the obscure by the obscurer.

I have set out some difficulties in standard arguments for supposing that we need a divine command meta-ethics to justify or explain morality. I now wish to consider a more sophisticated attempt to demonstrate the need for a divine command meta-ethics. In various articles Robert Adams has pointed to fundamental features of moral qualities which are best explained by saying that these qualities have their origin in the commands of loving God.[17] Primarily Adams has in view the thought that a statement such as 'Cheating is wrong' ascribes, to use his terminology, a 'quality' to an act which is objective, cognitively accessible and non-natural. The last feature arises out of the fact that moral 'qualities' bind the will in a manner foreign to mere natural ones. Adams then asks us to think of what would be the best causal explanation of the existence of such qualities attaching to features of our world. The answer is the commands of a loving God. The argument is not that we mean by 'wrong' what is contrary to the decrees of a loving God. Analogous to the search for whatever hidden nature best explains the outward characteristics of a natural substance such as water or copper, Adams reasons that the various properties of something like moral wrongness require explanation and that a divine command meta-ethics provides a wholly suitable explanation. It best explains why wrongness is objective, cognitively accessible and binding.

Two chief difficulties with this attempt to argue for the necessity of a foundation to ethics in divine commands will be aired.

Adams' divine command theory has to help explain how moral 'qualities' are cognitively accessible. If it works in this regard then reference to the commands of a loving God will better explain how moral agents make moral discriminations. He notes that the key notion of divine commands 'requires a theory of revelation for its adequate development'.[18] This is right. If by divine commands we think of things recorded in scriptures or relayed by prophets, it is absurd to suppose that ordinary, everyday moral knowledge is explained by reference to them. Since we hold normal, sane adult human beings to moral account for their actions, we must grant an ability to be aware of and to act upon moral distinctions to adult human beings as such. So Adams toys with ideas of general revelation and of a universal 'inner light' which might explain the necessary general awareness of divine commands (an awareness evidently possessed by those who have no belief in a divine commander). But far from such avenues appearing to be the best explanation of moral awareness, there appear to be better and more economical forms of explanation to hand, for it is surely possible to account for the moral awareness of normal adults by showing how it is a product of the possession of experience, self-knowledge and reason themselves and is built up from the resources of a normal human life.

A broadly naturalistic account of moral development need not be reductionist in the manner of Freudian theory, but can instead appeal to the fundamental experience of human beings having been born into and growing up in forms of morally structured human relationship. The human world is one that is normatively constituted. Many of people's interests are unintelligible unless we notice the way in which they grow out of their lives as beings related to others (as friends, spouses, sons or daughters, as partners in an enterprise, as teachers, as pupils, and so on) in ways which demand the acceptance of various forms of trust and obligation. Moreover, it is part of normal experience to see in others objects of standing and respect, whose acknowledgement of oneself as an agent and of one's projects as worthwhile is then capable of confirming one's sense of oneself as enjoying standing and respect. Fellow-feeling and sympathy are invoked by the normal experience of being brought up in social existence. Intelligent human beings are capable of making choices as to how to act and of learning how to act well through the experience of making choices. In these, and in other ways, we can explain how normal, adult human beings attain the reflective awareness of good and evil we call 'conscience'.[19]

These points suggest that, while it may be theologically appropriate in certain contexts to describe conscience as the 'voice of God', no appeal need be made to a tacit awareness of divine commands to explain conscience. Moreover, they point to a problem in supposing that one could become aware of moral distinctions by way of receipt of divine commands. This difficulty derives from Anscombe's assertion that

> One does not learn mathematics . . . by learning that certain propositions . . . are true, but by working out their proofs. Similarly one does not learn morality by learning that certain propositions . . . are true, but by learning what to do or abstain from in particular situations and getting by practice to do certain things, and abstain from others.[20]

The knowledge of good and evil is, in other words, practical or it is nothing. Our thought that someone's ability to mouth a moral judgement, rule or principle is an expression of moral knowledge is internally related to thoughts about how they have acquired this ability and what use they can put the judgement to. This is one reason for asserting the priority of the virtues as vehicles for moral knowledge over judgements, rules and principles, since to have a virtue is to have dispositions to act, dispositions embodying moral intelligence, awareness and discrimination. Such knowledge may be summed up in judgement, rule and principle but it does not consist in being able to utter such things truly. We can reflect on moral knowledge as practical skill by way of formulating propositions and such reflection – in the form of conscience – may be important in the development of awareness. But if moral knowledge is in essence intelligent practice, then it cannot consist in being given, as true and to be accepted, judgements, rules and principles. Thus, we cannot be given moral knowledge by being given divine decrees. The 'cannot' here is a logical one: no commands could give one the complex powers of perception, discrimination and choice underlying knowing how to act well.

The argument derived from Anscombe shows, strictly speaking, only that a set of divine prescriptions and proscriptions is not sufficient to explain moral knowledge. In and of itself it leaves open the possibility that divine command may be necessary in the explanation of morality. For example, might one not appeal to divine command as the only credible source of the grounding and awareness of the basic moral rules (such as 'Do not steal', 'Keep your promises') which are on most accounts a vital component in moral reasoning, albeit that such reasoning goes beyond them?

This potential reply on behalf of Adams is weak. We have already pointed to ways in which the building blocks of moral awareness are to be found in our development and presence as intelligent agents in a human society. Moreover, it is relatively straightforward to show how basic moral rules arise out of features and needs of social existence. For example, it is apparent that no stable, successful human society would be possible unless it honoured and taught some basic rules designed to combat those evils human beings are prone to and which threaten fundamental forms of social coexistence and co-operation. Hence we find as moral platitudes rules giving some protection to life and property, and some penalties for the breaking of promises and contracts.[21] Reference to God in this context seems poorer as an explanation of basic rules than reference to facts about human needs and inclinations. We have noted above, for example, how it creates problems about the universality of such rules. At best, a theistic argument might appeal to the divine for an explanation of human existence and its fundamental features (via the design argument, say), but this is to leave the precise territory of moral arguments for God's existence.

We conclude that Adams' theory does not best explain how moral 'qualities' are cognitively available. The second problem with his meta-ethics concerns its apparent redundancy. Adams insists that it is the commands of a *loving* God that might best explain rightness and wrongness. The reference to 'loving' is present to avoid the charges of divine and moral arbitrariness that the Euthyphro dilemma throws up for cruder versions of divine command theory. The need for the reference can be seen in another way. One of our intuitions about moral 'qualities' is that they are intrinsically related to the features of acts and their circumstances which surround them. We cannot judge one act right and another wrong if everything else about them is the same. There are numerous and competing philosophical attempts to explain this fact that moral 'qualities' are supervenient on other qualities.

The embeddedness of rightness and wrongness in features of acts and circumstances is not best explained by pursuing the origin of moral 'qualities' in divine decree; it threatens to make rightness and wrongness float free of what we think of as the morally relevant features of acts and their circumstances. Stipulating that it is a loving God who commands avoids these consequences by setting this God the task of seeking out which acts in their circumstances are enjoined or forbidden by love. There must then be features of acts and their circumstances for God to attend to which will engage with his love. But is it not then obvious that the divine decrees are redundant? Even without them we too can seek out what is loving and unloving (by, for example: seeking out what respect and care for others and ourselves as persons enjoins) and thence deem some acts right and others wrong.

The redundancy in Adams' theory lies in his admission that there are and must be things we ought and ought not to do even if there were no God, because the requirements of love lie independent of God. Surely we can take this further and say that given love's (that is, respect's and care's) requirements there are things we must do and must not do. Given the demands of love parents must stand by their children in want, illness or handicap. Adams may argue that the particular notions of 'obligation' or 'duty' attaching to moral right and wrong bring in reference to legislation and commands: they imply what is demanded or forbidden by some law. This could be accepted by the opponent of divine command theory. The concession, if made, amounts to seeing the language of duty and obligation as picturesque survivals from the days of dominance of divine command views of ethics. We might argue that we ought to return to a vocabulary of the virtues and that we lose nothing of substance in the process. However, I do not think even this concession is necessary. We are quite happy, as noted above, to talk of the demands of love, of what love requires of us. Obligation and duty language can slip back in through such a route. In addition much duty language ties in with the idea of the demands of the roles one plays or of the relationships one is in. The parents who reject and refuse to care for their child discovered to be handicapped fail in their first obligations and duties as parents. These duties and obligations are not rooted in legislation but in the requirements which are constitutive of the role of parent and of the relationship between parent and child. Even when viewed in theological terms, I suggest it is more promising to see such failure as a failure to meet to the demands of covenant, rather than the failure to meet the demand of law. This is because the failure, while being one to meet duty and obligation, is thereby primarily a failure in what is owed *to the child*. The parents have failed their child. It is not primarily a failure to heed some law-giver who has laid it down how we are to treat children. If some form of theism is true we might have an additional obligation of this kind to a cosmic legislator. But if parents, faced with the shock of having a handicapped infant, were to ask 'What do we have to do here?' and not direct their gaze at their child and what they owed it, they would already be on the wrong track. (Of course, one could argue that to be faced self-consciously with this question is in itself to be morally blind to a degree.)

The above points about moral failure can be the source of yet another general criticism of divine command theories of ethics, whether simple or modified. We may describe moral failure as if it were infraction of rules – using a tacit picture of failure to meet the requirements of legislation. But, when we do wrong, what we fail in is what we owe to others as human persons. If it is true at all that we in addition fail in keeping the terms of a real body of moral legislation, it is not the primary failing. If we fail some God and that is the morally salient fact about our failure, then we fail a God who is in the other human being.

So in response to these various metaphysical and epistemological arguments from morality to the existence of God, we have employed two of the critical principles outlined at the start of this chapter. We have contended that if there are facets of the epistemology and metaphysics of morals which are obscure, referring them back to a personal God might not help them become less obscure. We have also argued that, if they constitute genuine problems about morality, their primary solution has to come from within morality itself.

All of the above points can be made clearer by briefly considering an argument from Linda Zagzebski for the conclusion that without recourse to God we must become moral sceptics.[22] She notes the facts of moral diversity and disagreement and the doubt these throw up about whether any moral issues can be decided. Diversity in the absence of the means of resolving it rationally suggests no moral judgements are reliable. But recourse to the Christian God means that we have something more to trust than our own human faculties of perception, reasoning and intuition. We can rely on God's help. In particular, the theist has 'another source of moral knowledge in divine revelation and the teachings of the Church'.[23]

The last quotation from Zagzebski shows that she is in agreement with a general point made above: it is no use having a transcendent anchor for morality, unless that anchor manifests itself immanently within morality in ways which can readily be discerned – otherwise it is a cog attached to the moral scheme which merely turns idly. But Zagzebski is obviously not sufficiently attuned to the thought that what revelation might contribute to moral knowledge has to be more than a body of 'teachings'. If revelation (be it amplified by the 'teachings of the Church' or not) does not contribute at a deeper level to insight, apprehension and the ability to make judgements about the particular case, it does not sufficiently anchor claims to moral knowledge. But how could it provide these things? How could it provide the apprehension and discernment that consist in possessing the virtues? Moreover, we must ask what concretely lies behind the appeal to revelation and the teachings of the Church. There is more than one claim to be the source of true revelation and the true Church. Where there is agreement on those things, we can find disagreement over how they are to be interpreted. The fact of moral diversity itself encourages disagreements on what is religious authority and how it is to be interpreted. Finally, if Zagzebski is right, we should expect to find that those in receipt of true revelation on moral matters and those possessing the teachings of the true Church in this area should stand out as having greater moral knowledge than those less fortunate. These folk should stand out as the ones able to rise above disagreements and settle them. Their views are not subject to the relativities and uncertainties others are enmired in. Is there such a group of moral agents? Who are its members?

MORAL ORDER AND THE MOTIVE TO BE MORAL

Arguments to the effect that secular morality is crippled because it lacks a proper motivational background to pursue the moral good are legion. They trade on the general point outlined at the end of Chapter 1: on naturalist assumptions there is no guaranteed moral order to reality. Without that guarantee moral endeavour is pointless. Hence, we must suppose that there is a God who provides the requisite guarantee. We have already seen that this general line of thought is unlikely to yield the precise conclusion that there must be a personal creator. Other kinds of religious metaphysic can do the job. If these arguments against a naturalistic ethics work at all, they can then only go part way to establishing the reasonableness of belief in a God. But perhaps theistic apologists will be content with this limitation on the conclusion of their arguments.

Arguments for the use of the notion of 'God' from considerations of the need for belief in moral order are the staple of Kantian thinking about the relationship between religion and morality. Such arguments will accordingly figure largely in Chapters 3 and 4. The aim in this section is to give a preliminary survey of the general issues surrounding arguments from moral order.

The general stance of such arguments is clear: naturalist ethics can provide no guarantee that allegiance to morality is a means of promoting the human good, therefore it leaves morality without a sustainable motive. Straightaway we must set aside as misleading the crudest, if most popular, way of pressing home these claims, which depend on the idea that only God can guarantee that morality and self-interest do not ultimately conflict. If moral considerations and those of self-interest are not seen by moral agents to cohere overall, then those agents will have no motive to take account of moral considerations. Without a belief in a God who will reward the virtuous and punish the vicious in a life to come, there will be no effective stimulus to be moral.

It is worth setting out the errors in such reasoning in order to check that they are not repeated in allegedly more sophisticated versions of the argument from moral order. First, we note the tendency for the crude argument to change what it endeavours to support. Morality becomes a long-term insurance policy – a back door way of pursuing self-interest. The reality of action proceeding from virtue is denied. Someone who acts out the virtue of justice is one who is pained at doing an unjust act and takes satisfaction in doing justice. Second, we note the difficulty in enforcing the initial divorce between self-interest and morality the argument needs in order to invoke a mechanism to join them together in the long run. The point just made about virtuous conduct proceeding from a background of liking for the good and hatred of evil shows that it is at the heart of our development as moral agents that our interests are changed. To come to possess the virtues is to acquire new interests, new desires. The general picture of morality as providing a layer of restraint on top of a set of amoral personal interests is just naïve. Further to that, we have noted in the previous section how much of what people understand as their interests (and thus their identity as the persons they are) is bound up with the relationships that obtain between them and others. These relationships are constituted by forms of moral trust and obligation. So many of my most basic interests will in fact be inseparable from my existence as a moral being. Finally, we must query how the coincidence of morality and self-interest could be guaranteed in the long run by a religious mechanism. If it is by some version of the promise of the rewards of heaven, then our earlier points bite home. If those 'rewards' are worthy and credible ways of completing the good of a being who has taken moral considerations seriously, then they will be of a kind which only a being with interests modified and acquired through moral conduct will enjoy. But then they will not centrally appeal to those who, we are asked to imagine, have no interest in behaving morally but rather need to be told that so behaving will be in their self-interest.

Cumulatively, the above points show the crude argument to have little coherent idea of what motivation in morality may be like and what the 'self' is which allegedly needs a guarantee that morality and self-interest coincide in the long run. We will find that some of these points crop up again when we consider the Kantian arguments on this score. The failure of the crude argument should point us in another direction, namely to arguments which provide variations on the following theme: it is essential to morality's deep structure that moral conduct be seen as a means of attaining the human good. It is not an external means to this good but a constitutive means. Attainment of the human good cannot simply be thought to come after living a good life. Living such a life is one component of attaining that good, but there have to be other constituents as well to complete the picture. So, if morality does not lead to one's own good and the good of others then its deep teleology is thwarted; it lacks ultimate sense; and its background in human motivation is weakened. Now let us look at some of the variations on this theme.

For W. P. Sorley the key question to be asked of any purely naturalistic outlook is this:

> whether the facts of our experience and the course of nature as shown in this experience, can be brought into consistent relation with our ideas of good and evil, so that nature may be regarded as a fitting field for the realisation of goodness.[24]

This question must be answered in the negative unless the world as we experience it is taken to be part of a larger scheme of reality which is through and through moral. The world we live in, taken in isolation, is one where individual acts of goodness are possible but where fundamental barriers are found to living a good life and where those who make no effort to live such a life prosper. Only if this life is seen as part of a larger life where individual acts of goodness lead to a completed good life and where acts of evil are seen to take one away from such a life, can the overall purpose of morality be met. This means seeing this life as a preparation for further existence, a preparation which requires apparent haphazard goods and evils in order for moral virtue to be acquired. All this in turn demands that 'goodness belongs to the ground of reality, and that the realisation of goodness is the purpose and explanation of finite minds'.[25] Further arguments are offered for saying that the best way of conceiving how 'goodness belongs to the ground of reality' is through the idea of a personal God.

Sorley's argument appears to turn around the notion that the deeper teleology of morality concerns whether our individual acts of goodness are part of a process of attaining individual moral perfection. In the absence of belief in a larger and hidden moral order, there is much which suggests that they are not part of such a process. We can further specify why human beings are prevented from attaining complete moral perfection despite being able to perform individual acts of goodness. In the first place human sympathies and powers of understanding are limited. All of us therefore find it difficult, to say the least, to rise from doing individual acts of virtue to acquiring the characters of virtuous people who by second nature can be relied upon to act well consistently. Furthermore, the circumstances which surround our moral careers can make it practically impossible to attain such characters. A poor upbringing, crippling poverty, the debilitating effects of disease or handicap and the plain and simple barrier of dying before moral maturity: all these factors which reflect the contingencies of our human lot can prevent us becoming truly good people. Finally, we note the sheer cussedness of the human will: the deep propensity which all of us share in to prefer evil to good. For all the above reasons, human beings find it very easy to be less than fully good.

The idea of morality having a deep teleology can be broadened further, and with it the extent of 'the moral gap', that is the gulf which exists between what morality bids us to seek and what we are likely to attain.[26]

We can add to the above case the thought that individual acts of goodness must not merely be good and worth doing in isolation, but must be seen as increasing the amount of goodness in the universe. Morality must be seen to be 'efficacious', in Zagzebski's terms. Since we frequently have to sacrifice lesser goods in order to honour moral good, we must be confident that, overall, honouring moral good increases the total good.[27] But if we take the world solely as it appears, we cannot have this confidence. The total amount of good around us is not visibly increased, nor is the amount of evil decreased, by activities of good people. We need the idea of a God who guarantees that, in the long run and despite appearances, good individual acts will contribute to greater good in the universe as a whole. Zagzebski points to 'moral despair' as the upshot of abandoning this belief in a morally efficacious God. Adams points to 'demoralisation' as the possible result of regarding it as very likely that the history of the universe will be evil on the whole, no matter what we do.[28]

Another way of bringing out a deep teleology in morality is by arguing that not only must morally good acts and a life governed by the virtues be seen as the means to realising the morally perfect life, they must also be seen as the means of realising a satisfying life. Yet in a world with manifest and multiple examples of injustice, they cannot be so seen. The notion that to be complete a morally good life must be part of a satisfied life lies at the heart of the traditions of thinking about morality inherited from Greek philosophy. Independent support for it can be provided by reflecting on the fact that one of the basic thrusts of genuine moral concern is to promote the good of others. Much of morality consists in the enactment of a principled concern for the welfare of others. But our morally inspired efforts to meet the needs of others are always liable to be frustrated by the negative effect of the contingencies and evils of this world. So, if living in this world were the whole story, we might well come to see this concern for others' good as pointless. Moreover, if we are mandated by morality to be concerned with the welfare of other persons, this must be because we regard the welfare of persons as of great moral significance. Hence, we must regard our own moral welfare as of moral significance. So we must wonder about the point of morality if the acts of self-sacrifice typical of it do not in the long run turn out to be constitutive means of attaining a satisfied life. This argument is not at all committed to the reductionist view of human happiness characteristic of the crude reasoning with which we began this section. Its proponents can readily accept that part of what it means to live a good life involves acquiring the moral virtues and thereby becoming a certain type of person. But they will maintain that living a life that is satisfying and good overall does not wholly consist in acquiring moral excellence. The character of our concern for others' welfare amply bears this out.[29]

The above arguments will take us neatly to Meynell's conclusion about the moral despair facing the 'man of good will' who cannot believe in God:

> He must *want* it to be true that in the long run oppressors will not derive advantage from their oppression, that the innocent and righteous will ultimately achieve fulfilment at least approximately in accordance with their virtue. I conclude that the clear-sighted man of good will must wish that theism, or at least something with equivalent eschatological implications, were true; or at any rate that he cannot regard its falsity as less than a moral tragedy.[30]

The sophisticated version of the argument for God's existence is now in place. Morality has a deep teleology within it. The moral life has to be seen as the constitutive means to attaining the human good. The idea of the good includes: the moral perfection of the individual, the advancement of good over evil in the world's history and the fulfilment of human well-being. The natural order taken as it stands runs counter to, or is at best indifferent to, this deep teleology. It contains evil: undeserved harms. Good and evil are distributed haphazardly. Circumstance can cut off the journey to a morally perfected character, can swamp the effects of good actions by evils, and can lead to morally good individuals being deprived of satisfying lives. So: morality is pointless unless the given, experienced order is part of a larger order of justice which will fulfil the deep teleology of morality. The notion of God provides the best (that is, most intelligible, most reasonable) anchor for belief in this all-encompassing, hidden moral order.

Some preliminary critical comments on the argument from moral order to God will be offered at this stage, leaving deeper discussion to the treatment of Kant's systematisation of the argument in the chapters which follow.

In evaluating this moral argument for God, we can set aside the third critical issue of whether the religious metaphysics mandated by the argument must be based on the idea of a personal God. In Chapter 1 we noted that, *prima facie*, there are other religious metaphysics which will fit the bill. So we can take it that further argument, not to be pursued here, must be offered in favour of preferring theistic metaphysics.

Another of our critical issues in the appraisal of moral arguments for God's existence is: admitting that there are problems in anchoring facets of morality, are those problems made any easier by invoking God? And it is here that the naturalist can invoke the *tu quoque* prepared for in Chapter 1. The theist has found a problem of evil for any moralist: evil as ground for moral despair. The same facts behind that problem give the theist a problem of evil, namely why unjust harm exists at all if there is an all-powerful, all-good God. The moralist who is not a theist can accuse the theist at this point of a version of the sentimentality the theist sees in liberal reinterpretations of religion. John Kekes registers a sense of this when he characterises the desire to find a metaphysical, hidden moral order behind the natural world as an instance of 'false hope' or of the 'transcendental temptation': 'The transcendental temptation is to give in to false hope and suppose that behind what appear to be the essential conditions of life there is a deeper order that is favourable to humanity'.[31] Why is Kekes convinced that this is a false hope? Because any reason we might give for believing in a deeper order behind things must come from within nature, from the world as we experience it. To assert that there is such a deeper order may be consoling, but the assertion denies a basic feature of our world: it does not appear to be morally ordered. There may be much about our world that is unknown, but if we stick with our experience of it (and what else can we have?), we can have no ground for 'mythologising the unknown'.[32]

The theistic argument stands accused once more of replacing one mystery with another. How far this charge can be pressed home in

Kekes' direction depends on a range of factors. A proper treatment of the issues would review how far there were other considerations, drawn from natural theology, religious experience or revelation, for believing that there was a divine order behind the natural order. Could the moral argument be thus seen as supplemented by others?

We should also need to consider how far the fact that something we do *needs* a certain anchoring gives us any ground for supposing that it *has* that anchoring. Kekes' talk of 'false hope' and 'temptation' is an echo of criticisms of Kant's version of the argument from moral order to the effect that from needs of human reason nothing follows about what is the case. We ought to be struck by the *prima facie* oddity (not to say, invalidity) in arguing as follows: i. Morality commits us to certain goals; ii. Because of evil and contingency we cannot realise those goals without a divine supplement to human agency; iii. Therefore it is reasonable to believe in a divine source of moral agency. There appears to be no easy inference from the fact that we have a range of deeply cherished goals to the belief that the world must be such as to meet those goals. This can look like wishful thinking dressed up as argument.

Overall, we should need to examine how far there was to hand a satisfactory theodicy. 'Satisfactory' in this context refers to the extent to which a theodicy can give us an account of the relationship between the evil world we live in and the perfect moral order behind it which is both morally and metaphysically intelligible. It is not enough for the theist to wave a hand at the problem of evil facing morality by invoking the divine order of justice without telling us how the divine order relates to the experienced order. If that relationship is beyond our moral and metaphysical comprehension, the naturalist can justly say that we have not advanced much farther.[33]

Further points can be made in the area of accusing the theistic explanation of taking us from one mystery to another. Evil and contingency mean that morality bids us pursue a range of goods whose attainment it can by no means guarantee: moral perfection, the increase of good over evil, the attainment of fully good lives. To avoid crude reductionism, all agree that morality must be seen to be the constitutive means to attaining these goods. But the issue now to be faced is that the theistic interpretation of morality does not after all tell us that the moral life is crowned with these goods. It introduces an agency external to morality and modes of existence after the moral life is over to provide these goods. Peter Byrne's moral life cannot be guaranteed to lead to perfection in excellence in the here and now, but I am told that (as, without a doubt I am one of the elect!) moral excellence will be available to me in some life to come. But that does not do the job unless that life is both itself a moral life (one where the virtues are still required, exercised and honed) and a life which is a continuation of the moral life I am now living. I must live a life continuous with the moral struggles and moral experience of this one. If I do not, the goal of excellence through virtue embarked on has not been completed. How are we supposed to make any sense of all this? For example, I hope I have displayed in the present life the virtues associated with benevolence, kindness and love for others. But in so far as I have done so, it has been through the moral relationships connecting me with family and in my role as spouse and parent. If I am to continue with my moral life in the hereafter, am I to get a new family? Or wait for my old one to catch up with me? Or, if I have gone last, expect them to be up and running as a family and waiting for me? Or am I to be told that, sorry Byrne, your going to have a change of role here and rapidly acquire some new affections, responsibilities and objects of care (for I need all those if I am to exercise the virtues associated with benevolence)?

The general point emerging from the above argument is this: just because the goals of a moral life are embedded in it, and must be embedded in it, it is hard to see how it helps to suppose that the moral life we know is part of some larger scheme. To illustrate the point again, consider the way in which for someone who is morally excellent a life that is satisfying for them is bound up with goods external to the internal rewards of moral effort. Byrne's noble and perfectly virtuous moral efforts bring him some personal satisfaction. Such satisfaction is internal to those efforts. Yet they also bind him to goods external to those efforts: for example, the flourishing of philosophy, the flowering of King's College, the health and welfare of his family. Contingency and evil mean that these external goods cannot be guaranteed satisfaction and they are not wholly realised. So Byrne, though perfectly virtuous, is not perfectly happy. Now if *this man* is to be made happy by some agency independent of his own efforts it will be either in one of two ways. The first would be to secure the realisation of the external goods he is committed to. But that could only be in this life. There could be no starting again with these goods in some 'higher' state of existence (or at least, the thought is barely intelligible). The second way would be to tell Byrne: 'We'll start you on another set of external goods and since we are going to do it in an existence where justice does visibly reign, you won't face evils this time.' But this is to tell Byrne that the things he has been struggling for in this existence, and the desires which have hitherto partly constituted his identity and personality, are to be jettisoned: they offer no route to final happiness. Poor Byrne might regard this as more discomforting than otherwise. And it seems this is not a way of guaranteeing that the moral life – this moral life, the only one we know, and the one in which we have been constituted as persons with a given character and so on – is a means of escaping the vicissitudes of evil.

CAN WE BOOTSTRAP?

If the theistic antidote to moral despair arising out of evil has the above questionable aspects, is there some way we can respond to the problem of evil from within morality's own resources? Three ways will be considered.

The first, and most dramatic way, draws upon a tradition of reflection grounded in Socrates' famous statement recorded in the *Apology* 'that nothing can harm a good man either in life or after death'.[34] The thrust of this assertion is surely to imply that it is part of the function of moral values to provide us with criteria for judging what counts as harm and benefit. The good person will look upon the outcomes that the chances of life throw up differently as compared with the evil person. Good persons and evil persons will have different measures for success and failure, different desires and needs. Thus for the good person, the greatest evil to be endured will be the consciousness of moral failure.

Kant confronts a version of the above thought when he notes that, in different ways, both Epicurean and Stoic ethical theorists identified happiness with the state of being arising out of the attainment of virtue.[35] It will follow by definition that no one who is truly virtuous can be unhappy.

We have already noted the point that, in acquiring the virtues, the good person acquires a distinctive range of desires and goals. In what follows we shall see that there is indeed something in the notion that this reorientation of the self consequent on moral development gives the good person a certain freedom from the world's contingencies. But it is hard to accept that this freedom is so complete as to cut him or her off from any stake in goods affected by the evils of life. We have noted that the very business of moral endeavour will give the virtuous a stake in the flourishing of things which are the objects or scene of their moral endeavour, such as family, profession and the well-being of others in general. While it may seem to be part of becoming inward with the values of morality that one should come to take a different, lesser view of one's own personal welfare, those same values would seem to give one great interest in the flourishing of the objects of morally concerned behaviour. It would be odd if perfection in virtue lead one to become indifferent to the fate of others. But while one is committed to others' welfare one can most certainly be harmed by what happens in the world. Therefore, the good which we seek and which makes our lives of moral effort successful cannot simply consist in the effort itself.

The outcome of the effort matters and that is subject to chance, contingency and the destructive power of evil.

There is undoubtedly more to be said about the Socratic notion that the good person lies beyond the reach of harm. For example, both Gaita and Winch have tried to draw out the intelligibility and compellingness of the sense the supremely good person might have of having lived a life, which, for all its sufferings and vicissitudes, he or she can be thankful for.[36] But it is notable that both these defenders of the Socratic pronouncement see its moral point as lying not in a general verdict anyone can make about the good person, but rather as flowing out of an act of reflection which only the good can make upon their own lives.

A second and more straightforward way in which morality can 'bootstrap' itself in the face of evil has been developed by John Kekes.[37] His fundamental idea is that morality has its own resources for ameliorating the personal, social and natural factors which give rise to evil. For example, morality, socially embodied, creates institutions which provide rewards and punishments, establishing the human world as one where a semblance of justice reigns. Morality can encourage traits of character whose possession enables people to fight evil in their own persons and around them. Morality encourages the development of kinds of wisdom, modes of grasping practical complexities and problems, which add to the fight against evil. Kekes, in other words, bids us to face evil by way of developing the many resources within morality which will better enable us as individuals to defeat evil and which will help communities to make justice a reality.

A signal merit of Kekes' arguments is that they show how evil, far from encouraging an abandonment of morality as pointless, highlights the need for the institutions of morality in the human community. However, there are problems in seeing Kekes' account as sufficient as a response to evil.

The major difficulty with Kekes' response arises out of history. The forms of understanding and institution associated with morality have been around for a long time. Kekes proposes that our response to evil consists in laying bare the moral resources available to us in the hope that we can thereby work more effectively to combat evil. Now we can ask: what reason is there to think that any future progress in the human fight against evil can be expected unless progress in that combat has been observed in the past? On the assumption, which Kekes of course himself insists on, that there is no external moral agency riding in to rescue us, we must assume that the future of the human struggle against evil will be like its past. There is no reason to expect amelioration in the future unless we can see progress towards amelioration in the past. To illustrate: Kekes picks out what he styles 'essential conditions of human life' – in the form of the contingency of human existence, the moral indifference of nature, and the presence of destructiveness in human motivation – which give rise to human tragedy.[38] These conditions are not going to be removed from the human situation. But the resources of morality can be used to tackle them and mitigate their effects. However, the very effort to use moral resources in this endeavour will itself be governed by these 'essential conditions'. There seems no need to despair in face of these limitations if, but only if, we can discern a pattern in history which shows that they can be mitigated. So, Kekes' view is itself open to the charge of giving in to tempting, false hope unless it rests upon a plausible philosophy of history.

The suggestion arising out of this criticism of Kekes might be put in this way: his secular response to the problem of evil still requires a theodicy, where 'theodicy' now means an account of some purposive structure in the world which will ensure that evil will be overcome. A belief in progress in human history, a progress not grounded on an external, divine management of that history, will amount to a secular theodicy. These points will be seen to be important in the discussion of Kant in the chapters which follow. In Kant's later writings, particularly the *Religion within the Boundaries of Mere Reason* of 1793, the theodicy on offer appears to turn around finding a progress in human history. The response to evil is the belief that as a race we have been and are journeying towards the creation of an 'ethical commonwealth' on earth in which justice will reign over the human world at last. In developing this theme, Kant appears to be clearer than Kekes in seeing that, if moral effort itself is to be the response to evil, appeal must be made to a progressive view of human history in order to ground that response. Interestingly, we shall see that Kant thinks that some kind of reference to a transcendent agency is still required to buttress the belief in progress.

Progressive views of history might also provide individual moral agents with solace in the face of evil. Kekes does indeed recognise that moral and other kinds of effort yield satisfactions internal to them. There are internal goods in morality.[39] The thought that moral activity was a means of partaking in the progressive defeat of evil would naturally increase the sense that it was worthwhile. The third way in which morality can respond internally to the problem of evil builds upon the idea that morality provides satisfactions of its own.

This third route can begin from the Socratic pronouncement that the good person cannot be harmed. Within Aristotelian theorising about virtue lies a variant of that thought: though the entirety of the human good cannot consist in virtuous conduct divorced from supporting external goods, an essential part of the human good is to be found in acts which witness to the claims of good over us.

We have already drawn upon Aristotle's point that possessing the virtues means acquiring a disposition to find acts of virtue pleasurable and acts of vice painful. As he puts it, 'the man who does not rejoice in noble action is not even good; since no one would call a man just who did not enjoy acting justly, nor any man liberal who did not enjoy liberal actions'.[40] In other words, what the virtuous will come to desire is the activity of virtue itself. It will be a mark of having a virtue that one chooses to do its corresponding acts for their own sakes. There must therefore be something about virtuous acts which makes the activity involved in doing them worthwhile in itself.[41] Nancy Sherman sums up this point by making a distinction between actions which are ones of production and ones which are their own end.[42] An act of production has an external end and is worthwhile just in so far as it attains that external end. But an action that constitutes its own end, while indeed having an external end, is worthwhile even if it fails to realise the external end it is directed towards. There is no point in wanting to act justly by repaying a debt owed to another unless I want the payment to get through to the person to whom something is due and owing. But my action has a point even if I fail in this end. My action has an internalised end and in this respect it constitutes its own end.[43] The activity involved in doing it is supremely worthwhile independent of the external success of the activity. Here Sherman, following Aristotle, draws a contrast with vicious action. Despite the fact that some of the villainous savour the means of evil:

> Vicious actions do not seem to constitute their own ends in the same way. Their point and focus seem to remain on the external end – power, gain, deceit, avoidance of risk and fear. Promotion of these external ends are what counts.[44]

The claims we have made about the relation between virtuous acts and ends are not empirical generalisations but clarifications of the concept of virtuous activity and its component elements. So it is a necessary truth that this kind of non-contingent satisfaction may be found in virtuous activity. The reason why this kind of satisfaction is not available in acts which are not regarded as virtuous is that those acts do not by definition conform to the necessary truths arising out of the notion that virtuous activity is worth doing just for the sake of the activity involved in doing it. If a person were to do what is customarily identified as a vicious act with these thoughts about its non-contingent worthwhileness, then that would show they were treating what we style 'vice' as virtue. What is contingent in all of this is: whether or not there are any acts of which these necessary truths hold; what acts exemplify virtuous conduct; whether those who do them are satisfied by them regardless of outcome (they may not take the satisfaction which is available in virtuous conduct); whether the vicious are or are not dissatisfied in their careers of vice.

Despite the above qualifications, a number of important points flow from the realisation that virtue constitutes its own end.

First, we see that a life of virtue is part of the good for human beings and not merely something that might lead to it. A good for humanity that is morally worthwhile thus has somehow to complete the moral life rather than simply come after it. Second, we can see how virtue is not a complete good, though it is a non-contingent good. It is not complete because virtuous action has external ends, like the good of others, as well as internal ends and because the Aristotelian point does not entail that the virtuous person cannot suffer. But the good of virtue, being internal and consisting in the mode of activity itself, is in a manner eternal. Because the activity that is virtue is worth doing as an activity independent of its result, the virtuous person attains a good which is not dependent on the contingencies which affect the consequences of human action. (That and how morality provides an eternal good will be further discussed in Chapter 6. The notion is central to Sutherland's and others' moral interpretation of religion.) This suggests that, in respect of contingency, virtuous action is better off than vicious. All human action, good or evil, faces the problem that chance and external circumstance can frustrate it and prevent attainment of its external end. But it is activity that is motivated by a concern for the good that constitutes its own end and good as well as having an external end and good.[45]

We can sum up the points about virtue and the good by saying that morality can partially pull itself up by its own bootstraps. Virtuous activity can provide a consoling, non-contingent good even though it cannot provide the entirety of human good by itself. Kekes' points about the role of moral wisdom and institutions in directly tackling some of the evils which threaten us can add to the sense in which morality of itself offers a response to the problem of evil.

Yet that problem remains. The goods internal to moral action and the ability of morality to confront evil cannot of themselves guarantee: that morality leads to the human good; that the unjust state of this world is but a temporary phase of its development; or even that all will have the chance to develop their full moral potentialities in this life. For morality to be seen to lead inextricably to the human good or the conquest of evil something else must be added. This must be some kind of agency that sets the moral efforts of a given individual or a given human generation within a larger, successful purpose. Or, in other words, there must be a moral order to reality despite its apparent amoral character. Hence, the logic of the 'transcendental temptation' and the drive, which we have seen Kekes ridicule, to take the moral operation of our world to be evidence that true reality (as evinced by a God or by the human future) is quite unlike the world as it now appears. Present, morally imperfect reality is taken to point to a perfect reality which must lie behind it or which it must be leading up to. Our discussions suggest the somewhat paradoxical conclusion that this true reality must at once be an agency beyond the normal moral efforts of human beings, but yet somehow work to complete those very efforts. It must be beyond the moral life, yet somehow be working within it. We shall see that Kant's problems in articulating clearly how a reference to religious reality completes an account of morality arise out of this paradox.

This discussion can be brought to a close by returning to the original point urged against naturalistic ethics at the start of this section: such ethics must lead to moral despair because it cannot see moral effort as part of a process whereby good overcomes evil. In tracing the ins and outs of this charge one point has clearly emerged. Individual moral acts can be seen to have intrinsic point. If they do have such point, then they are worthwhile in and of themselves and not on the sole ground of being part of a successful triumph of good over evil. To rebut this reply the theistic apologist would have to maintain that individual acts of virtue were valuable only as part of a larger whole: the triumphant creation of the human good. There seems little independent reason to believe that is so.[46]

Reflections on the alleged need for moral activity to be supported by belief in moral order to reality undoubtedly present difficulties to a wholly naturalistic ethics, as I trust I have made plain; but these difficulties do not constitute an apologetic proof that in order to work at all morality requires theism.

NOTES

1. For a review and attempted rebuttal of their arguments see Bambrough *Moral Scepticism and Moral Knowledge*.
2. See Mackie *Ethics: Inventing Right and Wrong* for a sustained attempt in this direction.
3. See Byrne *Foundations of Ethics*, ch. 6, for argument on this score.
4. See pp. 88–93.
5. Taylor *Does God Exist?*, p. 92.
6. Devine *Relativism, Nihilism and God*, p. 82.
7. See Sagi and Statman *Religion and Morality*, pp. 23–4.
8. Devine *Relativism, Nihilism and God*, pp. 88–9.
9. Devine *Relativism, Nihilism and God*, pp. 86–7.

10. See Alston 'Some Suggestions for Divine Command Theorists' for a fuller attempt to identify goodness with the divine nature.
11. See Alston 'Some Suggestions', pp. 268–70.
12. Meynell 'The Euthyphro Dilemma' and Swinburne 'Duty and the Will of God' .
13. See Byrne *Foundations of Ethics*, ch. 4, for a survey.
14. See Byrne *Foundations of Ethics*, p. 30 ff.
15. Devine *Relativism, Nihilism and God*, p. 88.
16. Devine dismisses as inadequate the idea that moral imperatives may be 'thought of as immanent in the facts themselves': *Relativism, Nihilism and God*, p. 80.
17. Adams 'A Modified Divine Command Theory of Ethical Wrongness', 'Divine Command Metaethics as Necessary A Posteriori' and 'Moral Arguments for Theistic Belief'.
18. Adams 'Divine Command Metaethics', p. 116.
19. See Byrne *Foundations of Ethics*, p. 22 ff. for an expansion of this theme.
20. Anscombe 'Authority in Morals', p. 47.
21. For an extended deduction of the moral rules along these lines see Gert *The Moral Rules*.
22. Zagzebski 'Does Ethics Need God?'
23. Zagzebski 'Does Ethics Need God?', p. 302.
24. Sorley *Moral Values and the Idea of God*, p. 344.
25. Sorley *Moral Values and the Idea of God*, p. 350.
26. See Hare *The Moral Gap* for the notion of the moral gap.
27. Zagzebski 'Does Ethics Need God?', p. 299; a similar argument can be found in Hare 'The Simple Believer', pp. 412–14.
28. Adams 'Moral Arguments for Theistic Belief,' pp. 151–2.
29. For a version of the above reasoning about the good life see Mitchell *Morality: Religious and Secular*, pp. 142–3.
30. Meynell 'The Euthyphro Dilemma', p. 233.
31. Kekes *Facing Evil*, p. 27.
32. Kekes *Facing Evil*, p. 28.
33. It should be noted that Sorley endeavours to meet this demand and develops his own soul-making, Irenean theodicy from morality itself, but like all theodicies, it is open to fundamental objections as will be evident from the discussion of Sutherland in Chapter 6 below.
34. Plato *Apology*, p. 25, 41d.
35. Kant *Critique of Practical Reason*, pp. 229–30 [5/111–12].
36. Gaita *Good and Evil*, pp. 194–206, and Winch 'Can a Good Man Be Harmed?'
37. See Kekes *Facing Evil* and *Moral Wisdom and Good Lives*.
38. Kekes *Facing Evil*, p. 26.
39. Kekes *Facing Evil*, p. 20.
40. Aristotle *Nicomachean Ethics*, 1099a.
41. Hutchinson *The Virtues of Aristotle*, p. 115.
42. Sherman *The Fabric of Character*, p. 114.
43. Sherman *The Fabric of Character*, pp. 114–15.
44. Sherman *The Fabric of Character*, pp. 116–17.
45. There are other respects too in which virtuous action can be seen as superior for the agent to vicious; see Byrne *Foundations of Ethics*, pp. 127–8.
46. See Sagi and Statman *Religion and Morality*, pp. 108–9.

3

Kant on God and the Highest Good

INTERPRETATIONS OF KANT

In the numerous writings of Kant on ethics in the Critical phase of his philosophy we find repeated attempts to anchor the meaning and justification of the concept of God in belief in moral order. At the same time the concept of God is detached from its more traditional grounding in metaphysics and revelation and we are expressly forbidden to take the notion of the divine arising out of the need for moral order to be the object of any theoretical speculation. In contemporary literature there are at least two ways of viewing Kant's enterprise.

At either extreme are the views of Michalson and Green. We noted in Chapter 1 how Michalson regards the Kantian project as little more than an exercise in wishful thinking. Kant's revisionary moral interpretation of religion is of historical importance. It shows clearly what happens when the 'modern self' emerges and confronts traditional religious belief. The modern self lives in a world with which it feels 'disenchanted', for that world is shaped by the mechanistic vision provided by science. At the same time, it is aware of its own radical demands for autonomy. Given those demands, it can no longer accept the old supernaturalist forms of religion. So it searches for a new account of faith and transcendence somehow compatible with the disenchanted world and the self-defining subject.[1] As exemplified by Kant and the traditions of liberal theology he spawned, the 'modern self' engages in a hopelessly incoherent task. It is forced by the conditions of modernity to seek a ground for faith and relation to transcendence within itself (in Kant's case, within the logic of conscience). Yet it thereby faces a major problem. On the one hand it rejects traditional supernaturalist faith; on the other hand it is forced to use the language of traditional theology to express the faith it constructs. No stable religious view does or could emerge from this attempt. And thus Michalson portrays Kant's *Religion within the Boundaries of Mere Reason* (the major Critical work in which Kant sets out his moral revision of religion) as containing a series of conceptual 'wobbles' which are testimony to the divided cultural inheritance Kant struggled with.[2]

When viewed in this light, Kant on religion does not offer us a series of arguments which can be reconstructed and debated, but rather an historically important juggling of sensibilities.[3] We have already offered reasons for setting aside such an extreme reading of Kant's project. For we have found arguments, which at the least are worth taking seriously, for the conclusion that any reflective view of morality should hold on to belief in a moral order and teleology underlying the merely physical order. Yet we have also seen that there are some grounds for denying that traditional notions of religion serve as apt supports of belief in moral order and teleology. If we think there is anything to the considerations offered in Chapters 1 and 2 relevant to these themes, then much of Kant's 'wobbling' can be seen in a wholly new light. We can then sympathise with Kant's continued use of the traditional language for expressing belief in moral order and his practice of surrounding it with an interpretation steeped in agnosticism and mystery.

At the opposite end of the spectrum lies the reading of Green.[4] Crucial to this interpretation is the idea that Kant has laid bare the form of morality. Morality is as Kant described it: a body of universal, impartial and rational legislation. Moreover, the demands of reason in morality do occasion deep conflicts with the demands of reason coming from other areas of our practical life. These conflicts require a resolution, to be provided only by appeal to the transcendent and by the embrace of the mysteries of religion. On such an account, there may indeed be problems in the details of aspects of Kant's moral interpretation of religion – as for example in Kant's too ready assumption that only a theistic form of religion can guarantee belief in moral order.[5] But, overall, Kant has successfully uncovered a set of timeless truths about morality and a set of universal moral requirements which provide the major anchorage for religion. Kant has thus solved what many in the subject have seen to be the major problem of the philosophy of religion in its modern incarnation: the provision of a rational anchorage and interpretation of religious belief. Kant's discovery is specifically that this interpretation and anchorage is provided by moral reason.

In this and the next chapter I shall contend that this optimistic gloss on Kant's moral interpretation fails. I will show that Kant's arguments for his conclusions are not simply mistaken in matters of relatively minor detail, but fail at major points. If that is so, there is no philosophy of religion in Kant to be endorsed and taken over entire.

It is obvious that there is plenty of room for interpretations and evaluations of Kant's project which lie in between the two extremes outlined so far. Out of my discussion will emerge the thesis that there are indeed tendencies and needs in morality which Kant picks out for us and which have implications for religion. Moreover, Kant does go some way in indicating how a revisionary realism in religion might be coherent. However, there are major flaws in his claim that practical reason as such requires us to adopt belief in the attainability of perfected moral goodness.

On the view offered here, both Green and Michalson have part of the truth. There are needs in morality which are to be taken seriously and which point towards a religious teleology behind ethics (as outlined in the previous chapter). Yet Kant's claim that these needs have the absolutely pressing character of universal, rational demands does depend on contingent features of the outlook he inherited historically.

Lewis White Beck lists some of the features of the *Weltanschauung* Kant remained true to throughout his writing life.[6] From those features emerges Kant's commitment to key ideals of the Enlightenment: belief in the possibility of perfection for humanity via morality and rationality, and belief in the possibility of happiness only via such perfection. These ideals conflict with another facet of the *Weltanschauung*: commitment to the reliability of the scientific world view, and specifically the then current view of the world as a mechanical system. The scientific view tells Kant that the given world is not run so as to conform to the demands of moral teleology. So we have the key tension between, on the one hand, the conception of nature as non-morally ordered in its detailed workings and, on the other, the imperative goal of happiness-via-perfection-via-reason. This places the human subject in a situation of fundamental conflict: the subject is an embodiment of reason and must be governed by reason's demands; yet it is also part of a natural order which does not work so as to satisfy reason's demands. Typically, reason for Kant has an overarching concern to attain system and completeness in human thought. So reason as it operates on practical life will be concerned with completing our endeavours to be morally worthy and to satisfy our needs, hence the requirement to envisage a final human good as attainable. Kant's problem in the sphere of morality and religion is another instance of a general problem confronted in his mature philosophy: the gap between reason and nature.

The very *Weltanschauung* which creates these tensions provides Kant with a possible means of resolving them. For in that set of beliefs is the thought that, just in virtue of being machine-like, the world (nature) is not a product of chance but must be viewed as a teleological whole. This entails that any overall view of nature is able to see it as the product of purpose. The way is then open to offer a version of the 'refined supernaturalism' outlined in Chapter 1. Without disturbing the chain of natural causation, we are to see an overarching pattern in nature and history, one derived from viewing ourselves and the world as resting on a divine ground.

The possibility of reconciling the view that nature is a mechanistic process with the standpoint of supernaturalism is further supported by the inner logic of the transcendental idealism which arises out of the Critical philosophy. The fundamental problem facing that philosophy is the nature and status of metaphysics. Kant is concerned both to limit and give proper foundations to the claims of general and special metaphysics. General and special metaphysics are necessary and yet vexatious. General metaphysics arises out of the attempt to settle the general character of reality *a priori*. Its attempts to deduce the truth of general laws of reality such as 'All events are connected together by causal laws' are indispensable for the defeat of scepticism and for placing scientific enquiry on sure foundations. Yet those same claims place dogmatic restrictions on thought about matters relating to human destiny if they are taken to be true, without qualification, of reality as a whole. For when so taken they entail that reality in itself is mechanistic and material. The ideas of freedom, immortality and God are the typical objects of special metaphysics and all three must be rationally grounded if a coherent notion of a final human good via moral perfection is thinkable. Yet if their reality could be strictly proved then the claims of general metaphysics would be thrown into doubt, for the world would not then be governed through and through by causal laws.

The Critical philosophy offers to solve these tensions by means which at the same time put general metaphysics on a new, certain foundation. The claims of the general metaphysician about the general structure of reality are justifiable in so far as they represent how the world must be construed if it is to be an object of human knowledge. Human experience, empirical knowledge, has a form which can be determined *a priori*. That form dictates that certain conditions must be fulfilled if experience is to be possible at all. This fact in turn entails that any world we can gain experience of must have a determinate structure which will guarantee the possibility of a scientific exploration of its workings.

In the above fashion general metaphysics can be given all that it requires.

It is true to the extent that it describes an immanent metaphysics implicit in the structure of experience. Yet its pretensions are limited by this new deduction of its claims, for they turn out to be true of reality only in so far as we can gain empirical knowledge of it, or, as Kant puts it, they are true only of reality as it appears. What reality may be like independent of our ways of knowing about it, in particular independent of the conditions imposed by our forms of cognition, we cannot know. That is a tautology. This allows us then to think that there may be aspects to reality quite unlike those met in empirical, scientific knowledge. Given this, we can entertain the claims about the reality of freedom, an immortal soul and God as postulates. We make these postulates depend on the non-theoretical needs of human reason, particularly, though not exclusively, the needs of human reason arising out of the practical life and its completion in a final destiny for human beings.

We have summarised the movement of thought which leads Kant to declare 'I have therefore found it necessary to deny *knowledge* in order to make room for *faith*'.[7] Faith here refers to the 'pure rational faith' later to be outlined in the Dialectic of the second *Critique*. For the postulates which give us the skeleton of Kant's refined supernaturalism are not the objects of bare choice but reason, specifically reason manifested in the search for completeness in its practical operations. Thus are the conflicting claims of Kant's inherited *Weltanschauung* reconciled. The notion that the world is a mechanical system is supported properly for the first time, while the scope of the notion is reduced by relativising the reference of the word 'world' to those aspects of reality which are the possible objects of an empirical knowledge. This allows us to think that there are other aspects of reality, whose existence would meet the needs of reason in its practical employment. There is no final conflict between, or estrangement of, the realms of nature and reason. The realm of nature is *ex hypothesi* not to be equated with reality as a whole or as such. A supernatural meaning to reality is allowed to be thinkable, which meaning enables the key needs of reason to be met.

Kant's combination of naturalism and supernaturalism provides a perfect example of that movement of thought which we have noted Kekes castigates as giving into 'false hope' and 'the transcendental temptation'.[8] Pure rational faith in Kant demands that we think there is an order in which our deepest moral and religious needs can be met despite the apparent indifference, if not hostility, of nature to those needs. It is Kant's argument that, in the circumstances where we have no proof of the non-existence of the deeper order but have strong rational demands arising from the nature of morality itself, then we are more than entitled to indulge in the hope that behind nature is that deeper order which is through-and-through moral.

Kant describes three questions which face the human, rational agent: What can I know? What ought I to do? What may I hope?[9] His refined supernaturalism is an essential part of his answer to the third question. What I may hope is that human fulfilment via perfection in virtue is the destiny of all of us. Restrictions placed on any legitimate answer to the first question ('What can I know?') allow us to postulate realities that found this hope. The requirements of practical reason show us that we must have the hope. Kant would no doubt argue that it is only an un-Critical dogmatism that declares such a hope 'false'. Only failure to attend to the limits on knowledge found in the Critical examination of reason encourages Kekes' claim that how the world appears can be the only ground for thinking how it is. Kekes' argument that, since the world does not appear to contain a moral order or show signs of supernatural direction, we must conclude that there is no such order or supernatural agency, would be seen as dogmatic from the Kantian point of view.[10] The distinction between the world as appearance and as it is in itself (that is, minus the conditions on reality implied by the forms of empirical knowledge) seems to attack this argument of Kekes' head on. The distinction precisely forbids, as un-Critical dogmatism, any inference from the character of reality as it appears to the character of reality as it is in itself. Since reality may have many facets unknowable to any empirical knowledge, Kekes' inference would seem impossible. However, it should be noted in his defence that we have already quoted him as conceding that reality may be to a large extent unknowable. But where we do not know, we should not allow our hope to frame our guesses. We should not mythologise the unknown.[11]

This last challenge to Kant's attempt to bring in supernaturalism on the back of morality highlights two strands of his thinking. One is the positive dimension to the doctrines of transcendental idealism. Kant repeatedly makes the tempting transition from saying that we may conceive of aspects of reality beyond those that appear to an empirical knowledge like ours to saying that, since we know only reality as it appears, there must be a non-empirical reality of which that reality is an appearance. This non-empirical reality is then to be conceived as wholly intelligible and rational. A substantive, metaphysical idealism beckons. The thought, noted above, that a mechanistic world requires an ultimate teleological source chimes in with the full-blown metaphysics of transcendental idealism. The supernaturalism allegedly required by morality gains plausibility from such idealism.

If transcendental idealism understood in this way were the sole means of supporting Kant's supernaturalism, then that supernaturalism would be open to all the objections levelled at transcendental idealism.[12] The other strand in Kant's support for supernaturalism is his arguments from the very essence of morality for the postulates. These purport to show that moral reason itself requires all to believe in God and eternal life. It is to these arguments we now turn.

THE ARGUMENTS FOR THE POSTULATES

I shall concentrate on the arguments for the postulates of God and immortality and ignore that for freedom.

There are different versions of the argument for the postulation of God's existence in Kant's writings. All invoke supernaturalism to guarantee a connection of some kind between happiness and moral virtue. It is notable that in both the *Lectures on Ethics*[13] and the first *Critique* the connection is made at the point of the springs to moral action. Without a guarantee of the connection between virtue and action moral principles would be objects of approval and admiration but not 'springs of virtue and happiness'.[14] Making the connection in this way seems a clear violation of the teaching of Kant's mature moral philosophy that reason, in the form of respect for the moral law, is, and must be, the sufficient motivating factor in the performance of right acts. Accordingly, in the second *Critique* the argument turns around the rational necessity for all of the pursuit of a *telos* via moral action. This *telos* is the highest good or perfect good. The highest good is in turn the union of two goods: the supreme good and happiness. The supreme good is the complete realisation of a virtuous will: the 'complete conformity of dispositions with the moral law'.[15] Happiness is defined in various ways by Kant. Sometimes it is said to consist in an uninterrupted experience of contentment or agreeableness;[16] sometimes as the complete satisfaction of a finite being's desires or needs.[17] Within the perfect good, virtue is the condition for happiness: we are bound to seek the highest good via the route of seeking a virtuous will as a condition for, and in the expectation of, happiness. Happiness arising out of virtue is the perfect good for a finite rational creature.

Kant's argument asserts a necessary goal for morality in the perfect good, which in turn entails a necessary connection between virtue and happiness: virtue must be thought of as giving rise to happiness. But there is no way in which this necessary connection is founded upon anything analytic: it is a mistake, committed in different ways by both Stoics and Epicureans, to define happiness and virtue in terms of one another.[18] Where there is a necessary but synthetic connection between two ideas, we must seek a third term which guarantees the connection and the third term in this instance is God. There is no way we can see how happiness arises out of the pursuit of moral perfection if the mechanism of cause and effect in nature is all there is. We must suppose, therefore, that there is a cause beyond nature which can guarantee the exact correspondence between moral perfection and happiness. A moral causality, and therefore order, underlying the natural is thus posited. The traditional notion of a personal God with accompanying 'omni' properties is asserted to be the only means of picturing the character of the source of this causality and order. The argument is helped along by appeal to the principle that 'ought implies can'. Since we are under a rational necessity to pursue the perfect good, we must think it possible to pursue it and postulate the conditions which allow us to have that thought.

This is how the nub of the argument looks in Kant's own words:

> Now, the moral law as a law of freedom commands through determining grounds that are to be quite independent of nature and of its harmony with our faculty of desire (as incentives); the acting rational being in the world is, however, not also the cause of the world and of nature itself. Consequently, there is not the least ground in the moral law for a necessary connection between the morality and the proportional happiness of a being belonging to the world as part of it and hence dependent on it, who for that reason cannot by his will be a cause of this nature and, as far as his happiness is concerned, cannot by his own powers make it harmonise thoroughly with his practical principles. Nevertheless, in the practical task of pure reason, that is, in the necessary pursuit of the highest good, such a connection is postulated as necessary: we *ought* to strive to promote the highest good (which must therefore be possible). Accordingly, the existence of a cause of all nature, distinct from nature, which contains the ground of this connection, namely of the exact correspondence of happiness with morality, is *postulated*.[19]

In brief, Kant's argument has the following, simple form:

1. It is rationally and morally necessary to attain the perfect good (happiness arising out of complete virtue).
2. What we are obliged to attain, it must be possible for us to attain.
3. The goal of perfect good is only possible if natural order and causality are part of an overarching moral order and causality.
4. Moral order and causality are only possible if we postulate a God as their source.

    5. Therefore we are under a rational, moral necessity to postulate the existence of God.

This argument supports and is supported by the argument for the postulate of immortality. The latter's first premise states that 'The production of the highest good in the world is the necessary object of a will determinable by the moral law'.[20] We have already met its second premise: a component of the highest good is the achievement of a will wholly in accord with the moral law. By another application of the 'ought implies can' principle, we are told that pursuit of this 'holy will' must be possible, but since no 'rational being of the sensible world is capable at any moment of his existence' of attaining this[21] we must postulate a supernatural scene for the completion of this task. Completion is to be conceived as an endless progression to a complete fitness of the will with the requirements of morality, requiring the postulate of immortality to make sense.

There is an oddity about the argument for immortality which is immediately obvious: not even immortality will give us the goal of achieving a holy will. All it can secure is the endless progression towards such a will. Kant resumes the argument by bringing in the postulate of God: God is able to view the endless progression which those who are virtuous are embarked upon from a timeless perspective. From that perspective, God can see the endless journey as a completed whole and thus count us as having achieved the precondition for the perfect good.[22] This passage of argument looks forward to the way in which the tension between our aspirations to virtue and our actual condition as creatures (always tainted by evil to some degree) is resolved in the *Religion*. There we are reminded that we cannot rid ourselves of evil by human powers and yet we must be able to overcome it. The 'overcoming' involves a timeless, divine perspective upon our acts which is able to regard an improvement of our moral dispositions in the course of time as if it were the fruit of a complete reorientation of the timeless ground of all our willing.[23]

Before attempting to evaluate these arguments we must ask what force Kant meant them to have. They are clearly based upon the premise that morality has an underlying teleology without which it would be null and void. Even after Kant had abandoned the thought that the elements of the teleology are required to transform moral laws from objects of contemplation into springs for action, he still insists unequivocally that if the highest good were deemed impossible of attainment the moral law ('which commands us to promote it') would be fantastic and inherently false.[24] The problems which suggest that the necessary teleology of morality cannot be realised stem from the paradoxical position of human beings as finite embodiments of reason. As creatures of reason, the completeness of a will in accord with the moral law is demanded of them; but as finite they cannot attain this completeness, indeed as human they are tainted by a radical evil which they can never wholly shake themselves free of. As finite rational creatures, their perfect good cannot consist simply in attaining moral perfection and enjoying the contentment which flows from that. It consists in attaining their finite ends, and thus happiness, by way of acting morally. But as finite creatures they know that frequently the pursuit of happiness conflicts with the heeding of moral demands and thus that the latter is not the means of attaining the former.

The force Kant sees behind the postulates is best interpreted as follows: the postulates present the only means of avoiding a practical absurdity arising out of the conflict between equally rational demands. The rational demand we face as moral creatures is to attain the supreme good. The rational demand we face as finite creatures is to attain happiness. These demands are in conflict only given the assumption that the world is not morally ordered through and through but is as it appears to be. We postulate God's existence in order to remove the assumption that puts reason in conflict with itself. In the special case where theoretical reason has nothing to say for or against such postulation, we are rationally required to bring in reference to supernatural realities underlying the given world.[25] This is the ultimate ground which a defender of Kant would cite for saying that his supernaturalism is not a giving in to *false* hope or a transcendental *temptation*.

There is an element of paradox in this way of presenting Kant's case. For in order to avoid antinomies arising out of the very structure of practical reason as embodied in finite creatures, reason requires us to employ ideas which, in virtue of being supernatural, are non-rational – when judged from the standpoint of theoretical reason. Green is precisely right in saying that, for Kant, religion is 'the effort by a rational being to act in a rational manner'[26] but the effort succeeds by reason helping itself to ideas which not only have no theoretical proof, but which are resistant to proper explication by reason. Religious ideas have a source in reason, but in a human reason which must transcend itself in order to complete its work. It is this fundamental paradox of 'rational non-rationality' which goes a long way to explaining why there is so much else in Kant's moral interpretation of religion that is paradoxical, providing ammunition for critics like Michalson to complain of Kant's 'wobbling': his frequent, infuriating appeals to the concepts belonging to a supernatural world view while setting aside the precise religious beliefs on which their application appears to rest. It is notable that Kant himself is ready to use the notion of 'mystery' to categorise some of the elements of the supernatural world-view reason must borrow to avoid practical absurdity.[27] Religion, then, represents a sphere into which reason must enter but whose notions are rationally problematic and opaque. Hence, it is right to see Kant's interpretation as a form of highly revisionary religious realism.

REVISIONARY, PRACTICAL REALISM

Chief among the many critical questions to be raised about Kant's moral deduction of the necessity of supernaturalism is how far that super-naturalism can be taken seriously. Kant does indeed say at one point in the second *Critique* that the arguments for the postulates give us a form of cognition of God, but he immediately qualifies this 'but only with a practical reference'.[28] This means that there are no theoretical inferences to be drawn from holding the postulate of God's existence. It is not a basis for any further speculations as to God's existence, nature or influence upon the world.[29] The implications of supernaturalism lie in our practical lives, and even there they give us no new obligations or ends. Supernaturalism merely affects the way in which we pursue ends already implicit in the moral law. It is true that morality leads inevitably to religion and that religion is the recognition of all duties as divine commands.[30] But to say this is not to say that we should look to divine commands to determine our duties. It is to say two things: first, that the requirements of the moral law are to be regarded as holy, with a due and proper reverence; second, that they are to be seen collectively as the constitutive means whereby the overarching goals of morality are to be realised, which goals in turn enshrine a religious destiny for humankind. But we are not to seek out special religious duties or goals. Even though in Book IV of the *Religion* Kant admits prayer, church attendance and the like as parts of the life of the person moved by moral reason, it is only because he can interpret them so that they have a function in supporting moral agency. What the supernaturalism does is make us obey moral commands with a special reverence and pursue the goals arising out of those commands with a confident hope. We are to get no additional goals but rather we are to pursue the overarching goals of morality in the complete confidence that they will be achievable despite appearances to the contrary.

In particular, the supernaturalism of Kant by the time we get to the *Religion* of 1793 boils down to a confident hope that human history will proceed so as to realise the ultimate purpose of morality: the creation of a commonwealth on earth wholly run by moral laws. Here the complete good is conceived in immanent fashion as the triumph of morality in human life. In the ethical commonwealth justice will reign and the

conditions which at present mean that the pursuit of happiness is one thing
and giving respect to morality another will vanish. The supernatural
machinery is invoked only to do what we saw Kekes could not do:
guarantee that through individual and collective moral effort the fundamental conditions making for evil in this world will be overcome. With the
machinery we can be confident that the historical order will eventually
coincide with the moral order, indeed that the underlying order of history
is the moral order. Morality determines the answer to the question 'What
ought I to do?' Religion answers the question as to what I may hope by
affirming that ultimate good can be achieved by doing what I ought to do,
and only by doing it. Kant himself provides the perfect summary of this line
of thought when he writes that 'Moral theology is thus of immanent use
only. It enables us to fulfil our vocation in the present world . . . .'.[31]

The idea of a set of religious notions with their characteristic transcendent reference nonetheless having only an immanent employment in
morality and only on the basis of moral requirements may be paradoxical, yet it exactly captures the spirit of the moral interpretation of religion.
But now we must face the charge against Kant that the moral interpretation of religion is a species of non-cognitivism or reductionism. What has
happened to the religious object, the religious referent?

In certain crucial respects we can say that the religious object has gone.
One of the main reasons for concluding that the postulates are not an
invitation to elaborate speculative theories about the supernatural is that in
Kant the postulates do not rest on reasons or evidence which derive from
contact with the objects cited in them. Their basis is subjective, in the sense
that they arise from the needs of the person, though indeed they are
universal needs arising for all rational, finite agents as such. They derive
from the force of the rational demands facing the conduct of personal
agents. They do not derive either from traces or perceptions of the activity
or the character of the putative referents of religious ideas. So Kant is able
to say that 'I must not even say, "*It is* morally certain that there is a God,
etc.", but "*I am* morally certain, etc"'.[32]

The ready confession that the putative religious object plays no part in
the justification of our speech about it shows that Kant's account of
religious language departs from realism as that is understood by many
contemporary philosophers. For they understand realism in the light of the
claims of a causal account of knowledge. Referential success grounds
realism and is a mode of cognitive contact between speaker/knower and
reality. If success and contact is genuine, then the symbols or states of mind
that display it should be explicable as arising out of causal relations
between the knowing subject and the object cognised. We should be able to

say at least that if the object had not existed, the linguistic, symbolic items that refer to it would not have arisen. If the relation between subject and object of cognition is in part causal, then religious realism entails the thought that religious language is in part explicable as arising out of causal contact between the human religious subject and the transcendent. Kant's realism cannot be of this sort.

How far his view is realist can be further questioned when we consider that for Kant there are severe limitations surrounding how the content of the ideas employed in the postulates present their objects. The content of the idea of the agency that guarantees moral order and progress to the perfect good is the traditional notion of God as the supreme personal agent possessing the 'omni' properties. Kant may be criticised for his failure to see that religious ideas with a different content could perform the job of guaranteeing belief in moral order and progress equally well. Yet this criticism chimes in perfectly well with the thrust of his own comments about the content we give to the symbols referring the supernatural agency required by moral reason. On Kant's own account this content cannot be assumed to offer a true portrait of the character of this agency. The symbols we use can be judged as correct only in so far as they help us to keep in focus the thought that there is such an agency, which in turn keeps alive the hope required for unstinting moral effort on the part of rational agents. This general stance encourages the thought that we might appropriately think of the agency in non-theistic terms provided the same ends can be accomplished thereby. These symbols are not accurate pictures of an object of cognition:

> The attributes . . . we ascribe to the Being in question may, objectively used, involve a latent anthropomorphism. Yet the object we have in view in employing them is not that we wish to determine the nature of that Being by reference to them – a nature which is inaccessible to us – but rather that we seek to use them for determining our own selves and our will.[33]

In both the *Critique of Pure Reason* and the 'Critique of Teleological Judgement' Kant argues that, while we are constrained to view the intelligible mechanism underlying nature in terms of appropriate analogies drawn from the mundane, we know that a condition of using them to refer to ultimate reality is that we cancel out all the connotations which attach to them as mundane analogies and which provide their very content. Kant's view of religious language in these two works can be seen as re-using a distinction familiar from Aquinas' account of how descriptions of

God gain their meaning. This is the distinction between *what* our descriptions of ultimate reality might refer to and *how* they refer to that reality.[34] In the first *Critique* Kant asserts that we must affirm that there is some reality distinct from the world which contains the ground of the world's order:

> If, in connection with a transcendental theology, we ask, . . . whether there is anything distinct from the world, which contains the ground of the order of the world and of its connection in accordance with universal laws, the answer is that there *undoubtedly* is.[35]

So that language about God refers to some reality of a transcendent kind is not open to question. In this respect Kant's philosophy of religion is unequivocally realist in intent and neither reductionist nor non-cognitivist.

Kant says in both *Critiques* that in order for the idea of God to play its role in practical life it must be given some content – beyond the bare notion of a something we know not what which is the ground of order. In the context of the practice of science, we need to pursue the vision of the given world as a systematic, economic whole. In the context of morality, we need to keep alive the hope and demand that each and every moral action is a constituent means of attaining the perfect good for humanity. For reason to function in pursuit of a systematic science and moral good, it needs a concrete representation of how the completeness it seeks is possible.

> But why should it be of any consequence to us to have a theology at all? . . . it is quite obvious that it is not necessary for the extension or ratification of our knowledge of nature or, in fact, for any theory whatever. We need theology solely on behalf of religion, that is to say, the practical or, in other words, moral employment of our reason, and need it as a subjective requirement.[36]

Reason must call the imagination to its aid. It draws up a concrete representation of the ground of order by relying on models drawn from experience. Thus the reality, whatever it may be, which is the ground of all appearances must be modelled after appearances and its relation to the given world and be understood by analogy with the relation one item in the given world has to another. Yet we know that the concepts employed to do the job of modelling have no application to realities beyond the world of spatio-temporal things. They 'are empty titles for concepts . . . when we thus venture with them outside the field of the senses'.[37]

Kant thinks that, in giving content to the bare idea of an unknowable ground of the given world, we inevitably resort to anthropomorphism. We use the notion of God as supreme person and as possessing human perfections to an ultimate degree. We also know that we cannot think that the ground of things has the mode of existence and attributes of a person. Our concepts cease to function as vehicles of understanding if we attempt to apply them to such a reality. Kant's account of knowledge means that he is implacably agnostic about the actual character of ultimate reality. What it is like in itself we cannot know.

> For this being is posited only in the idea and not in itself; and therefore only as expressing the systematic unity which is to serve as a rule for the empirical employment of reason. It decides nothing in regard to the ground of this unity or as to what may be the inner character of the being on which as cause the unity depends.[38]

So the content we give to our notion of this reality is human, one derived from our own reflections and needs. In this respect, Kant has a projective account of the nature of religious symbols. Their content does not reflect awareness of a supersensible object, but rather human needs and humanly rooted images. But that there is some supersensible reality or other to which these images correspond is not a matter of human projection, but rather a truth vouched by reason.

Kant sums up this conception of religious language in the third *Critique* by affirming that we can *conceive* of the ultimate source of order as a divine, personal being, but cannot thereby *cognise* it.[39] The distinction between conception and cognition is that the latter provides us with knowledge of an item, while the former does not. The various facets in our conception of the divine derive from the needs of human reason. They cannot reflect the known characteristics of any object which might correspond to that conception. Our conception of God serves only to regulate our rational activities as a result. It does not constitute an object of knowledge. We do not know of a divine object through our concept of the divine. All that we know is that there is something related to the given world as the guarantor of its hidden moral order. As Yovel puts it, all we know through the concept of God is 'that the given world is the highest good *in potentia* and that human praxis can make it so actually'.[40]

In Chapter 1 the moral interpretation of religion was linked to revisionary realism. In what sense is Kant's understanding of religious language a form of revisionary realism? It is realist in respect of retaining an extra-human reference for religious language. It is revisionary in two respects. The warrant for the reference is largely found in morality, and not in more traditional sources such as revelation or metaphysics. In addition, the referential intent of religious language is divorced from the customary idea that we can construct assured descriptions of the character of the divine. The content of those descriptions is rather said to be based on the human imagination. So, Kant's realism is one that spells the end of theology as a putative science of the character and intentions of the divine.

There are ways in which Kant's revisionary realism can be presented as a major break with the philosophical and theological tradition. Thus Yovel describes the root convictions of moral faith as consisting in the following beliefs: that there is something about the world which makes the world capable of moral transformation; that the worlds of human freedom and of nature are not alien to one another; that history and the universe are not meaningless but have a moral meaning and direction. He then infers that these convictions 'have no theological import. The postulate of the existence of God tells nothing of God, only of man and the world, and the Kantian theory of the Deity remains strictly humanistic'.[41] In this verdict Yovel seems to pass over the distinction between the transcendent reference of religious language and the human content of that language. This is no doubt because he sees the mechanism, whatever it may be, which is capable of grounding Kant's moral teleology as being immanent in the given world. It is certainly true, as noted above, that by the time Kant writes the *Religion* he has perceived that any worthwhile good resulting from a moral teleology in history and nature has to be manifested in history and nature. But does that mean that he has abandoned the thought that the mechanism which guarantees the teleology must be a transcendent ground of the world of appearances?

From another perspective Kant's approach to revisionary realism can be seen to continue a tradition set out in Aquinas' account of analogical speech of God. In question 13, 8 of the *prima pars* of the *Summa* Aquinas gives as the primary intent behind the use of 'God' the desire to refer to that which exercises a wise providence over all things. It seems Kant can sign up to the referential, realist intent of this minimal notion of God. There is a moral teleology in the universe and 'God' refers to whatever it is that is the ground of this teleology. Aquinas insists in those early questions that we can not know what God is, only what he is not. In question 13, 8 the meaning of 'God' is expanded as referring to the whatever it may be that is the source of all things, above all things and distinct from all things. That is to say, the primary definition of 'God' is negative and relational. Kant too could follow the tradition in giving realist force to a negative, relational conception of God. Where he departs from the tradition is in his denial that there is either a metaphysically given or revealed order which enables us to discern a relationship between the divine and the human, such that we can then be sure that certain human-rooted perfection terms are true of the divine nature. Kant's realism remains too agnostic to allow such positive predications of the divine. This is no doubt because he allows only one sure relation between the divine and the human: the divine is whatever it may be that is the ground of that moral teleology which we assume and try to make real in moral conduct. That divine-human relationship is too thin to allow a positive theology; theology remains an anthropocentric exercise in image construction.

Our examination of Kant's account of religious language shows that he can easily escape a dilemma which his critics frequently throw at him. Either, it is said, Kant is merely saying that we must act as if there were a God, or he is saying that there is a God who is to be proved via morality. If he says the former, he does depart from traditional theology, but in the direction of a radically reductionist or non-cognitivist account of the content of faith. If he says the latter, he has saved some worthwhile content to theism, but he cannot exclude what is saved from being a stepping stone to, or an element in, a traditional attempt to construct a theoretical account of God's nature.[42]

But it is perfectly possible for Kant to have his cake and eat it. The postulate of God's existence is not a route into traditional theological speculation because no content we give to the notion of a transcendent ground of order can be a reliable basis for inference in speculative thought. But we must take it to be the case that there is some ground or other to moral order. Our answer to the question 'What precisely is the source of moral order?' is and has to be an imaginative construct. Nothing but the imagination could be at work in producing a detailed, concrete conception of divinity. If you like, we act as if something real corresponds to any such imaginative construct. But we are committed to thinking that there is some source or other of moral order. This means faith is left making an existential claim.

When we turn to the character that Kant's moral faith assumes in the light of his account of religious language, we see grave problems in interpreting faith's precise nature. Is it a species of 'faith in' (*fiducia*), or 'faith that' (*fides*), or does it combine both of these? Allen Wood does indeed argue (on the basis of Kant's remarks in the *Lectures on Ethics*) that faith is understood in the Critical philosophy as including an element of personal faith in God.[43] But this can hardly be Kant's mature view of the matter. While moral faith may be personal in the sense of arising out of each individual's daily struggles to realise moral goodness, Kant's account of religious language rules out there being available any object for us to have a relationship of *fiducia* to. In so far as we conceive of the divine as a person we also know that conception to be humanly generated and to yield no reliable portrait of the character of the divine as it is in itself. Wood is on firmer ground in later presenting moral faith as a species of 'faith that', specifically the faith that reality is as the Critical philosophy's *Weltanschauung* presents it.[44] It is the faith that a final human good can be realised in a world which can also be described by science, the faith that the world of freedom and morality and the world given to us through empirical knowledge are but aspects of the one reality.

We have already noted one important oddity for Kant in moral faith. Morally grounded faith that there is a God has a warranted referential component but its content is not reliable. So, believing that there is a God is an odd and in some ways problematic belief for Kant. There is a further, much debated, oddity in moral faith, thought of as containing a belief that there is a God. In the second *Critique* Kant gives due prominence to the objection to moral faith that no belief that something is the case can be founded upon a human need. There is no inference from 'We all need p to be true' to 'p is true'.[45] Moral faith, in other words, seems to be no more than the dressing up of a grand piece of wishful thinking. (We are back again to Kekes' transcendental temptation.) Kant's reply to this objection is that reasoning from need to belief is appropriate if two conditions are fulfilled: first, that the needs in question are universal needs of reason; second, that there is nothing in the way of evidence against the belief thus arrived at.[46]

Kant can be accused of not taking the measure of the above objection. The precise problem is this: to believe that p involves taking up a positive stance towards the probability of p. To believe that there is a God involves believing that it is more probable than not that there is a God. There would be some kind of pragmatic contradiction in saying both 'I believe that there is a God' and 'It is not more probable than not that there is a God'. To affirm the second of these propositions would normally be taken as a way of denying that one believed that there was a God. It surely follows from all this that I may not recognise any considerations as being reasons for believing that there is a God which I cannot at the same time recognise as reasons which raise the likelihood of there being a God. Now, let us put Kant's universal need of reason for adopting moral faith at its strongest: there will be a contradiction at the heart of human, practical reason unless there is a ground of moral order underlying the given world. How could that be a reason which adds to the likelihood of there being such a ground of order? It can surely only be such a reason if we believe it is likely in some degree that the world will be such as to meet our deepest needs and allow human reason to flourish in it. But to hold this last belief is already to be committed to the world view of the Critical philosophy, and so we have gone round in a circle. Kantian moral faith still appears to be a monumental piece of wishful thinking.

One way out of this problem is to reinterpret Kant's argument for the postulates of practical reason after the style of the arguments discussed in Chapter 2 above. The character of moral faith would change accordingly. Viewed in this light we would see the postulates resting upon a *fact*, one pertaining to human experience. It appears to us that morality is a meaningful enterprise. On pain of moral scepticism, we must assume that it is, which means assuming that the world will allow the completion of the ends of morality, and so on to the hypothesis of God's existence. The problem with this way of interpreting Kant is that we might now have considerations bearing upon the likelihood of God's existence but at the cost of removing the distinction between theoretical, probabilistic arguments for God's existence and the distinctive route to postulates of practical reason. Moral faith becomes a species of theoretical belief, grounded in the veridical character of moral experience and the improbability of moral scepticism.

If we reject the above reinterpretation of Kant, there is another way of interpreting and defending the character of moral faith: understanding moral faith that there is a God as not entailing belief that there is a God. So understood moral faith need not bring with it the view that it is more probable than not that God exists. And it might have proper grounds which do not add to the probability of God's existence. This interpretation of moral faith arises out of recent discussions which stress the links between 'faith that' and 'hope that', downplaying the links between faith and belief at the same time.[47] While I can find no clear evidence that Kant held the interpretation I shall now outline, it does conform with his dual emphases on moral faith as an answer to the question 'What may I hope?' and on the rational demands of practice as the source of moral faith.

We can note many uses of 'faith that' locutions where faith that p does not entail belief that p. If a mother has lost her child, she may have faith that she and her fellow searchers will find it unharmed without believing that this will be the case. If her faith is dashed, this will not amount to showing that she had a belief which turned out to be false. The grounds she may have for her faith in a successful search may be quite other than grounds for thinking that success is more probable than not. She may have faith even though she believes that success is not overall likely. Her faith may grow out of and be supported by practice and values. It will be more than hope. One may hope that many things will be so without having faith that they will be so. One can hope that something is the case without acting in order to bring it about or actively relying on its being the case. But one cannot have faith that something is the case and at the same time not recognise practical demands that one should help to bring it about or place no reliance on its being true. If I have faith that this book will be finished and will be an excellent product, my faith if at all sincere will undergird my behaviour. As well as having a practical dimension, 'faith that' is cognitive, even though it does not entail 'belief that'. It is cognitive in so far as its object is a putative fact. It can be rational or irrational. If one has proof that something is not the case, one may not have faith that it is the case.

'Faith that' is bound up with what one can hope for and strive for or rely upon. Crudely, we might say that 'faith that' is rational, non-idle 'hope that'. Kant can then be interpreted as meaning by a moral faith that there is a God: a commitment to the existence of something corresponding to 'God'; which falls short of holding this existence to be more probable than not; which arises out of the demands of practice; which is not irrational; and which undergirds daily moral striving. It does not amount to knowledge that there is a God. Nor is it a tentative opinion that there is a God. Nor yet is it merely acting as if there were a God. One may act as if something is true, while believing firmly, indeed knowing, that it is not true. Acting as if something were true may be a way of merely pretending that it is true. In contrast, moral reason demands commitment to an active, whole-hearted faith in there being an appropriately grounded moral order in things. That commitment is continually reinforced in moral practice.

NOTES

1. Michalson *Fallen Freedom*, p. 2.
2. Michalson *Fallen Freedom*, p. ix.
3. Michalson *Fallen Freedom*, p. 140.
4. See Green *Religious Reason* and *Religion and Moral Reason*.
5. See Green *Religious Reason*, p. 100.
6. Beck *Early German Philosophy*, pp. 427–9.
7. Kant *Critique of Pure Reason*, Bxxx.
8. Kekes *Facing Evil*, p. 27.
9. Kant *Critique of Pure Reason*, A805/B833.
10. Kekes *Facing Evil*, p. 28.
11. Kekes *Facing Evil*, p. 28.
12. Compare Strawson *The Bounds of Sense* with Allison *Kant's Transcendental Idealism* for opposing views on the plausibility of Kant's idealism.
13. *Lectures on Ethics*, p. 73.
14. Kant *Critique of Pure Reason*, A813/B841.
15. *Critique of Practical Reason*, p. 238 [5/122].
16. *Critique of Practical Reason*, p. 56 [5/22].
17. As in Kant *Critique of Pure Reason*, A806/B834. Kant appears to have taken these two formulae to be equivalent. Later, in Chapter 4, we shall see that they are not and thereby reveal a major problem in Kant's arguments for supernaturalism.
18. *Critique of Practical Reason*, pp. 229–30 [5/111–12].

19. *Critique of Practical Reason*, p. 240 [5/124–5].
20. *Critique of Practical Reason*, p. 238 [5/122].
21. *Critique of Practical Reason*, p. 238 [5/122].
22. See *Critique of Practical Reason*, p. 239 [5/123].
23. See *Religion*, p. 92 [6/47–8].
24. *Critique of Practical Reason*, p. 231 [5/114].
25. For this reading see Green *Religious Reason*, pp. 70–3, and Wood *Kant's Moral Religion*, pp. 29–30.
26. Green *Religion and Moral Reason*, p. 15.
27. *Religion*, p. 164 [6/137].
28. *Critique of Practical Reason*, p. 250 [5/137].
29. Though Kant indeed does hold that for the postulate to do its work in the practical context we must use the conception of God as omnipotent, omnibenevolent, etc., even while we are not to do anything speculatively, theoretically with this conception – Kant *Critique of Practical Reason*, p. 252 [5/140].
30. Critique of Practical Reason, p. 244 [5/129].
31. *Critique of Pure Reason*, A819/B847.
32. *Critique of Pure Reason*, A829/B857.
33. 'Critique of Teleological Judgement', p. 127 [6/457].
34. Aquinas *Summa Theologiae*, 1a. 13. 3, pp. 57–9.
35. *Critique of Pure Reason*, A695–6/B723–4.
36. 'Critique of Teleolgical Judgement', p. 159 [6/482].
37. *Critique of Pure Reason*, A679/B707.
38. *Critique of Pure Reason*, A674–5/B702–3.
39. 'Critique ofTeleological Judgement', pp. 126–8 and pp. 160–3 [6/456–8, 6/483–5].
40. Yovel *Kant and the Philosophy of History*, p. 121.
41. *Kant and the Philosophy of History*, p. 121.
42. See O'Leary-Hawthorne and Howard-Snyder 'Are Beliefs about God Theoretical Beliefs?'
43. Wood *Kant's Moral Religion*, pp. 161–2.
44. Wood *Kant's Moral Religion*, p. 249.
45. See Kant *Critique of Practical Reason*, p. 254 [5/143].
46. *Critique of Practical Reason*, p. 255 [5/143].
47. See Audi 'Faith, Belief and Rationality' and Pojman 'Faith without Belief'.

4

Kant and the Demands of Reason

HAPPINESS AND RATIONALITY

We have seen that Kant thinks there is a *reductio* argument for the key principles of religion. We must postulate a moral order behind the given world which will then guarantee the attainment of the highest human good via moral effort. The form of the *reductio* is this: without this postulate practical reason faces absurdity in the form of a contradiction between two of its necessary ends (that is, the pursuit of happiness and the pursuit of moral perfection). But if Kant cannot make good the assumption that these are both necessary ends of reason, then the argument for the postulate fails. The moral interpretation of religion would not inevitably fall with the proof of the postulate of God. It might still have some degree of plausibility but it could not be said to be *the* means philosophy must adopt for interpreting religion. It is time to test the assumption that reason does have the goals of happiness and perfection as necessary ends.

Kant makes a distinction with regard to happiness. Pursuit of happiness by a finite, rational agent is rationally required, though not a duty.[1] This presumably means that a failure to pursue one's happiness is not a breach of obligation. Yet it is a breach of a rational requirement, for on a number of occasions Kant affirms that all finite rational creatures are under a rational necessity to seek their happiness.[2] Indeed, the reason why the pursuit of happiness is not a duty is because 'every man (by virtue of his *natural* impulses) has *his own happiness* as his end'.[3] Kant assumes that if we are bound by our natures to do something it cannot at the same time be an obligation for us. The imperative to act so as to gain happiness is 'assertoric': it can be assumed 'a priori and with assurance' that all rational, finite agents have the end of gaining happiness.

There is an obvious objection to these claims about happiness. Experience shows us countless cases where individuals consciously forgo or sacrifice their happiness in the interests of doing right by others. In order to give this point any precision, we must analyse what is meant by 'happiness'. I follow the account of Tatarkiewicz which distinguishes four things denoted by words synonymous with 'happiness' in modern European languages:[4] experiences of the greatest joy; satisfaction with life as a whole; success; and possession of the highest good.

The first item in this list is a powerful and often short-lived emotion. It is happiness in this mode that radiates from Byrne's friends whenever they see him. Satisfaction with life as a whole introduces happiness as in part a verdictive notion. Happiness in this mode is not an emotion divorced from judgement. One judges one's life to be happy. Past and present emotional states may be evidence for this judgement and a judgement that one's life is happy or unhappy will occasion the rise and fall of emotions. Judging life to be happy is bound up with finding it rewarding, and satisfying, so in these ways it is more than simply approving of one's life, even though it includes a verdictive element. As to the third notion of happiness, Tatarkiewicz notes that in many languages other than English, words for 'happiness' also have the connotation of 'good fortune' or 'success'.[5] 'Happy' used of someone in this way is also connected with the idea that someone's goals have been achieved. The final use of 'happiness' is found in translations of the Greek *eudaimonia*. It has the connotation of 'blessed'. A happy person is one who lives well and fares well, who possesses the good. The word then refers to something analogous to Kant's perfect good. We have already noted that he in fact objects to this Classical fusion of the ideas of doing well and faring well into one notion, on the grounds that such a merger tends to make virtue and happiness (as joy, satisfaction or success) analytically connected, when they can only be synthetically connected at best. Underlying this criticism is his major objection to the Classical tradition: since what will make human beings happy (that is, will give them lives with which they are satisfied) will be almost infinitely various, we cannot build an ideal of happiness into a single standard of the mode of living that is morally choiceworthy.[6]

In what follows, where 'happiness' is used without qualification it is happiness in mode two that is in question – happiness as a life found satisfying. I take it that in so far as we aim at happiness or regard it as a component of the highest human good, it is happiness of this kind that is in question.

Kant himself provides us with two ways of defining human happiness. He uses these in the same texts and often in close proximity to one another; so we can assume that he regarded them as equivalent. That they are not will be seen to create major problems for this theory. In one mode of definition, happiness for Kant is 'satisfaction with one's condition'.[7] This looks four-square to be an instance of happiness as satisfaction with one's life. Sometimes Kant gives essentially the same definition with the overtone that such a satisfaction will inevitably occasion sentiments of a joyful kind, or that a verdict of 'satisfying life' arises when one is conscious of agreeable sensations having accompanied all of one's existence.[8] I shall assume that this extra gloss is not significant: Kant has in mind happiness as satisfaction with one's lot, with appropriate trimmings and accompaniments.

Kant also defines happiness as the 'entire satisfaction' of our 'needs and inclinations',[9] thereby ushering in happiness in mode three – success. More strikingly, but in this same vein, he defines happiness as that 'state of a rational being in the world in the whole of whose existence everything goes according to his wish and will' which 'rests on the harmony of nature with his whole end'.[10] Happiness is the satisfaction of needs/preferences/ends and the mark of the successful pursuit of ends by a rational, finite creature.

There are crucial ambiguities in Kant's version of the happiness-is-success theme. I will show that these, together with the ambiguity arising from the fact that he also defines happiness as satisfaction, destroy his claim that happiness is the necessary end of any finite rational creature.

If we take happiness as success to consist in the complete satisfaction of an agent's ends, we can easily see how in Kantian terms it might seem to be a necessary goal of finite reason. Reason in general is that faculty which seeks harmony and unity in the objects of cognition. As practical but finite creatures, we have many ends arising out of our pursuit of limited goods in this world. It is the necessary task of practical reason to seek the highest unity among these ends. Leaving aside Kantian terminology, we might agree that, at any one time, the overarching goal of any agent has to be the maximal satisfaction of the goals that agent has set him or herself. Not all goals will be capable of co-realisation, but it would be a mark of irrationality in conduct to have a set of ends to be pursued in conduct and yet deliberately to act so as not to achieve as many as are conjointly achievable. (Something like this claim is what Kant's theory needs. In fact, the claim ignores our ability to rank some ends as very much more important than others.) Rationality as consistency bids us to avoid ends which cannot be conjointly achieved and a set of ends once decided upon gives us sufficient reasons to act upon them.

Even if the above points are accepted, they will not yield the substantive claim that every agent necessarily desires happiness. For many agents will have active, intention-informing ends which are not directed to their happiness, considered as a satisfying life. A person who resolves to give up career, friends and outside interests in order to care for an elderly relative may act so as to satisfy consistently all the ends of his or her conduct. But those goals entail the non-satisfaction of tastes, interests and ambitions. Here we find the obvious ambiguity in the Kantian formula for happiness as an existence in which everything goes in accordance with 'wish and will'. Our self-sacrificial carer may have a life in which his or her wishes and will are satisfied if we mean by 'wish and will' 'intentions and plans'. But many wishes and desires must have been abandoned in order to arrive at his or her enduring intentions and plans to act as a long-term carer consistently and conscientiously.

The example of what is forced upon people who, with full resolution, heart and mind, act out the role of carer is not extreme or out of the way. Many, many thousands of people act thus. But this kind of case should make us initially highly sceptical of the kind of claim supporters of Kant maintain when they state such things as: 'If we are to endorse whole-heartedly the long-term shape of our lives, we have to see this shape as consistent with our own happiness'.[11]

Allen Wood endeavours to support the line of thought rebutted above by pointing out that Kant's conception of happiness depends on the idea that a human being's finite nature 'imposes' upon him or her 'certain natural needs, or "natural ends"'.[12] Happiness is the idea corresponding to the satisfaction of the totality of these natural needs or ends. But this defence of Kant is also beset with crippling ambiguities. Needs are not ends. Nature may give me certain needs, as for food, shelter, security, companionship and the like. But whether these are ends of mine depends on the way I form my intentions and on the goals I set myself. Indeed it is hard to see how nature can give me ends at all, if this means impose on me without choice things which are intentions (key elements in my life as a planning, practically rational agent). Moreover, 'natural' could have at least two senses in Wood's reconstruction: that is, 'non-reflective' or 'non-moral'. Consideration of this ambiguity shows that there can be no simple contrast between the totality of natural ends and the totality of moral ends. Many of the ends and needs our self-sacrificial carer gives up will be ones which grow out of projects and desires that are the product of intelligent reflection: for example, this person's career goals and the needs arising out of the shape of that career. These are not imposed by nature and they involve elements of reflective valuation in choosing them. They will be underwritten by a sense that they are worthwhile. But they are not thereby moral ends, if that means determined wholly or mainly by thoughts of duty or the requirements of a life manifesting the virtues. Nor yet will they be wholly divorced from an agent's conception of what is morally demanded. As reflective ends, their pursuit will occasion the exercise of moral values and their adoption by the agent will show the influence of moral values upon him or her.

The more we reflect on the ambiguities involved in appeal to an agent's allegedly natural ends and needs, the more it will be seen that they do not help to clinch the case for saying that finite, rational agents necessarily have happiness as their goal.

Green's reconstruction of Kant's argument for the postulate of God may be seen as an attempt to get round the difficulties just aired. In contending for the claim that happiness is the necessary goal of all agents, he employs the 'economic' notion of rationality current in many parts of the social sciences. Rationality in conduct consists in the maximal satisfaction of preferences – maximal because not all of a person's preferences will be conjointly satisfiable given human circumstances. The notion of preferences may seem a commendably more precise version of Kant's 'needs and inclinations'. On this economic understanding, rationality is internal to the preference set of any given agent. Conflict between preferences in that set may call for preferences not to be acted upon, but alleged goods external to the agent's preferences have no claim on the agent's rational deliberations unless such a good becomes the focus of a member of the agent's preference set. Rationality is now relative to the preference set whose optimum satisfaction is in view, but that is of course quite compatible with Green's insistence that whether a given course of conduct is optimally preference-satisfying for this agent is a matter of objective fact and thus subject to public judgement.[13] It is natural to define happiness as the maximal, optimum satisfaction of someone's preferences. Happiness is after all the satisfaction of one's desires.[14] This yields a new proof of Kant's point that what happiness consists in for creatures of our kind is unavoidably diverse: we have different preference sets. But we have seen reason to define rationality in conduct as the optimum satisfaction of preferences. So now it is analytic that everyone necessarily pursues happiness if they are rational. The *absurdam practicum* that any moral agent is involved in emerges starkly: reason in one mode says that I must strive for my happiness, while in its impartial mode it tells me that to do so is frequently wrong.

'Happiness is the optimum satisfaction of an agent's preference set' might seem to be a good way of fusing the notions of happiness as satisfaction and of happiness as success. A life in which my preferences are maximally satisfied would be the epitome of a successful one. And how could it fail to be felt and judged satisfying overall?

On reflection we shall find that the appearance that the economic conception of rationality solves Kant's problems is wholly illusory. First, we note that talk of an agent's 'preferences' trades on some of the ambiguities noted above. By 'preferences' we may mean an agent's felt desires, cravings or longings. Or we might mean by 'preferences' an agent's goals and ends as they are fixed in his or her intentions. If we concede, temporarily and for the sake of argument, that maximal satisfaction of preferences as desires or cravings is related to the realisation of happiness, it is not even plausible to suppose that rationality in conduct consists in such an optimum satisfaction of preferences so understood.

Preferences as desires and longings are not yet formed intentions. As rational agents human beings have, and must exercise, the means of deciding which of their desires and longings are worth satisfying. What they do when they exercise that power is reflect on the worthwhileness of the objects of those desires. We may note that we have a felt desire for something and rationally choose to pay no heed to that desire if it is directed to something which on reflection is not worthy of pursuit. What the model of rationality as optimum desire-satisfaction does is set arbitrary, *a priori* limits to rationality in conduct by insisting that, when a desire is set aside in forming intentions, this can only be because of the heed given to some other desire or desires whose fulfilment is incompatible with the one ignored. But this view contains a false emphasis on the inwardness and passivity of practical reason in human beings.[15]

If we view preferences as formed goals and ends embodied in an agent's intentions, then the thought that rationality consists in the optimum satisfaction of preferences has greater plausibility. At the least, it points us to the need for agents to act on consistent intentions and to act up to their settled intentions. These are certainly necessary conditions for rational action. But this is hardly a complete account of rationality in conduct. It leaves out of account all that we have alluded to in the above concerning how rational powers are exercised in choosing what actively to pursue and avoid, what intentions actually to form. It is evident also that there is no guarantee of happiness as a satisfying life to be got from the idea of the optimum attainment of an agent's goals and ends. We have noted above that circumstances may, and frequently do, force agents to abandon the pursuit of goods connected with their deepest ambitions, their most cherished interests. They may then act optimally to fulfil the intentions formed in the light of this renunciation. Their conduct is thus rational in a minimal sense, and may be rational in a deeper sense too, if their intentions are formed after due deliberation about what conduct is choice-worthy in the light of their settled conceptions of what is of central concern and value in their lives. Yet in these cases, the intentions of agents, though rationally formed and acted on, amount to abandoning the pursuit of happiness as a satisfying life.

So far the preference conception of happiness and practical rationality seems to be no advance in cementing the case that there is an *absurdam practicum* in finding that happiness and moral perfection are not jointly attainable, and in particular in showing that everyone is rationally bound to pursue happiness as a goal. We can now explore yet more difficulties in Green's reconstruction of Kant with a view to further clarifying the nature of happiness as a goal.

We have seen that the maximal satisfaction of preferences-as-desires does not yield a definition of rational conduct. Now we can see that it will not even yield a definition of happiness. First, we can note that satisfying even a strongly felt desire does not always bring satisfaction or happiness in mode one (that is, a feeling of joy). Fulfilling some deeply felt desire does of course bring the satisfaction of that desire, and there may be some felt satisfaction in no longer having a craving which is unmet. But that is not to say that if we satisfy lots of desires, we are bound to have lots of joyful experiences; still less does it mean that we will thereby be satisfied human beings and have happiness in mode two (a satisfying life). There is no commoner experience in human life than desiring something but finding it unrewarding once we attain it. There is a strong tradition in modern moral philosophy and action theory which wants to deny this. It preaches that the good for any human being is what that human being wants. This tradition can accept that false beliefs mean that what we want frequently does not satisfy us when we get it. For example, I might want to slake my thirst by drinking the glass of water in front of me. But drinking it will not satisfy me if, unbeknownst me, it has been spiked with salt. However, such argumentative manœuvres are feeble. People may find what they antecedently desire dissatisfying for all sorts of reasons. No reasonable view of the facts can ignore that frequently they are disappointed by virtue of having desired what is undesirable and bad for them. Our desires are frequently mistaken not because they are based on false factual beliefs, but because we desire the wrong things. It is part of life's education to learn better what is worth desiring through the experience of attaining the object of our desires. No amount of improved belief short of that experience could tell us whether such desires were for the desirable. The truth of this last point is a mark of the difference between being an actor in the world and a mere spectator of it. To know what is choice-worthy and desirable, we need the experience of those who make choices and act upon their desires. Such knowledge cannot be gained theoretically.

So far I have suggested against the preference view of happiness that maximally satisfying preferences cannot be a sufficient condition for happiness, since whether preferences are preferences for humanly satisfying objects and pursuits is not solely or mainly a matter of the internal relations between our preferences, but rather of the nature of those objects and pursuits themselves. These points will also work to show that preference satisfaction is not a necessary condition for happiness. We often are forced by circumstance to accept what we did not antecedently prefer and frequently find it satisfying. That is another way in which desire gets educated. Happiness just is not a matter of getting what you want and wanting what you get.

Green has tried to give more precise expression to Kant's thought that happiness consists in an existence in which 'everything goes according to wish and will'. The preference theory of the good allegedly does that and also provides a convenient definition of happiness. The failure of Green's attempt is the failure of an internalist, narrow and spectator-based conception of reason and happiness. This failure shows that Kant is guilty of a similar error to that he finds in the Stoics and Epicureans. He has two notions within his conception of happiness: contentment (happiness in mode two – a life found satisfying) and everything going according to one's plans (happiness in mode three – success). He thinks that they are analytically connected, so that pursuit of the one is necessarily pursuit of the other. But they are synthetically connected, if connected at all. Thus if we can link one conception to the minimal conditions for rational conduct, it does not follow that we can link the other to those conditions for rational conduct. The first part of Kant's *absurdam practicum* falls to the ground.

HAPPINESS AS A GOAL

The above discussion still leaves unclear what happiness might consist in and the precise nature of the demand that we act so as to secure happiness.

The central conception of happiness we want here is happiness in mode two: the reflective sense that a life has been overall a satisfying one. It is at best a substantive view about the life found to be satisfying (though, it appears, a false one) that it consists in the frequent possession of powerful experiences of joy. Likewise it is a substantive view about the satisfying life that it consists in success in achieving life's goals. This latter view is at least partly false, for the reasons given above – success in endeavour is not a sufficient condition for satisfaction in life. We might concede that at least some measure of success in endeavour was a necessary condition for happiness as satisfaction.

Kant is no doubt right to insist that it is a substantive view that happiness as satisfaction consists in *eudaimonia* – the fusion of faring well and cultivating the virtues. We cannot make true by definition the thought that happiness consists in *eudaimonia*. We cannot legislate that the pleasures of virtue are the only true ones. But this does not ditch the entirety of the Greek tradition's attempts to argue that the satisfying life for human beings is the life which realises the intellectual and moral virtues. There are, in writers such as Plato and Aristotle, arguments for the substantive claim that happiness for beings of our type is realisable only through cultivation of the virtues. Moreover, Kant's other favoured reason, noted above, for dismissing this tradition is weak. The fact that individuals have different goals and desires may suggest that what is a satisfied life will be different from case to case. But this is not to say that a common feature of all will not be the infusing of those concretely different lives by the same virtues. For the virtues may be realisable in concretely different styles of living, and give a common form to those styles. The virtues may be necessary to the realisation of a happy life even if such realisation takes manifold concrete shapes. Thus, to live a satisfied life may involve the virtue of courage, but one can display courage in many styles of life: in being a nurse, a teacher, a parent, a friend, and so on.

It is beyond the scope of this section to discuss the view that the satisfied life is also the virtuous life. Instead my target is the opposition in Kant's thought between the two orders of reason which produce the alleged *absurdam practicum* behind the postulate of God: the order of impartial, rational demands arising out of morality and the order of personal reasons arising from the search for happiness. Further reflection on the concept of happiness may show that the opposition between these orders of reason may be misplaced.

The key question is 'How, if at all, could happiness, as a life judged to be satisfying overall, be a goal of conduct?' It is only by thinking about happiness as a goal that we could think how the pursuit of happiness might or might not conflict with the pursuit of moral rectitude. The answer to our question lies in Dent's discussion of how agents may govern their lives by reference to a 'stable sense of significance'.[16] Happiness can only be a goal if agents have a conception of how their lives ought to be lived if they are to be lived satisfactorily. This will entail agents standing back from the press of any immediate desires and reflecting upon where their overall concerns, goals, ambitions and the like lie. This implies a standing back from desire both with a view to separating short-term from long-term concerns and with a view to distinguishing central from peripheral objects of pursuit. Moreover, if the objects pursued by an agent are not worthwhile in some way, agents may still fail of happiness even if they succeed in acquiring and acting on a stable sense of significance in their lives. Such a conception of an overall shape given to life by way of identification of worthwhile, central objects and pursuits may take many years to acquire and may undergo change once acquired, as, for example, agents gain knowledge of what genuinely satisfies them. But, for all that is difficult to attain and hold on to, a conception of an overall shape to life seems necessary if it is to be more than a jumble of satisfactions and disappointments following each other willy-nilly. Such a conception enables a thought of what an agent's happiness consists in and allows that thought to be acted upon. Reflection resulting in a conception of this kind will identify central interests and goals an agent holds dear. The pursuit of happiness as a satisfied life will be the pursuit of these interests and goals.

Now it is true that the interests and goals arising out of the stable sense of significance which may govern a life will connect the agent to many goods which are external to morality, in the manner set out in previous chapters. Virtuous conduct will be displayed in the way in which these central goals are pursued, but the ends in question will extend beyond those internal to the exercise of the virtues. So acting virtuously cannot guarantee that a satisfied life will be attained. Nonetheless it can be seen that action in pursuit of a reflective concern of this kind is typically dependent on factors of a moral kind.

A controlling sense of significance will depend on many of the things associated with development of the virtues. It will depend on the direction and education of the agent's desires. (Virtues like continence and temperance will thus be important.) It will depend on the intellectual, deliberative virtues and on the ability to display some wisdom in identifying what the agent truly finds desirable among the many claims competing for his or her attention, and in deciding how such things are to be gained. Once we have an agent set on identifying and pursuing long-term and central goals, then an executive virtue such as courage will be important as trials and temptations hindering pursuit of those goals are faced.

The above may go some way to show that the Kantian picture of two orders of reason – morality being slapped on top of an amoral rational pursuit of happiness – is false. This point can be reinforced by reminding

ourselves of the thought set out in previous chapters that many interests of
the typical human agent will be unintelligible outside of moral ties that
bind that agent to others. If I endeavour to reflect on what my abiding
central concerns are, I will identify many that arise out of my relation with
others. My interests as this person's friend, that person's business partner,
this other's parent will be fused with the interests of these others. I will
have these interests only because I share a life with them. This is indeed one
reason why my satisfaction is bound up with goods external to my own
strivings. I do not need a moral order in society solely or mainly for the
purposes of pursuing my interests without fear of interference from others.
I am a member of a moral order in having the interests I have, because as a
person I am constituted in some of my central concerns through my
relationships to others.

The point about the dependence of the self with its interests upon the
moral order can be strengthened by reference to a further insight about the
self's dependence on membership of a moral order found in a whole range
of authors. This is the insight that for agents actively to grasp and pursue
their own conception of the good, they must be possessed of a sense of self-
respect or self-worth. But such a sense of self-worth is only possible if I see
myself as someone who matters in the eyes of others. That I am a *person*, a
being whose interests and good matter, consists in it being true that my
concerns are to be taken account of when others pursue their ends. I am not
just an object which can be ignored or used as others think fit. I deserve and
gain recognition from others as a being who matters. My sense of standing
and worth grows, and could only grow, out of my awareness that others
recognise me as a creature deserving of respect. In the love, esteem or
respect others accord me I find confirmation of my desire to see myself as a
something that matters and not as mere nothingness.

Thus my sense of self-respect and self-worth depend on my membership
of a moral community, that is a society of agents prepared to grant each
other respect and concern.

What do the above arguments on the self and the moral order establish?
They do not show that wickedness is impossible, still less that none of the
wicked will prosper (though they do point to the instability of wickedness).
They still allow that some individuals may perceive a pervasive divorce
between the claims of self-interest and those of morality.

Despite the above, our reflections on the nature of happiness and self-
worth do suggest that there is no appropriate general contrast between two
orders of reason: the one derived from the internal demands of preference
satisfaction and happiness; the other derived from the claims of morality
and impartial right. Happiness as a life goal, if possible of fulfilment at all,

will demand some of the disciplining of desire and choice typical of a virtuous life. Moreover, we are constituted as beings with a set of interests and sense of self-worth and respect through relations with others and through our membership of a moral order.

Green tries to defend the *absurdam practicum* argument for the postulate of God by stressing the pressing character of the question 'Why should I be moral?' Having dealt with the question 'Why should there be morality at all?', which might lurk behind 'Why should I be moral?', Green takes it to be a question about why it should be rational for *me* to be moral. This question gets its force because there is a persistent tension between self-interest and morality, a tension connected with the fact that reason has two employments which are essentially distinct: the prudential and the moral.[17] We have seen how this doctrine is enforced by the preference account of reason and the good. With that account 'Why should I be moral?' becomes for Green the question 'Does paying heed to moral demands maximise the satisfaction of my preferences?' The fact that this question sharply conflicts with the question 'What do the demands of impartial right tell me to do?' generates the *absurdam practicum* which then leads to the invoking of supernatural mechanisms which ensure that in the long run both questions can be met with a list of the same set of actions.

This section has raised doubts about this entire approach from three directions. First, prudential reason directed towards determining and pursuing what my happiness is will be concerned with something very different from the maximisation of satisfied preferences. It will be concerned with establishing a sense of my deepest concerns, which will in turn evoke reflection about the worth of many of my preferences and disciplining and moulding of those preferences. All this shows the continuity between prudential and moral reason. Second, many of my preferences will in fact arise out of, and be conceptually dependent on, morally structured relations with others. Third, the self which seeks to satisfy the requirements of prudential reason will have status, worth and thus an antidote to self-doubt and despair, only because it is bound in a web of mutual recognition with others. Because of this it must recognise a range of basic moral requirements. And it must do so wholeheartedly: it cannot say 'I need, in general, a moral ordered society to give a stable background to the pursuit of my own prudential goals, so I will go along with many moral demands so as to sustain this society'. It must recognise the moral standing of others in order to count their recognition of itself as worthwhile. If the encouragement to self-respect I gather from others' recognition of me as more than a mere object is to be genuine, I must regard those others as persons in their own right. If I regard them as objects of contempt, having a use value only, then the recognition they give to me is worthless.

So, for these reasons, the divorce between prudential and moral reason is wildly overblown in Green's reconstruction of Kant's *absurdam practicum*. The most forceful presentation of the basis of Kant's argument for the postulate of God thus fails. I shall return in the last section of this chapter to the question of what rational force might remain in the desire to have a supernatural guarantee of happiness. But before that topic can be broached we must turn our attention to the other half of reason's demands on the moral agent: the duty to be morally perfect.

KANT AND THE DEMAND TO PURSUE MORAL PERFECTION

We have seen that Kant's complete good for human beings is happiness as the accompaniment of moral perfection. He contends that we are required to promote the highest good and a component of that is 'the complete fitness of dispositions with the moral law'.[18] So we are obliged to pursue this morally perfected state. The 'ought implies can' principle yields the sub-conclusion that it must be possible for us to pursue or attain this perfected state and then we have swift recourse to the notion of an after-life as the only way of making such pursuit intelligible.

This argument is open to obvious objections. One objection arises out of the deliberate ambiguity in my summary of Kant's reasoning: is it our duty in reason to *pursue* a morally perfected state or to *attain* it? The individual bent on attaining human virtue must endeavour to become more and more virtuous. Must he or she become virtuous, on pain of failing the requirements of moral reason? Robert Adams' comment on this issue seems eminently sensible: 'In any reasonable morality we will be obligated to promote only the best attainable approximation of the highest good'.[19] Applied to the demand to seek moral perfection as the condition for attaining happiness, Adams' point leads on to the following observation: surely all that our obligation to seek virtue entails is that it should be possible to engage in this pursuit, not that we should be guaranteed ultimate success. Kant himself says at one point that it is our duty to strive for perfection not to achieve it.[20] Provided that there are frequent occasions when something counts as choosing virtue over vice, and thus as strengthening virtuous dispositions in us, then perfection in virtue can be pursued. Such a pursuit would be impossible in practice, and therefore not mandated if we accept the 'ought implies can' principle, only if our state were commonly like this: we are for the most part faced with choices which are only between one evil act and another. Very rarely, or not at all, can we choose to express and strengthen virtuous dispositions and weaken vicious ones. I presume we can accept that this utterly bleak picture of the human condition is false overall (even though some dire human circumstances answer to it).

It may be objected that this way of dealing with Kant's demand that we be morally perfect does not meet his claim in Book I of the *Religion* that all of us suffer from a primordial guilt. We show, according to Kant, a predisposition to subsume moral considerations under amoral ones. It is as if we have all made a prior choice for evil and against good. So the problem we face is not simply that we cannot attain perfect goodness in this life, but rather that we seem unable to throw off evil. Yet we face the constant demand to choose the good. Hence, we are confronted with the moral gap: the gulf between the 'ought' that confronts us daily and the 'can' which points to our moral inability to meet that 'ought'.[21] Since we ought to throw off evil we know we can – otherwise the 'ought' would be out of place. We know, however, that we cannot do so by our own efforts. Therefore the machinery of the postulates is engaged.

Putting Kant's argument about moral perfection in terms of the need for us to escape from evil does not increase its cogency in my view. Its logic invites sending the argument into reverse: since we ought to escape from evil, we know we can and we know therefore that we do not need external aid in so doing. We cannot at once be said to suffer a deep moral guilt and at the same time be said to be powerless to choose against evil. For we cannot be guilty of that which is beyond our control. Moreover the notion that we might bear a primordial guilt is one that already seems to involve a relationship to a religious reality. We are indeed guilty of individual infractions of the moral law. But the claim that we should feel guilty over and above these for some primal fault is unlikely to appeal to anyone who does not already use religious categories, who does not already think that, over and above wrong to oneself and other human beings, we also do wrong to a commanding God when we do evil. The points arising out of Adams' comments on the main Kantian argument on moral perfection still seem to stand. So long as we are still faced with choices between good and evil (and not between evil and evil) and can conceive of ourselves making better choices than in the past, then we can hope for a closer approximation to goodness in the future.

The obvious criticisms of Kant just aired gain even more force from the fact, noted in the previous chapter, that when Kant presents the postulate of immortality in the second *Critique* it transpires that the after-life does not guarantee that we shall attain virtue, but merely that our endless progress will continue. God's perspective on our acts is required to ensure that this progress can be counted as if it were complete. In the *Religion* the timeless, God's-eye view of our fundamental dispositions takes over completely from the progress to virtue in the after-life to explain (albeit, most mysteriously) how we can deem ourselves worthy of happiness. We are left with a rational demand that we conceive of some perspective on our fundamental moral orientation whose possibility enables us in turn to count ourselves worthy of happiness. The concept of God provides the means whereby we can give the notion of this gracious view upon ourselves some content.

The problem with these thoughts is not just their inherent unclarity, but, more importantly for present purposes, whether they can be seen to be the result of the demands of reason. Moral reason does demand that I act virtuously when occasion arises and thus that I mature in virtue. Some substantive, if minimal, beliefs about our human condition do seem to be presupposed by that demand. If life forever presented me with choices only between one evil act and another, then the demand would be out of place. But what we don't yet see is how, in the other half of the alleged *absurdam practicum*, we face a rational demand to attain perfected virtue.

We clearly have a settled element in Kant's *Weltanschauung* which reflects an ideal for moral striving centring on the notion of human perfection. Human beings are to have natural and moral perfection as an ideal before them. The thought of happiness accompanying human life that is not perfected is regarded as intolerable. There are numerous duties, perfect and imperfect, arising of the goal of natural and moral perfection.[22] Kant is clearly an heir to a long philosophical tradition linking morality to the ideal of human perfection. Equally clearly, he has difficulties in reconciling the demands of that tradition with the Augustinian teaching within German Protestantism which teaches the radical evil of humanity, an evil which infects the human will.

In pursuit of whatever may help us to see perfection as a necessary goal, we can note that Kant does teach that the categorical imperative is a necessary requirement on all rational conduct and at the same time reads the ideal of human perfection into some of his formulations of it. The first formula of the categorical imperative in the *Groundwork of the Metaphysics of Morals* is 'act only in accordance with that maxim through which you can at the same time will that it should become a universal law'.[23] This is said by Kant to be equivalent to two other formulae which contain strong elements of the ideal of perfection: 'So act that you use humanity, whether in your own person or in the person of any other, always at the same time as an end, never merely as a means', and 'all maxims from one's own lawgiving are to harmonise with a possible kingdom of ends as with a kingdom of nature'[24] These formulae link the idea of morality as consisting in respect for the demands of universal, impartial legislation to the idea that morality is the means whereby we respect human beings as ends in themselves and whereby we can create a community in which all of us flourish harmoniously as ends in ourselves. The formulae dealing in the idea of human beings as ends have an obvious teleological element. They imply a view of human agency as something whose nature possesses inherent value, which therefore contains a good which should be promoted and perfected. Thus Kant is happy to illustrate the second formula by considering the wrong in committing suicide. One who acts thus violates human nature considered as an end: 'I cannot dispose of a human being in my own person by maiming, damaging or killing him'.[25]

In this discussion I have followed those who have taken the second and third formulations of the categorical imperative to be treating human agency as an absolute value, whose nature and flourishing morality is there to respect and promote.[26] Kant thinks these formulations are equivalent to the first. Such equivalence can be seen if we contend that the formula of universal law-making also has a central concern with the value of agency. The formula is not to be interpreted as giving us the simple test 'What would it be like if everyone acted like me?' Rather it expresses the thought 'Let me test my maxim by asking if it could be freely adopted and accepted by everyone'. A maxim allowing me to kill, hurt, deceive or deny aid to others could not be thought of as likely to be adopted by others. I could act on such maxims only if I do not give others the chance to accept them and if I hide from them my own adoption of them. I thereby do not respect their agency. The acts that flow from such maxims will typically assault the agency of others, impairing their ability to act as agents with their own projects and plans. In this way the universal law formula links up with those bidding us to respect others as ends in themselves and to aspire to live in a community in which all can flourish as ends.[27]

As I read Kant (with the help of Herman and O'Neil), we have to attribute to him a substantive belief in the inherent value of human, rational agency to make the formulae of the categorical imperative equivalent and thereby allow his ethical system to work. It will not do, for example, to interpret the formulae to do with ends after the fashion of contemporary social contract theory as implied by Green.[28] On Green's account (which he derives from Rawls), moral principles are those everyone would accept if constrained to judge impartially. We imagine everyone joining together to agree on rules to govern a society and being forced to judge impartially by passing through a veil of ignorance. This deprives them of knowledge of who they are and thus of the particular preferences they have. All they know about human nature are its generic features and the range of interests human beings can have. It is then argued both that whatever rules would be agreed on in this situation would be the moral rules (for they would embody universality, free consent and a radical kind of impartiality) and that these rules would be the ones we take to be typical of social morality. All these antecedent co-legislators would accept customary rules forbidding violence, harm and deceit towards others and mandating basic forms of benevolence and co-operation. But this cannot be all that Kant has in mind by the test of the categorical imperative, for it is notorious that the contractarian approach leads to principles designed to grant the maximum liberty to each, compatible with leaving the liberty of others undisturbed. Since no substantive, rich human goods are allowed to mould the thinking of the co-legislators (if they did this would not be a contractarian deduction of ethics), only principles of social morality restricting conduct which interferes with the liberty of others' pursuit of their own private preferences come out of the procedure. So Kant's panoply of perfect and imperfect duties to oneself, reflecting the requirements of natural and moral perfection, are absent. Perfectionism is precisely left behind. For on the minimal requirements of impartial rationality embedded within the contractarian picture, the aim is to promote the maximum liberty of each to pursue his or her preferences. Neglecting myself or even destroying myself in an act of suicide are not wrong if so acting does not violate others' interests. By the same token, actions of mutilation, assault or what have you committed by one person on another are going to be difficult to rule out should the victim permit or request them.

Further debate is of course possible on how far the apparently formal principle that is the first formulation of the categorical imperative will or will not allow one to deduce the perfectionist ends and principles of Kant's ethics. That he has these ends and principles and that they are close to the heart of his understanding of his ethical system is evident from the *Groundwork* and *The Metaphysics of Morals*. My provisional verdict, naturally rebuttable, agrees with that provided by Keith Ward: 'To understand his ethical theory, one must . . . penetrate behind the terminology in which it is expressed . . . to the underlying teleological view, which is frequently and unmistakably outlined in his many published works'.[29] That teleology involves the substantive belief that morality is concerned, amongst other things, with natural and moral perfection. In calling this a 'substantive' belief, I am registering my judgement that these concerns cannot be deduced from the demands of impartial rationality as such. Kant interprets those demands in the light of inherited, perfectionist teleologies. If I am right about this, then we have further ground for doubting Kant's claim that reason as such demands that we pursue the perfect good and adopt a world picture which will enable us to see how that perfect good is attainable.

THE STATUS OF KANT'S MORAL INTERPRETATION OF RELIGION

We are now in a position to assess the force and value of Kant's moral interpretation of religion. We have found a mixture of strength and weakness.

Kant's account of the function and meaning of religious language in relation to morality is one of the stronger parts of his account. Kant offers a revisionary realist portrayal of religious language which has many advantages. It embodies, we noted, a sharp version of the ancient distinction between what our words for the divine signify and the way they signify it. The content of our symbols for the divine are human, in two important respects. The symbols draw upon human analogies for conceiving the divine, and human interests, particularly moral ones, control and shape the use of these symbols. Yet these symbols putatively point beyond themselves to a transcendent ground of the given world whose nature we cannot know. But we do not need to know it, since the legitimate role that this postulate can play in our lives is in the area of practice, in particular in giving us the confidence to pursue good and justice with hope of ultimate success. In giving religious language this role, Kant thereby connects it with the permanent and vital interests of humankind and tries to show that it is not an optional extra in human discourse.

The advantages of this account will be seen by those who cannot accept an unmodified, unqualified realist view of religious discourse yet who wish to avoid the alternatives of reductionism or non-cognitivism. Realism, unvarnished, must among other things embody the thought that the important aspects of the content of religious discourse are best explained by the hypothesis of contact between speakers and divine reality. It is very tempting indeed to see the chief facets of human talk of the divine as anchored in human interests and as lacking any signs of a reality beyond those interests – herein lies the strength of accounts of religion's development in human terms alone.[30] The Kantian portrayal avoids the burdens of explaining religious language as the outcome of cognitive commerce between humanity and a divine reality. Yet we have seen it also affirms that this language is a necessary element in articulating human concerns and preserves the idea that such language is intended to point beyond the human world to something which transcends it.

We have found the weakest part of Kant's moral interpretation to lie in his arguments for saying that we are all under a rational necessity to use this language. We can concede, in the light of the discussions in Chapter 2, that important human interests are reflected in Kant's postulates of the existence of God and of immortality. Those who respect morality and its claims will feel that morality calls us to conquer evil and that morality's point is threatened if the hope of triumph over evil is lost. Yet we have seen that the Kantian arguments for the postulates do not really establish that we are rationally bound, on pain of otherwise living with a contradiction at the very root of practical reason, to believe that there is an extra-human mechanism which will guarantee the defeat of evil. Kant's arguments trade in too many questionable assumptions about the nature of happiness and goodness to allow us to say that he has shown that belief in a moral order behind the given world is rationally required of us.

Let us return to a point made at the beginning of Chapter 3. We have tried to steer a middle course between two appraisals of Kant's moral interpretation. Michalson would have us believe that the works setting out the moral interpretation are valuable as testimonies to the divided, fractured thought of their age. They unwittingly tell us something about the predicament the 'modern self' has got into, and that is all. Green would have us believe that Kant has discovered the universal, necessary and rational links between morality and religion. Kant has shown why finite rational agents as such are committed to the use of religious symbols and has displayed the true meaning of religious symbols wherever and whenever we find them.

As against Michalson, we have shown that Kant has a version of revisionary realism in the interpretation of religion which is at least viable in its broadest terms (ignoring the details of Kant's account of specific symbols such as the Atonement and the Incarnation in the *Religion*). There are good reasons why Kant's account should leave us with mysteries in the precise explication of religious symbols, mysteries which arise out of Kant's version of 'the thing signified versus the way it is signified' distinction. Genuinely human moral and religious interests and dilemmas lie behind Kant's nuanced, practically based religious realism. As against Green, we have argued that the postulates rest on arguments which are a clear reflection of key items in Kant's *Weltanschauung*, but not a reflection of any inescapable demands of moral reason as such.

Part of what is involved in rejecting Green's appraisal of Kant is the denial of Green's portrait of 'Religious Reason' as the universal core of religion throughout history and the chief, if hidden, mechanism which determines the shape of the various religions. In both of his books on this topic, Green opts for an 'essence and manifestation' view of the nature of religion. Such a view tells us that there is an invariant core to religion and that the surface features of religion are to be explained by virtue of the setting of this core in the varied social and historical circumstances of humankind. Religions as historical, manifest entities are the result of the interaction between the essence of religion and the particularities of social and historical life. Thus Green writes of there being a 'deep structure' to human religion.[31] He lists 'the requirements of pure religious reason'.[32] These correspond to the rational, moral requirements on religion Kant's writings defend. The general character of the doctrines of particular religions and specific, key episodes in the development of religions are then explained by virtue of the deep structure and the requirements of religious reason. In this way, moral philosophy, and Kant's moral philosophy in particular, provides *the* hermeneutic for rendering the sense of religion. This thought is self-consciously modelled on the details of Kant's *Religion* where a close correspondence is postulated between items of Christian symbolism and doctrine on the one hand, and the requirements of moral philosophy on the other. It is noticeable that in the *Religion* Kant says that there is but one religion though there are many faiths.[33] The one religion is the inner awareness of the demands of moral reason which may be variously manifested in different ecclesiastical/historical entities. He says that a scripture such as the Bible has in effect two meanings. One historical scholarship can elucidate and relates to the surface meaning the text had in the context of its time and place; another the moral philosopher reveals and that moral meaning of the scripture is the primary and true meaning.[34]

In the view that it reveals the essence of religion, the moral interpretation of religion gains an extra dimension. It is one which has the implication that the philosopher of religion is the primary interpreter of religion and the religions. Now these pretensions attaching to the moral interpretation must fall if it is not after all demanded by reason. If human beings are not rationally compelled to give religious symbols the meaning Kant gives them, there is no ground to say that their one and only true meaning is that dictated by Kantian philosophy of morals and religion. The motive to see the moral interpretation as uncovering the essence to religion collapses.

Despite the above criticism of Green's (and Kant's) procedure, we can save part of the intent behind his argument by considering some trenchant criticisms offered of these Kantian efforts to find an essence to religion.

These are to be found in a critique of Green by Michael Levine.[35] Levine offers some general criticisms of attempts to find an invariant essence to religions. Such approaches are too prescriptive and *a priori*. They will favour just one discipline in the study of religions and deny the need for methodological pluralism. But Levine has a specific complaint against the Kantian approach: the stress on moral reason as the primary determinant of religion hides the truth that religions are primarily systems of cultural-linguistic symbols. To see them as such is to see them as reflecting and caused by a variety of factors beyond the demands of reason in a people's life. It is to see them as bound up with the rest of their culture, arising out of it and helping to shape it. Thus philosophy cannot pretend to be the primary interpreter of religion. Other disciplines such as anthropology must be given equal or greater weight.

Levine's case is unobjectionable so far as it goes. However, we find that it unexpectedly uncovers a strength in the Kantian approach to religion when it draws on the writings of one of the key sources of the cultural-symbolic approach to religion: Clifford Geertz. Geertz too sees religions as primarily systems of cultural-linguistic symbols and he is famous for his observation that it is the primary purpose of this particular kind of symbolic system to integrate the world view and the ethos of a society.[36] By 'world view' Geertz understands a society's picture of the structure of reality. By 'ethos' he understands those values it lives by. A religion is a set of symbols which establishes in the mind of its adherents a meaningful relation between the values they hold dear and their picture of the general order of existence: 'Sacred symbols thus relate an ontology and a cosmology to an aesthetics and a morality: their peculiar power comes from their presumed ability to identify fact with value at the most fundamental level.'[37] In thus bringing a particular value set in congruence with a metaphysics, religions enable the authority of the one to lend support to the authority of the other. Without this felt congruence, people face a problem of motivation and meaning, arising out of the many occasions when pursuit of the goals mandated by their value system is frustrated by the contingencies of existence. So elsewhere Geertz is able to define religion by reference to the way in which it establishes 'powerful, pervasive, and long-lasting moods and motivations'. These 'motivations' are vested with authority and reality by being related to 'conceptions of a general order of existence'.[38]

The reason why critics of the Kantian interpretation of religion feel able to cite Geertz's cultural-symbolic conception of religion as evidence in their favour is as follows: Geertz naturally sees the content of the symbol system that is any given religion as arising out of the historical and cultural life of a given people. The notion that there is something called 'religious reason' which generates similar patterns of thought across all religions is thus questioned. However, Geertz's general approach does suggest a minimal, common form to all religions and that common form is closely related to Kantian themes. The form arises out of the need to close the gap between value and reality, between the world as it ideally should be given human values and the world as we find it. In Kant's system the world of values is the world of reason. The world as we find it is that revealed by science and history. These two worlds appear to conflict. The sheer givenness of the second world seems to prevent completion of the task of creating in external form a world to match the requirements of reason. Religion embodies the faith that these two worlds can ultimately be reconciled. But this matches the Geertzian picture closely: the moral interpretation of religion locates its minimal essence in the thought that the deepest human values and the most fundamental ontological structures cohere. This coherence allows us to think that a project of pursuing human good is viable.

The Kantian interpretation of religion can indeed be seen to cohere at a deeper level still with the anthropologist's understanding of the cultural rootedness of religious symbols. For once we have set aside his arguments for saying that the concept of a God with the 'omni' attributes is normative, Kant's account of religious language allows us to recognise that many different symbol systems can be used to relate value to ontology in the manner required. Kant's revisionary realism leaves as finally unimportant what precise imaginative content surrounds the thought 'Reality as a whole is such that the gap between value and the given world will be overcome'. Thus it can appreciate the historical rootedness of religious symbols systems. Moreover, Kantian interpretation provides a way of filtering out what, from a developed moral point of view, might be seen to be the harmful consequences of the use of symbols of the most real to buttress a people's ethos. By telling us that no reliance can be placed on any particular religious symbols as pictures of religious reality, Kantianism purges away the temptation to let the power of such symbols weaken human effort to realise values in the given world. That temptation is, of course, the one manifesting itself in the idea that the gods might be manipulated or persuaded to bring about our moral goals for us.

The upshot of the above links between Kantian and anthropological theorising about religion is this: while recognising the weakness of the claim that Kant has uncovered detailed demands of 'religious reason', his interpretation of religion is a philosophical gloss on what appears to be a necessary and foundational element in the nature of religion.

So, my conclusion on Kant's moral interpretation of religion is this. It fails to show that the postulates of God and immortality (or any equivalents of them) are rationally necessary for human agents. But it does succeed in relating religion to fundamental human needs and in articulating in a sophisticated fashion a common thread in religion as such. Moreover, it does offer an interpretation of religion which retains a minimal realism, while yet removing the necessity of judging the precise, imaginative content of any set of religious symbols to be true.

Examination of Kant confirms a thought pressed from the beginnings of this study onwards. Religion is rooted in the human response to evil. By 'evil' here we mean those factors in human nature and human circumstances which militate against attaining a full, assured form of the human good. Religion responds to evil by offering a metaphysical, ontological commitment made through the means of imaginative symbols. It contains some version of the thought that the given world, with its structures of agency and causation, is not all that there is but masks deeper levels of reality, agency and causation which will not ultimately block the attainment of human good. There seems to be reason for saying that without this thought nothing could count as a religious view of reality. If that is the case, then a moral interpretation of religion which abandons it leaves religious realism behind and enters the territory of reductionism or non-cognitivism. Kant remains faithful to this thought, essential to the defining of a religious outlook. His value as an interpreter of religion lies in two things. First, he shows just how exiguous this thought of an ontological mechanism buttressing morality can get yet still survive, thus allowing the philosopher imbued with a large measure of religious agnosticism to retain it. Second, he shows why this thought needs to have a cash value which is immanent within the human moral struggle if it is not to undermine that moral struggle.

Now we are in a position to sum up what is at stake in opting for the moral interpretation of religion. The moral interpretation will be plausible to those who think we have good grounds (philosophical and historical) for a radical religious agnosticism, but who think we cannot abandon the minimal postulation of a mechanism in reality buttressing moral effort. The general issues at play in the plausibility of radical agnosticism have been aired in Chapter 1. The gravest objection to the second component of the moral interpretation is that aired in Chapter 2 deriving from John Kekes' characterisation of it as giving in to 'false hope' and a 'transcendental temptation'. I found reasons for questioning Kekes' dismissal of the belief in a transcendent support for moral agency in Chapter 2. Our discussion of Kant highlights and adds to those reasons. We have seen that

Kant can divorce commitment to the reality of moral order from commitment to the literal truth of any given religious symbol set. We have seen that his notion of the ethical commonwealth can root the pay-off of the commitment to something within the ethical life. These two points should tell against Kekes' implication that the moral interpretation licenses something akin to myth making. Moreover, Kant's distinctive notion of moral faith points to the way in which the commitment behind the moral interpretation can survive while lacking the force of a well-evidenced belief, so that it does not have to be seen as an inference from the facts of the given world (which is then deemed improbable *ex hypothesi*). Finally, Kant's reflections on the relation between the minimal metaphysical commitment of the moral interpretation and history reinforce the argument for the inadequacy of Kekes' own response to evil. Let us appeal, Kekes argues, to the institutions of morality in order to create a human response to evil. Kant on history highlights the point that such a response is naïve unless backed up by a sense of history's progress, which sense will in turn introduce the metaphysical commitment Kekes wishes to eschew.

NOTES

1. Kant *Critique of Practical Reason*, pp. 214–15 [5/93].
2. See, for example, Kant *Groundwork*, p .68 [4/415–16].
3. Kant *The Metaphysics of Morals*, p. 517 [6/385–6].
4. Tatarkiewicz *The Analysis of Happiness*, pp. 1–7.
5. Tatarkiewicz *The Analysis of Happiness*, p. 4.
6. *Critique of Practical Reason*, p. 161 [5/28].
7. *Groundwork*, p. 49 [4/393].
8. As in *Critique of Practical Reason*, p. 156 [5/22].
9. *Groundwork*, p. 59 [4/405].
10. *Critique of Practical Reason*, p. 240 [5/124].
11. Hare *The Moral Gap*, p. 88.
12. Wood *Kant's Moral Religion*, p. 53.
13. Green *Religious Reason*, p. 16.
14. Green *Religious Reason*, p. 61.
15. For a critique of the inwardness and passivity of this account of reason in conduct see Byrne *Foundations of Ethics*, pp. 102–7.
16. Dent *The Moral Psychology of the Virtues*, p. 112; I draw on pp. 106–29 in what follows.
17. Green *Religious Reason*, pp. 4–5.
18. Kant *Critique of Practical Reason*, p. 238 [5/122].
19. Adams 'Moral Arguments for Theistic Belief,' p. 151.
20. Kant *Metaphysics of Morals*, p. 567 [6/446].
21. See Hare *The Moral Gap*, p. 23ff. for a reconstruction of Kant's argument along these lines.
22. See Kant *Metaphysics of Morals*, p. 565ff. [6/442ff.].
23. Kant *Groundwork*, p. 73 [4/421].
24. Kant *Groundwork*, p. 80 [4/429] and p. 86 [4/436].
25. Kant *Groundwork*, p. 80 [4/429].
26. See Herman *The Practice of Moral Judgement*, pp. 236–9, and O'Neil *Constructions of Reason*, pp. 126–44.
27. See O'Neil *Constructions of Reason*, pp. 138–9.
28. *Religious Reason*, pp. 21–4, and see Byrne *Foundations of Ethics*, p. 89ff.
29. Ward *The Development of Kant's View of Ethics*, p. 118.

30. For elaboration of the above points see Byrne *Prolegomena to Religious Pluralism*, ch. 7.
31. Green *Religion and Moral Reason*, p. 3.
32. Green *Religious Reason*, p. 109.
33. Kant *Religion*, p. 140 [6/107–8].
34. Kant *Religion*, pp. 143–6 [6/112–15].
35. Levine 'Deep Structure and the Comparative Philosophy of Religion'.
36. Geertz *The Interpretation of Culture*, p. 127.
37. Geertz *The Interpretation of Culture*, p. 127.
38. Geertz *The Interpretation of Culture*, p. 90.

5

Iris Murdoch's Moral Platonism

THE GENERAL CHARACTER OF MURDOCH'S APPROACH

Our discussion of Kant on the moral interpretation of religion has revealed both profit and loss. On the credit side, we can see in Kant the basis for a portrayal of religion which is metaphysically agnostic but which holds on to a minimal religious realism. We have seen, in addition, that through the use of Kant we can present the moral interpretation as giving us something which is close to the essence of religion. On the debit side, we noted the weakness of Kant's arguments for the conclusion that religion when reinterpreted in moral terms is rationally inescapable.

We now turn to contemporary philosophical writings to trace the current state of the moral interpretation of religion. Here we will be concerned to match the Kantian account of moral faith against the accounts of moral faith offered by living writers. The aim will be to see both if they are true to the essence of religion as this has apparently been laid bare by Kant and if they offer alternative ways of grounding the moral interpretation to Kant. Iris Murdoch's writings are important for our purposes because they have attracted attention as a contemporary moral interpretation of religion and because they ground moral faith not on an account of the demands of practical reason but upon a phenomenology of morals.

Starting with her early work on vision and choice in morality,[1] Iris Murdoch has been concerned to explore the phenomenology of morals. This exploration has led her to question the subjectivist and prescriptivist accounts of moral language and epistemology long dominant in post-war moral philosophy. In their place she substitutes an account of morals turning around the linked notions of reality and vision. Moral judgement is seen as arising out of the subject's vision, not his or her will. The object of that vision is moral reality. The themes of vision and reality in her work introduce a religiously loaded description of the moral life. The kind of vision required for moral discovery is likened to religious mysticism. The reality that is the object of this vision acquires some of the attributes of the divine: transcendence, supreme perfection, necessary existence.

While all the components in the above sketch need to be expounded and explored at greater length, we can already see the justice in Gordon Graham's description of Murdoch's account of the ethical as 'spiritua-lised morality'.[2] This spiritualised morality is articulated by the terms of what Graham styles as Murdoch's 'moral Platonism'. The correlative notions of vision and reality in Murdoch's account of morality are given richer expression through the link she makes between them and the notion of the Good, conceived of along the lines of a Platonic form. What moral vision strives for is a right perception of the Good – something immanent in the circumstances of moral perplexity and yet transcending them. Through moral vision we see the given world as mediating the Good towards us. So, Murdoch invokes the language of Platonist metaphysics to characterise properly the relation between vision and reality in the moral life.

Graham sees Murdoch's moral Platonism as having three key features.[3] First, the idea of the Good that features in it is thought of as independent of the human will: something abstract yet real which we do not create or control. Second, the Good commands our attention and draws us towards it. Third, we need to go through a process of moral purification in order to see the Good aright. Perception of it arises out of virtue and ethically correct apprehension. Thus the form of the Good as it is so tellingly portrayed in Plato's metaphors of the Sun, Line and Cave in *The Republic* is reused by Murdoch to express her spiritualised vision of morality.

So the object and form of moral apprehension acquire a religious dimension for Murdoch. She is able to use a religiously rich vocabulary in characterising the moral life. Via this vocabulary she suggests the conclusion that morality is at least an important way in which religious apprehension manifests itself in human life. But further, in Murdoch's hands morality becomes *the* interpreter of what is permanently valid in religion. This is not to say that she dismisses manifestations of religion that are not immediately moral (in such areas as: liturgies, art and forms of spirituality). Rather, the redeeming sense of religion is given by spiritua-lised morality. Murdoch's writings on morality and religion help them-selves liberally to the notion of myth, and she comes to distinguish between religion proper and myth, which may be the vehicle of religion.[4] Religion proper is then defined in moral terms: 'Religion is a mode of belief in the unique sovereign place of goodness or virtue in human life'.[5] The use of 'myth' to characterise other elements of religion beyond spiritualised morality is indicative of the many adverse comments Murdoch makes in her writings about the permanent value and detailed truth of those religious symbols which purport to go beyond what she defines as religion proper.

The reader should recognise in the above the very strong affinities between Murdoch and Kant on the essence of religion.

The way is now open to see how Iris Murdoch offers a moral interpretation of religion which is, in intention, a version of revisionary realism and which is therefore within the broad tradition of Kant. To see this more clearly, we should note how, even while praising the project of 'demythologising' traditional religious thought-forms, she firmly distinguishes her spiritualised morality from the interpretation of religion offered by Cupitt in his *Taking Leave of God*. Cupitt's account of the reality of God in that book is based on the postulation of a religious requirement or imperative in human beings. This is an autonomous yet authoritative demand upon us to pursue spiritual growth and enlightenment. 'God' is not the name of an object, external to human life, towards which the spiritual quest might be taking us. It is rather the name of a reality created in human life, in human consciousness by the operation of the religious imperative:

> We chose to be religious because it is better so to be. We must strive with all our might to become spirit, and what God is appears in the striving to answer this call. God is, quite simply, what the religious requirement comes to mean to us as we respond to it. A religion is a cluster of spiritual values.[6]

Though she welcomes some aspects of Cupitt's attempt to rethink the idea that 'God' refers to a transcendent, personal being, she criticises him for being an 'expressive voluntarist'; for his denial of any transcendent goal for human thought and transcendent reference for religious language; for his reliance on Nietzsche and Derrida and above all for his anti-Platonism.[7] Whatever is wrong with 'mythological' religion for Murdoch, it is not that it has tried to transcend the self. Murdoch affirms:

> all religions make use of our ability to express and experience spiritual and moral aspiration by taking particular contingent things

as symbolic of, or signals toward, a reality thought of as more or less veiled from us by our own egoism.[8]

Murdoch's moral Platonism is precisely a way of saving some kind of transcendent reference for religion not a Cupitt-style rejection of it. (In this regard, her heavily critical discussion of Derrida in chapter 7 of *Metaphysics as a Guide to Morals* is very telling.) What precise form of transcendence she is interested in saving remains to be determined.

The apposition of Murdoch and Cupitt makes it timely to bring out some further detail from Sprigge's discussion of the difference between piecemeal and refined supernaturalism.[9] This detail will enable a sharper picture of the character of Murdoch's religious philosophy and will, in subsequent sections, form the basis of major criticisms of elements in that philosophy.

Sprigge's basic contrast is between, on the one hand, those outlooks which hold that there is a supernatural reality active in the world and therefore closer to some events in its history than others, and those outlooks, on the other hand, in which the supernatural provides a layer of meaning to experience, history and reality as a whole. Refined supernaturalism severs the thread between a transcendent source of meaning to human life and specific historical events or stretches of 'salvation history'. So it is obviously to be associated with nineteenth- and twentieth-century attempts to 'demythologise' traditional religious symbols. Sprigge goes on to distinguish two sub-types of refined supernaturalism: the scientific and the mystical (or metaphysical). The first sub-type is exemplified by the likes of Cupitt and R. B. Braithwaite; the second Sprigge illustrates via the views of F. H. Bradley. The former accepts the completeness of the scientific description of reality. It is content that all the objective truths about the world are contained, actually or potentially, within the natural sciences. It maintains that there is nothing in the world or related to it which cannot be characterised and explained in terms of the natural sciences. The supernatural enters into reality only as something expressed in the language and behaviour of human beings, for example certain emotions or morally invigorating fables. This form of refined supernaturalism does not challenge the scientific view of the world, but rather leaves religion purely as a function of human anthropology, albeit an important and permanent one. In contrast, metaphysical or mystical supernaturalists wish to give a religious meaning to reality as a whole and thus deny that the natural sciences have a monopoly on the determination of all facts about the world. The natural scientific account of reality is not the complete account of it. As Sprigge points out, it is characteristic of these forms of supernaturalism to refuse to attach the transcendent or supernatural in some special way to specific events in history because they see all reality as having a pervasively spiritual character. The attitudes of human beings we call religious (including in that the moral) are called forth by this pervasive character or are appropriate to how things are.

It should be apparent from Chapters 3 and 4 that Kant rejects scientific, refined supernaturalism. On his view science does not describe the world as it is in itself. The possibility that reality contains aspects or dimensions beyond those discoverable by science is at least thinkable. Moral experience grounds a commitment to what is real beyond the world as investigated by science. Murdoch can initially be viewed as supporting mystical or metaphysical refined supernaturalism. She offers descriptions of the human phenomenology of morality and religion, but it is evident that she wants to see that phenomenology as pointing to something beyond itself. Her paramount notion of the Good is that of a perfect and necessary reality which *invokes* and *draws forth* acts of human attention. Moreover, she does not isolate the transcendent. It is not just episodes of religious and moral experience that bring the transcendent close to us. It is experience as such – or as she puts it, 'the ubiquitous moral nature of experience'[10] – which does this job. Science itself contains modes of experience which embody the morally structured and disciplined attempt to grasp the real, in turn showing the human response to and pursuit of the Good: 'We can experience a "transcendence" at any time in our relations with our surroundings'.[11] The forms of spiritual discipline and apprehension centrally displayed in religion and morality are then implicit in all attempts to apprehend the real honestly, hence the need to invoke metaphysics (of a Platonist kind) to serve as an adequate guide to morals.

Later in this chapter we shall have to raise the question of how far Murdoch is true to her offer to provide a metaphysics of reality as the background for morals. For the moment we must concentrate on two matters: how she comes to her spiritualised view of morality and why she rejects the terms of traditional theism.

SPIRITUALISED MORALITY

We have noted already that Iris Murdoch gets to her spiritualised morality by way of a critique of subjectivism and prescriptivism in ethics. What begins as an exercise in pointing to areas of the moral life allegedly ignored by such accounts develops into a fully religious interpretation of the moral life. In this interpretation moral discovery and experience are likened to the mystical and spiritual quest typical of religion, and the object of the quest, moral truth and reality, is likened to the reality spoken of by religion.

Moral experience becomes something involving loving attention to realities outside one's own ego and entailing the daily fight against the ego's demands and perceptions and for spiritual purification. Moral reality becomes something mediating a transcendent, perfect and necessarily real object of attention.

The kind of account of morals which is Murdoch's prime target she finds paradigmatically displayed in the moral philosophy of R. M. Hare. On Hare's account as she interprets it, three notions are central to the foundations of moral thought: fact, principle and decision. Reality is thought of as consisting of a realm of facts whose character is to be established by common sense and scientific investigation. The world of facts contains no values. Facts become morally relevant only when human moral agents bring principles to bear upon them. The fact that my conduct will gratuitously harm others in itself is morally irrelevant, but becomes relevant if I espouse the principle that gratuitous harm is wrong. Moral value, not lying in the world, is created by human decision: specifically the decisions of principle to link the circumstances and consequences of action to notions of what is to be prescribed or proscribed.

So: fact and value are thought of as separate. Value is not in reality but is ascribed to facets of reality by the human will. Out of the ingredients outlined so far comes an emphasis on action as crucial to morality. A morality is thought of as primarily a series of action-guides (prescriptions and proscriptions) and it is the function of principles and decisions of principle to make facets of reality relevant to the determination of how we should act.

Murdoch's first line of attack against this account consists in stressing the importance of moral vision as the precursor to moral understanding. That is to say, she criticises the notion that there can be a realm of easily apprehended 'fact' which is the background to moral choice. She points to the need for moral agents to exercise responsible vision in order to discover what is salient and relevant from the moral point of view in the circumstances which face them. It is no use having principles of, say, beneficence and justice, if one cannot see that occasions to help others or to mitigate injustice are in front of one. She stresses throughout her writings the difficulty in having a correct view of our moral situation. That difficulty is a moral one. It is a moral task to see the world aright as it confronts in making ethical decisions. Two insights she takes directly from Christianity bear on the difficulty of attaining right moral vision: goodness is difficult to attain and sin is universal.[12] The barriers to goodness in universal sinfulness are regrounded in Freud's pessimistic view of the human psyche as a system of egocentric energies making objectivity and unselfishness in perception and action difficult for human beings. Correct moral vision is everywhere clouded by the demands of the 'fat relentless ego'.[13]

From the stress on moral vision as the required but hard to attain underpinning of the moral life follows the demotion of action from the centre of the moral stage. Murdoch points to the many instances where the moral struggle for human beings consists in the effort to gain a just and loving view of the people and circumstances which surround them. So the area of moral endeavour extends well beyond the concern with how to act well. Her crucial example to illustrate the demotion of action is the problems facing a woman in her attempt to overcome negative, dismissive thoughts about a relative.[14] Murdoch insists on the complexity and effort involved in such an attempt to form a just view of someone's character, and on how the endeavour could be morally pressing even though the other person had moved away from the reach of one's actions.

The demotion of action and the promotion of vision in morality is taken further by Murdoch's attempts to argue that where a fullness of moral vision has been attained there is no room for the human will then to operate. The typical phenomenology of morals is not, in her view, that of patient attempts to see the morally neutral facts aright, followed by the exercise of a decision of principle to act this way or that. Rather the struggle to achieve right moral vision, which might engage the will in the fight against self-serving motives and preoccupations, is, if successful, rewarded with a sense that I *must* act thus and so: 'The idea of a patient, loving regard, directed upon a person, a thing, a situation, presents the will not as unimpeded movement but as something very much more like "obedience"'.[15]

The notion that moral action involves obedience to something thought of as beyond the volition of human individuals will need to be taken up later, but let us note another facet of Murdoch's moral phenomenology which emerges from the above quotation: the stress on moral vision as the work of attentive love – something Murdoch borrows from the writings of Simone Weil. Murdoch states at the very beginning of *The Sovereignty of Good* that love is a central concept in morals and she criticises moral philosophers for their neglect of this concept. Love is central to her notion of moral vision because of its role in revealing what is morally relevant and salient in the circumstances around us. Those moral circumstances are typically ones where moral relevance and saliency are tied to the relations between ourselves and our putative attitudes and actions, on the one hand, and the feelings, needs, interests and sensitivities of other human beings, on the other. 'Love' for Murdoch denotes the respectful, caring attention to the reality of the other human person. The work of love is both vital and difficult in attaining right moral vision because it engages by way of opposition with the system of preoccupations and perceptions arising from the ego. To see aright morally we must attend to the other in love, which entails fighting the ego. The emphasis on love reinforces the Murdochian notion that morality exhibits a spiritual quest and invokes spiritual disciplines.

We are now well on our way to seeing how Murdoch links the phenomenology of morals to religion. Indeed, she frequently describes moral experience as a form of 'mysticism' in order to highlight this link.[16] We have in morality, and in all experience concerned to gain access to the real and thus transcend the individual ego, a pursuit of true vision which in turn arises out of something analogous to spiritual perfection. Such vision is completed in a state which attains obedience to values which are apparently independent of and transcending the subject, values not created by us but calling us to act.

Murdoch's account of the phenomenology of morals as quasi-mystical finds parallels and echoes in a number of other writers. It is set out and defended as inescapable in the first four chapters of the Charles Taylor's *Sources of the Self*. Something very similar provides the entry point to F. R. Leavis' account of the religious value of literature. This account is based on the manner in which great literature explores, defines and celebrates the moral sense. Leavis' *locus classicus* for the illustration of this 'moral mysticism' is the passage in D. H. Lawrence's *The Rainbow* where Tom Brangwen realises he is called to marry 'the Polish lady' – a call that is one to lead a higher kind of life.

> And then it came upon him that he would marry her and she would be his life . . . But during the long February nights with the ewes in labour, looking out from the shelter into the flashing stars, he knew he did not belong to himself. He must admit that he was something fragmentary, something incomplete and subject . . . So he sat small and submissive to the greater ordering.[17]

Such passages show, for Leavis, Lawrence's discovery that human beings respond to their deepest values and commitments as though they 'do not belong to themselves' but are responsible to something that transcends the human individual.[18]

For Murdoch, art, both in respect to its creation and its appreciation, provides an epitome of moral spirituality. Much art, she affirms, may be no better than fantasy gratification. But at its best, artistic creation is the effort to portray the real by way of a vision which has silenced and escaped the ego.[19] The one who appreciates art is likewise called to exercise a spiritual discipline to attend to the real (an order of meaning outside of oneself) through leaving the ego's preoccupations behind. Murdoch describes the experience of beauty in art and nature as a spiritual exercise and as 'a completely adequate entry into (and not just an analogy of) the good life, since it *is* the checking of selfishness in the interest of seeing the real'.[20]

What is distinctive of the art object (or of an example of natural beauty, such as a hovering kestrel[21]) is that it is a purposive unity. Each part or aspect of the whole takes its place in an order of meaning. To attend to the work properly is to experience the items that make up the whole *not* in terms of their relationship to one's own concerns and preoccupations but as parts of that meaningful whole which is independent of oneself. The structure of my experience becomes the structure of the object contemplated. This is paradigmatic of the 'unselving' generally found in correct, attentive vision of the Good and is a proper exemplar of the attentive concern for another human being which is love and which closes the gap between self and other. The analogies with aesthetics Murdoch uses turn out to be important in establishing her Platonic theme that knowledge (of the appropriate sort) is virtue.

In drawing this connection between morality, religion and art, Murdoch is not only explicitly linking her work to aspects of the Platonic corpus. She is also implicitly linking her thinking to a Romantic tradition of writing about religion which sees aesthetic consciousness as proto-typical of all experience and sees all experience as potentially religious.[22] It is this tradition which ultimately lies behind Leavis' thought that the experience of value is our primary route into the religious and is to be found paramountly in responsible artistic creation.

So far, we have shown how Murdoch's moral Platonism connects morality and religion at the level of phenomenology. The connections at the metaphysical level come about through her use of the concept of the Good as a substitute for the notion of God.

We may be initially puzzled as to why she thinks herself entitled to move from the phenomenological account into the metaphysical realm. It may seem that to balance the notion that analogues to spiritual disciplines and mysticism are found in morals she needs only the vague thought that value is somehow objective in the world. In general, language drawn from Platonic accounts of the Forms is helpful to Murdoch's phenomenology. For the Forms are standards which are once immanent in everything which partakes of their natures yet which transcend all contingent particulars.

They are to be known by way of attending to particulars but through a kind of vision which at the same time looks beyond those particulars. Still we might ask: 'Why talk of goodness in a way which leads on to the concept of God?' There are three, interconnected, themes which support this transition: unity, attractiveness and perfection.

Murdoch defines 'God' as a 'single perfect transcendent non-representable and necessarily real object of attention'.[23] She uses 'the Good' to stand in place of 'God' in her moral interpretation of the religious. Such a use would be fruitless if there were no unity within our experience of value. There are many passages in *The Sovereignty of Good* affirming that moral and value experience exhibits at least preliminary intimations of, and calls forth a drive towards, unity. She affirms that the thing we have knowledge of in virtue can, 'given the variety of human personality and situation, only be thought of as "one", as a single object for all men, in some very ideal and remote sense'.[24] While she recognises that the notion of a single source or focus of value can give rise to false ideas of consolation, she states that much moral reflection involves a search for the best solution to, the right meaning in, matters of practical perplexity.[25] There is a unity in the virtues,[26] a unity shown in their being varied manifestations of love.

Murdoch is keen to use the notion of the Good to anchor the sense that we are *drawn* to the effort to escape the ego and to attend to others and the world. The idea of the Good promotes the sense that we have in 'spiritualised morality' a 'field of force',[27] 'a transcendent magnetic centre'.[28] The Good figures in Murdoch in the role Taylor describes as a 'moral source': 'something the love of which empowers us to do and be good'.[29] Murdoch even describes it at one point as a creative source in our lives [30] – though we shall see below that there are problems in ascribing creativity to the Good as she conceives it. Finally, we have in Murdoch's account of the phenomenology of morals the idea that the endeavour to attain a right, loving gaze on others and upon reality is never-ending. Murdoch takes over from Plato the notion that the Good is non-representable and indefinable. The unceasing demand to purify our moral vision of the limitations of ego is then represented via the image of all value-experience as united around an endeavour to see such a Good in and through immanent things.

The grounds of Murdoch's talk of God as a 'single perfect transcendent non-representable and necessarily real object of attention' are linked to her enthusiastic endorsement of the ontological proof (notably in chapter 13 of *Metaphysics as a Guide to Morals*). The ontological proof is taken by Murdoch to be a proof of the necessary reality of something matching her definition of the divine. The proof as traditionally known moves from the premise that 'God' is to be defined as that than which no greater can be conceived to the conclusion that a most perfect conceivable being must exist. The proof fits into standard theistic apologetics through identifying the most perfect conceivable reality with the entity which exemplifies the traditional attributes of deity. This last step is the one, of course, which Murdoch rejects.

Murdoch notes the use of reasoning parallel to that embodied in the traditional proof in contexts where it is not used to support traditional theism (as in Plato and Simone Weil). She intends to transform the argument, initially by severing its sub-conclusion that a supremely perfect reality exists from its customary theistic gloss. Further, she invites us to see it, not as a deductive argument, but as a concealed argument from experience. The proof draws upon our unavoidable and ubiquitous experience of good and evil.[31] It moves from that to point to the 'unconditional structure' revealed therein.[32] This unconditional structure has been imaged through the notion of God, that is, a supernatural person. But what the proof directly shows is that Good is necessarily real and omnipresent in our awareness of value. The Good corresponds to our search for perfection, for the right vision and response called for in moments where matters of value are in question: 'What is perfect must exist, that is, . . . the object of our best thoughts, must be something real, indeed especially and most real, not as contingent accidental reality but as something fundamental, essential and necessary'.[33] The experience of value, then, points to absolute, unconditional perfection as the necessary focus of vision and quest in matters of value and as something corresponding to 'the sense of a pure untainted source of spiritual power'.[34] Perhaps the best summary of how the ontological argument works for Murdoch is given by the character Plato in her dialogue *Acastos*: 'If we have the idea of value we necessarily have the idea of perfection as something real'.[35]

The proof as viewed by Murdoch repeats the argument that the phenomenology of value brings with it the idea of the Good. It underlines the thought that the Good is a necessary reality and it contains what Taylor describes as a 'best account' argument.[36] That is to say, we are to take as real whatever has to be postulated as the best account of those experiences we think we can rely on. What Murdoch is telling us, via her version of the ontological proof, is that the best account of moral experience demands postulation of a perfect, non-representable reality.

GOD, THE GOOD AND THE REAL

We begin the task of critical exploration of the coherence of Iris Murdoch's moral Platonism by pursuing a question important for the themes of this study. How far is her picture of morality as the interpreter of religion capable of a realist interpretation? If we have doubts about this, then much of the interest of her views will disappear, and her pretensions to have provided a 'de-mythologised' form of religious outlook which avoids the subjectivism of Cupitt will have been brought into question.

We have already met her criticisms of Cupitt's approach. Her discussion of the ontological proof reinforces the sense that she requires metaphysics to be the guide of morals, in that out of moral phenomenology comes a reference to a putatively real transcendent entity – God or the Good. Her rejection of what it is customary to style 'non-realist' interpretations of religious symbols is shown in her critical strictures on Wittgensteinian interpreters of religion. She takes them to be saying that the reality of God is indeed necessary and unconditional only within the 'language game' of religion. She criticises this conception on the grounds that it leads to the idea that there is something called 'religious language' which is expressive and not descriptive. Religion is thereby made optional – 'put in a corner as one possible mode of proceeding'.[37] Murdoch's rejection of the 'language game' approach as she understands it is connected with her emphasis on the unconditional character of the reality pointed to by the traditional notion of God, the Platonic notion of the Good and the Kantian Categorical Imperative.[38] She means by these reflections to point to the Leavis/Lawrence recognition that 'we do not belong to ourselves': the pull of ideas of perfection and value is not to be gainsaid and is an experience of something that stands over and apart from the human will. Hence, we noted as the first item in Murdoch's Platonic creed an apparently referential and ontological claim which would entitle Murdoch's view to be interpreted as a form of religious realism: 'the good is something distant, abstract and ideal, an independent existent that is not a function of or the outcome of human will or desire'.[39]

On this interpretation, Murdoch is a revisionary realist. She may object to the way in which traditional religious symbols (those of a personal God) have depicted religious reality, but she affirms that there is a something or other, extra-human and transcendent, to which these symbols can refer. This is the direction in which the affirmations and images of *Metaphysics as a Guide to Morals* seems to take us. However, there is another way of interpreting Murdoch whereby her use of 'Good' and 'God' as apparently referring expressions is but a manner of speaking. In a passage in *The Sovereignty of Good*,[40] Murdoch states that the claim 'Good is a transcendent reality' means that 'virtue is the attempt to pierce the veil of selfish consciousness and join the world as it really is'. If this is *all* that 'Good is a transcendent reality' means, then talk of the Good is no more than a way of representing the demand that we overcome the barriers preventing us from having a just and loving perception of our moral circumstances with a hint that this demand places a never-ending task upon our vision. What it does not yield is the idea that there is an object, in metaphysical space, which we are aware of in and through our just and loving attention to particulars. What difference might the ontological and referential claim make here? Surely this: if the notion of the Good has referential and metaphysical import, then something is postulated which might explain the pull towards the just and loving vision Murdoch's phenomenology of morals documents. The notion of the Good's attractiveness then has some explanatory role to play. Murdoch's view appears to be that love requires a transcendent object which energises the self to undertake the spiritual and mental effort required for right vision.[41] Moreover, as we noted above, the alleged unity of the demands of right vision gets some kind of explanation.

There is much, then, inviting us to see Murdoch as endorsing a Platonic ontology. She has been taken by at least one commentator to be declaring that morality (with the aid of art) is the best route to an 'ultimately mysterious, transcendent and unknowable ground of being',[42] with the caveat that we can presume that this reality is not personal. Hence, we substitute the idea of Good for God. Like Kant, she can then be interpreted as saving a reference for 'God', albeit a problematic one since perfect reality is unrepresentable and achieved knowledge of it is always a task and never finally completed. Like Kant she may be setting aside the content of the notion of God as imaginatively useful though descriptively unreliable, while yet affirming that it is referentially indispensable.

The question which must now be faced is whether this putative revisionary realism can survive the reasons Murdoch offers for rejecting traditional theism. These reasons can be discussed under three heads: history, the Euthyphro dilemma and the rejection of teleology. We shall see that the third type of reason for rejecting theism does indeed throw the apparent realist thrust of Murdoch's interpretation of religion into doubt.

The first of these reasons is represented in those passages in Murdoch where she implies that traditional 'supernatural' religious beliefs have been and must be superseded by scientific and technological perspectives. For example, she tells us that the ontological proof 'speaks with an especially apt voice now when traditional supernatural religious beliefs fade, and seem to be *inevitably* superseded by scientific and technological conceptions of human existence'.[43] As Graham points out, Murdoch gives every appearance of being committed to a version of the secularisation thesis whereby belief in God and the gods is now impossible for 'us', that is modern, Western intellectuals.[44] There is a ratchet of intellectual history driven by the rise of science which cannot be reversed and it has made belief in supernaturalism impossible for 'us'.

Graham styles the above line of thought as the 'chief' presupposition behind Murdoch's revisionary account of religion and points to the grave difficulties in adequately supporting it.[45] He repeats the now commonplace criticism that such theses about the inevitable secularisation of the 'modern mind' do no more than absolutise a particular set of beliefs about history which in turn belong to a particular wing of the European Enlightenment and its successors.

It is certainly true that this line of thought in Murdoch shows that she pays no attention to those contemporary theistic philosophers who have developed apologetic strategies for the defence of traditional theism. That such strategies flourish certainly shows that there is no 'inevitability' about the demise of theistic outlooks in the modern world. It can be said in defence of Murdoch that there are features of 'modernity' which do put traditional religious symbols on trial. It is a fact that we now know more about the historical roots of religious traditions, their scriptures and their claims to revelation than we used to. This knowledge stresses the rootedness of those traditions and their symbols in contingent cultural patterns. This rootedness is reinforced by knowledge arising from the social scientific study of religion. The result is inevitably to stress the humanly based character of religious symbols. With other appropriate forms of argument (such as one might glean from Kant) in favour of religious agnosticism, the character of our modern awareness of religion could provide support for Murdoch's attempt to treat traditional notions of the transcendent as imaginatively useful but metaphysically unreliable.[46]

The second type of reason for rejecting traditional theism behind Murdoch's Platonism is implicit in her frequent insistence that perfect reality is 'non-representable and indefinable'.[47] This is connected with her equally frequent affirmations that the demands of the Good are unconditional and absolute. When she states that no empirical thing can be God (that is, the God we need) and no necessary thing can be God (that is, the personal God of traditional theism), she has in mind that our image of the transcendent should take us towards the unrepresentable source of absolute and unconditional demands. Yet, of any concrete thing that embodied goodness we could always intelligibly ask 'Is it good after all?' The statement 'X (a concrete, representable thing) is good' may be true but the 'is' in such a statement can never be the 'is' of identity. This point holds even if the something in question is the creator-God who has the omni-attributes. This conclusion is implicit in the reasoning behind the

Euthyphro dilemma. We cannot say that the will of a creator is (identity) what is right or good, for that makes rightness or goodness metaphysically arbitrary. Moreover, it seems to produce the gross paradox that it means nothing to say that God is right or good. For if God is identical with rightness or goodness, then to say that his will is right or good is to say no more than 'God is God'.

The reasoning that lies behind the Euthyphro dilemma is in essence that which lies behind G. E. Moore's intended exposé of the 'Naturalistic Fallacy' in ethics. And it is noteworthy that at the start of *The Sovereignty of Good* Murdoch sums up and endorses Moore's essential points about the indefinability of the Good. Traditional, personalist theism is thus to be rejected because it endeavours to define the Good, that is identify it with a concrete existent.

This underlying movement of thought in Murdoch's revisionary enterprise shows why she has recourse to the categories of Platonism. For the Forms in Platonic thought enjoy the peculiar status of both being existents, at least in the sense of being objects of reference akin to particulars, but not being concrete entities. Hence arises their puzzling status, the impossibility of making them out to be denizens of our spatio-temporal world and the difficulties in thinking of them as objects of knowledge. They are both like and unlike concrete particulars and like and unlike qualities. This status has made belief in the Forms the subject of intense and damning criticism from Plato's own day to the present, but we must take Murdoch to be affirming that there is an experiential demand, channelled by the Euthyphro and Moore arguments, for postulating at least one such paradoxical entity: the Form of the Good.

Debate between Murdoch and the defenders of what we have styled 'traditional theism' on the above issues might take many forms. I shall concentrate on two possible lines of response. First, we should note the head-on attack on Platonism in morals contained in Alston's paper 'Some Suggestions for Divine Command Theorists'.[48] Alston describes some of the problems in making out God to be identical with goodness while construing God as an individual, personal being. However, he contends that we can retain the notion that goodness is identical with God if we distinguish two types of predicates. There are those Alston styles 'Platonic predicates' which are applied to particulars in virtue of their common participation in some general idea or principle, which might then be construed as a Form. There are 'particularistic predicates' which are applied by reference to the relationship particulars have to individual things taken as paradigms of the genus in question. Alston notes that there are some readings of the logic of natural kind terms which have it that such kind terms are defined essentially by reference to given examples. So we might say that 'Gold is any sample of metal like these', pointing to the paradigmatic samples of the kind. Then the statement 'These samples are gold' said of the paradigmatic, defining samples would be a necessary truth and it would make no sense to ask the Moore-like question 'But are they gold after all?' But we would be here dealing with a significant necessary truth and the Moore question would indeed be foolish given the way in which the predicate had been introduced in the language. In the same way, it is an important tautology to say of the Standard Metre in Paris that it is a metre long. Alston's suggestion about 'good' is then two-fold: it is a particularistic predicate and the paradigm for its meaning and application is God, an existing individual. To say of something apart from God that it is good is to say that it is like God. To say 'God is good' is to utter a tautology with the force of 'God just is the standard of goodness'.

Alston notes and responds to a number of objections the Platonist will have to his proposal. Will not this conception of the meaning of 'good' make goodness arbitrary, especially as there is a stipulative element in many particularist predicates? How can 'good' have a meaning fixed by reference to the standard set by God's nature when God is not an item of inspection in our world? Further, we might wonder if the Platonist could not reintroduce his or her main contentions by asking what explanation could be given of an instance of goodness being 'like' the paradigm of goodness that is God. A notion of similarity is introduced, a notion of the paradigm and the members of its class sharing a common nature or properties. So there is something that is both one and yet participates in these many individuals (good things and God). Could this be room for reintroducing the idea of a Form of Goodness? These questions do not amount to refutations of Alston's account at all; they point to the areas in which debate between Platonists and non-Platonists might flourish.

A second line of response to Murdoch's Euthyphro-based critique of the idea of God would consist in pointing to a movement of thought within what must be otherwise styled 'traditional theism' which denies that God is a being and which affirms that God is precisely a reality partaking both of the character of a universal and a particular. I refer here to the traditional doctrine of divine simplicity as this was advanced by a host of medieval theologians, Christian and non-Christian.[49] In Aquinas we find the assertion that God is both unlike an individual substance in being pure form as opposed to a union of matter and form and yet unlike a form in being a subsisting individual.[50] This tradition is one pointer to the ways in which dominant and influential traditions in Christian, Jewish and Islamic theology have greatly modified the extent to which 'God' is the name of a person. Hand in hand with that has gone radically qualified accounts of religious language, which as we saw in Chapter 3 sharply distinguish what our words might refer to when we speak of God and how we refer to that being.

There may then be more affinities between her ideas on the Good and traditional theology than Murdoch is able to perceive and thus more from that tradition that is salvageable even given the limits she imposes on what is religiously acceptable.

When we turn to Murdoch's third reason for rejecting the traditional God-idea we face the many instances where she disavows any moral teleology to the world as we know it. This refrain in Murdoch is connected with two others: the notion, discussed above, that 'we' must accept that we live in a world about which science has the final say; and the idea that belief in a personal deity is a means of providing ourselves with a false consolation. The most striking affirmation of Murdoch's abandonment of teleology is in the following passage from *The Sovereignty of Good*:

> Human life has no external point or *telos* . . . There are properly many patterns or purposes within life, but there is no generally guaranteed pattern or purpose of the kind for which philosophers and theologians used to search. We are what we seem to be, transient, mortal creatures, subject to necessity and chance.[51]

The connection of this bleak vision with science is made in the assertion that the idea of human life as self-enclosed and purposeless is 'the natural product of the advance of science'.[52] Looking to a personal God who will provide a *telos* to human life of happiness or blessedness is linked to the desire to furnish ourselves with consolation, the kind of consolation which amounts to abandoning a realistic, unselfish vision of the world: almost anything which consoles is a fake.[53]

It will be seen at once that this rejection of teleology places sharp limitations on the metaphysical import of Murdoch's moral Platonism. Not only does it distance her ideas from the implications of traditional theism, it also shows that she departs from the way in which Kant gives his moral interpretation of religion a minimal realist thrust and metaphysical reference.

Consider Murdoch's proposition that postulation of a moral teleology surrounding human beings is inevitably consoling and inevitably corrupting. Undoubtedly these beliefs of Murdoch are partly shaped by her reading of Freud and the power of the picture in *The Future of an Illusion* of God as the fantasy-gratification of our wishes. We might say that Murdoch is obsessed with the human tendency to fantasy-consolation. She says that almost all art is a product of this drive, even while it has the potential to overcome it in selfless realism.[54] The objection to consoling pictures and teleology is connected with her assertions of the pointlessness of virtue. It seems that for Murdoch goodness can only be seen in the human world if we are sure that it is good for nothing and is thus patently set in a world in which everything is subject to necessity and chance. This implies that we positively require good acts to produce no visible good for anyone in the long run, especially not ourselves, in order to see them as good.

I find it hard to give weight to Murdoch's strictures on teleology inevitably leading to fantasy-consolation. It is evident that there are dangers inherent in searching for a human-friendly order in the world around us. This search may just be the result of the fat, relentless human ego at work again. It is equally evident that the Freudian critique of religion strikes home against some manifestations of religiousness. But once we have noted the dangers, we do not have to accept that every religious conception which provides for some hope of good to arise out of the exercise of goodness in action is a fantasy consolation – unless we are already convinced that there is absolutely nothing to reality apart from blind physical processes. If we think we have reasons for believing in forms of moral teleology, then, though that belief may be consoling, it is not only consoling and it will not be the result of fantasy. The view that a good act is only genuine if it is pointless appears just as extreme and wrong as the counter view discussed in Chapter 2 to the effect that a good act is only genuinely good if it permanently adds to the total amount of good we see around us.

If we accept the vision that all that happens is the product of nothing other than necessity and chance, we have little response to the problem of evil which confronted Kant and is raised by other writers: on what assumptions can we hope that the human good will be attainable through doing good acts? Murdoch's moral Platonism turns out to provide no answer to this question because she has dismissed it before she starts her constructive work.

The central problem which emerges from Murdoch's rejection of teleology is that the concept of the Good seems to refer, in her system, to something which is inert. It is a commonplace to say: that which is real is that which has causal power. To test whether 'the Good' makes a reference to something which is real, and which exists independently of our conceptions of it, is accordingly to ask if there are phenomena which this postulation might causally account for. There should be something the Good *does*. Refined supernaturalists have of course given up the idea that specific events in history are to be seen as the outcome of what the divine does, but they can still postulate facts about the world's or history's general character to be explained in terms of what the divine does. In abandoning any belief in a moral teleology to the universe and its history, Murdoch has cut off her notion of the divine from any such function.

It might be argued in her defence that the Good as a transcendent object of reference does have some explanatory power. There are facts about the moral phenomenology of human life (such as: the alleged unity of the virtues, the pull of the demand for purity of moral vision) which are to receive their explanation through the Platonic metaphysics of morals. In reply, we might query how far the putative reference to the Good can explain such facts of our moral experience unless such reference goes hand in hand with the belief that the Good exists independent of our perception of it. If it has that kind of reality, then it exists as part of what is there outside the world of human moral perceptions. But then it should also exist as the source of powers in the world beyond the human realm; in which case we cannot leave that world to be wholly described by the sciences. What science reveals about the world we inhabit cannot be the whole story. Whence then the meek acceptance that all that surrounds human choice is chance and necessity and that there is no external *telos* beyond us? Murdoch wants to say that we need metaphysics to complete the world of morals but yet leaves that world to the devices of the most rampant scientism.

This complaint against the metaphysical and realist credentials of Murdoch's account can be reinforced by asking in what sense we are to take her repeated claim that aesthetic and moral experience gives us access to reality? If we abandon the world outside of human choice and moral experience to the descriptive resources of the natural sciences and those alone, then the sense in which moral experience reveals the real is extremely attenuated. If our experience of value is credited with the capacity to show us what is so about the world independent of our specific perceptions of that world, then we surely cannot allow the natural sciences to have the last word on what is. This is part of the logic of refined supernaturalism as that kind of view has been set out for us by Sprigge.

In the light of the above points, we can see the misleading character of the interpretation of Murdoch given by Scot Dunbar.[55] As noted above, he takes it that Murdoch's language about vision, the Good and the real amounts to an experiential argument for belief in God of a revisionist kind. The postulate of a personal God has gone, for that will lead to consoling fantasy. Instead, Murdoch's portrayal of the centrality of the Good in human life, according to Dunbar, turns the concept of God into a '*symbol for some kind of impersonal ground of all that is*'.[56] But it appears evident that Murdoch's moral Platonism precisely has no implications for what we think about being and its ground. Being, outside of *human* being, is left to science. The coherence of this move is open to question. If we say that the world outside of human being is everywhere governed by necessity and chance, this surely should have implications for our thoughts about the character of the human. Human beings are not merely the creatures of necessity and chance according to parts of Murdoch's account of the moral. She affirms they can pursue and move towards attaining a vision of perfect reality. The world they live in is rich in moral and evaluative meaning. But what coherent view of reality can assert all this about the human world and yet leave the surroundings and setting for this world to the bleak vision implicit in Murdoch's abandonment of teleology and her embrace of the sufficiency of the scientific view of things? Here, Murdoch seems unable to relate anthropology to ontology. She appears to fall into the same trap as the existentialist philosophies whose weakness she so unmercifully unmasks. This is the trap of abandoning the world to mechanism while hoping to preserve a 'high' doctrine of the human. Only a radically dualist view of the human self's relation to the physical world supports such a divided conception, but such dualism fits in ill with much else Murdoch preaches (as, for example, is shown in her stress on natural beauty as the exemplar and mediator of value and reality).

If something like the Good were the ground of being, then the structures of being would reflect the power of the Good and we would not abandon the extra-human world to the devices of natural science. At the very least, and like Kant, we would place limits upon the sufficiency of the scientific account of reality, limits which would then enable us to think that our moral efforts might be going along with the grain of reality's ultimate structures.

That Murdoch has abandoned thoughts about what the character of the ground of being might be further questions the sense in which she brings in metaphysics as the completion of morality. It cuts her off from one of the most important aspects of Plato's concept of the Form of the Good, for that concept is surely in Plato a gesture towards ontology as well as epistemology. At the crucial point, where the relation between the world in which we act and the alleged transcendent reality that is the Good is in question, Murdoch leaves the transcendent with no contribution to make to the structure of reality. One must then question how far she can pretend to have preserved anything like the spirit of the ontological proof. For it is not enough to assert in this connection that we can retain the idea that perfection and value have necessary existence. Perfection and value turn out not to have the kind of existence which would put them at the heart and ground of all else that is. Surely it is some such minimal thought which makes the proof a pointer to divine things.

The criticisms of the coherence of Murdoch's moral interpretation of religion and of its religious and metaphysical credentials can be taken further by noting the extent to which its terms depart from Plato himself. We have seen how apt Graham's epithet 'moral Platonism' is as a label for her views. Yet the abandonment of teleology in Murdoch is also the abandonment of much that is characteristic of Plato. Mitchell has noted that to abandon an external *telos* behind human life is to reject a common presupposition of the entire tradition of pagan philosophy.[57] The metaphysical and teleological implications of Plato's doctrine of the Forms are usefully highlighted in Michael Despland's study of Plato.[58] Despland notes that the postulation of the Forms has cosmological implications, implications connected with Plato's central concern for how the good life as he conceived it to be might be possible in our world. Among these implications were the ideas that the mental was not the mere product of the material; rather the Forms guarantee that mind or intelligence is at the heart of reality and holds sway there.[59] Plato has a concern to see that justice is upheld in the universe so that a life reflecting its demands is possible and capable of realising the human good.[60] Despland makes much of the fact that in dialogues after the *Republic*, such as the *Laws* and the *Timaeus*, belief in the Forms is connected with belief in deity, with the aim of thereby depicting a creative mechanism in the world which will ensure that it reflects the Forms and thus constitutes an intelligible order in which human good can be realised.

All the above features of Plato's cosmology are, of course, swept away in Murdoch's abandonment of teleology. What does impress Murdoch is that part of the Platonic inheritance which insists that being oriented towards the Good is not merely a causal means to living a good life, but rather a present constituent and realisation of the good life. Despland quotes from *The Sovereignty of Good* in a context where he is making the point that, for Plato, contemplation of the Good is not good in merely leading to good in some utilitarian fashion. He says: 'it is good for us, not because of what it does to us, what appearances it wins for us, what rewards it delivers, but because of what it is'.[61] These Platonic thoughts chime in with what we have affirmed in Chapter 2 about virtue being a constitutive means to the good life and about virtuous action constituting its own end. Murdoch adds an extra, important dimension to such ideas by bringing out the modes in which 'virtue' involves more than action but also vision, discernment and the like. Her strictures on teleology and consolation can be seen as vivid ways of pointing out the intrinsic worthwhileness of virtue, considered as vision and action. They point to the dangers lurking in outlooks which tempt us to see virtue as the non-constitutive means to the good life. But all this being said, it is evident that Murdoch has no answer to the question raised by John Kekes: how can good lives be possible given that the world contains manifold forms of evil? It is evident that the Platonic dialogues (at least some of the later ones) can answer this question by appealing to a vision of reality which holds out the kind of transcendentally grounded hope Kekes dismisses. Now it is important to see that Murdoch implicitly confronts the Kekes problem and responds by maintaining the unblinking affirmation that there is no metaphysical unity in human life and that all is subject to mortality and chance.[62] Her work, then, amounts to offering the answer to Kekes' problem which consists in affirming the self-sufficiency of the realisation, through action and vision, of virtue.

I have summarised in Chapter 2 the reasons why I do not think we can rest with a solution to the secular problem of evil which affirms the Socratic position that to be virtuous is in and of itself to have attained a good which is complete and invulnerable.

So, to what extent is Murdoch's moral Platonism an instance of what we have styled revisionary realism in the interpretation of religion or of what Sprigge categorises as mystical or metaphysical refined supernaturalism? The alternative is to see Murdoch as offering us no more than a phenomenology of morals. In this phenomenology religious and spiritual categories are used to good effect, but they have no metaphysical or referential implications – not even of the problematic, exiguous Kantian kind explored in the previous two chapters.

I argued in the previous chapter that a necessary condition of anything's counting as a religious view of reality is that it should provide some picture of things which enables the individual and/or society to overcome the gap between value and reality. A religious symbolic system is one which integrates ethos and world view, which enables the thought that reality answers to our deepest values. The Kantian reinterpretation of religion preserves this necessary element of a religious outlook even while it abandons much else and is heavily agnostic about the nature of religious reality. It is this element which enables a hope to be kept alive which will in turn answer the secular problem of evil. Now we have found that Murdoch's spiritualised morality does not provide a religious vision on this understanding of the religious. She *appears* to have a religious vision –

the employment of the Platonic vocabulary suggests a neo-Kantian revisionary realism, in which morality's structures will provide *the* backing for a metaphysical referent of religious symbols. This referent will show us that the ultimately real corresponds to our deepest moral perceptions. But it turns out that the reality of Murdoch's putative religious reality is in doubt, since it is causally inert. And it is debarred from playing any role in our future expectations about the goals to be achieved in human moral striving of the kind which might solve the secular problem of evil.

Murdoch's departure from what we have argued to be the canonical moral interpretation of religion which retains metaphysical realism can be brought out in another way. Recall the neo-Kantian account of the essence of religion as the overcoming of the divide between value and reality: religion provides a symbolic, imaginative means of overcoming the gulf between self and world. Now I take it that it is the very thrust of Murdoch's comments on consoling fantasy and the need to see the pointlessness of virtue against the background of a *telos*-free world that she would deprecate any attempt to overcome this gap. Part of what she understands by 'realism' is the vision, bound up with the pointlessness of virtue, that all such efforts are yet further ways in which the fat, relentless ego distorts our perceptions. We have noted above how she in part allies herself with a Freudian interpretation of religion as an illusion-driven attempt to overcome the gap between self and world in her frequent uses of the notion of consoling fantasy in relation to the concept of God.

Part of the argument between Murdoch and the properly Kantian interpretation of religion is going to be a moral-cum-psychological one about the extent to which the minimal essence of religion, as Byrne stipulates it, is on a par with wishful fantasising, as *The Future of an Illusion* would have us believe. Such an argument would in part turn around the character of the difficulty raised by the secular problem of evil and how much intellectual weight should be placed upon the dilemma it confronts us with. It would turn, further, around how far a Kantian approach could deliver on its promises to make effective, real use of its postulated religious mechanisms and yet not to corrupt the human struggle for good. Kant thinks that his religious minimalism, which is grounded in his particular account of religious language, enables him to fulfil both promises. (We return to these issues in Chapter 7.)

I offer no verdict on how such a debate might go. What I have affirmed is that in the last analysis Murdoch's writings fail to offer a moral interpretation of religion which avoids reductionism. My criterion for reductionism in this field amounts to this: to avoid reductionism any revisionary account of religious belief must preserve a minimal metaphysical realism. What counts as minimal realism relates to how far the secular problem of evil is taken seriously by the revisionary account in question and how far it maintains a commitment to some, however exiguous, teleological outlook which addresses the gap between value and reality.

IRIS MURDOCH: FURTHER CRITICISMS

The main criticism I have directed against Murdoch's spiritualised morality has been that it does not provide sufficient referential force to the notion of God to allow the moral interpretation of religion to proceed. Her work has attracted a range of further criticisms we must now briefly explore.

Some of these tell against all endeavours to provide a purely moral interpretation of religion. These are to be noted now but dealt with when we come to sum up the profit and loss of the moral interpretation at the close of this study. For example, Basil Mitchell has argued vigorously that Murdoch's account of the moral life is broken-backed: it implicitly relies on conceptions dependent on traditional Christian theism to work while explicitly rejecting them. Specifically, he charges that Murdoch's central emphasis on morality as the loving attention to others only makes sense if we give to people the unique, unconditional worth attaching to them in the tradition of Christian ethics. But this stance towards the human individual arose out of a theological belief in human beings as the product of divine creation and the objects of divine love and is unsustainable without that theological background. It is just this background which Murdoch's rejection of traditional theism destroys.[63] This is a powerful critique, but it tells, and is meant to tell, against any version of the idea that we can maintain a 'high' conception of the moral life, use that on its own to justify a religious perspective on reality and yet keep clear of traditional theological affirmations. It would apply as much to Kant's ideas as Murdoch's. So we shall postpone discussion of it to Chapter 7.

More pertinent as a specific criticism of Murdoch is Stewart Sutherland's point that a moral interpretation of religion which uses the notion of the Good as a substitute for the traditional concept of God will inevitably reproduce the same metaphysical conundrums which led to the search for a moral interpretation of religion in the first place. Sutherland takes it that Murdoch wishes 'to regard the transcendent Good as an object of attention' – which is to conceive it in some sense as a particular.[64] Sutherland then points to a two-fold difficulty with the idea of the Good as so employed by Murdoch. First, we have the problems of making intelligible its character as a determinate thing which yet transcends the world – just the problems we might have in thinking of God as an individual yet beyond space and time. These will include problems in making intelligible the causal relations such an object might have with the given world. Second, we will be tempted to see the Good as an external agency, one only contingently related to the dynamics of moral vision. Thus we may take our attention away from the necessary intellectual and practical tasks facing us as moral agents. For example, we might come to think that right attention to the Good was an alternative to right attention to others.[65]

These strictures seem to me to flow from a misunderstanding of Murdoch's intentions. I can find no evidence in her writings that she thinks the Good can be a separate object of attention distinct from other human beings, art-works and facets of the natural world as objects of attention. This I take to be the message of the sympathetic, yet critical discussion, of Buber's *I and Thou* in chapter 15 of *Metaphysics as a Guide to Morals* (published of course well after Sutherland's comments). The Good is an object of attention in Murdoch only in and through the loving attention to others. To use the language of the Good is better to represent features of the experience of moral vision directed at things in the given world.

Since, as we have seen, we cannot take Murdoch's references to the Good in a realist fashion, the problem of conceiving its causal relations to the world does not arise. Nor does it, therefore, have any potential to introduce elements of heteronomy (as: in the false reliance on external moral agency to solve problems which are for us to tackle). So here too I think Sutherland's comments are wide of the mark. We should note, however, a general issue Sutherland's critique of Murdoch raises. It is vital for understanding the character of his own moral interpretation of religion. Behind Sutherland's strictures one might see the following problem for the moral interpretation of religion: it can only construe religious language as having a reference to a metaphysical object on pain of embroiling itself in the endless struggles of traditional philosophical theology to give a detailed and intelligible account of the nature of that object. Now I take it that we have seen in Kant's account of religious language the means to dissolve this problem. We took from Kant a three-fold analysis of the dynamics of references to a putative, transcendent object which is the source of moral order: i. the content of the images and concepts we use to frame such a reference; ii. the conviction that there is something, we know precisely not what, corresponding to such images and concepts which in turn is the ground of moral order; iii. the support which this conviction gives for our active hopes in continuing the moral struggle. If we attend to the nature of these elements of talk of the transcendent as plotted for us by Kant, I think we can avoid the problem Sutherland poses.

It would be more pertinent to criticise Murdoch's apparent hypostatisation of the Good by questioning those features of moral experience which it is required to explain. We have noted that chief among these is the apparent unity of the demands of virtue. Her language of the Good reflects the perception we allegedly have that the demands of moral vision stem from, or lead us to focus on, a single source of value. As against this presumption, it can be argued that a persistent and inescapable feature of moral experience is the facing of moral dilemmas where we meet incompatible yet equally valid, compelling requirements and values. Murdoch's moral Platonism encapsulates monism and realism. Monism, as the view that value is unitary, is disproved by moral conflicts between equally compelling moral values. Realism – as encapsulated in Murdoch's claim that, given that I have attained right vision of my moral circumstances, I see what I must do and have no choice as to what is demanded of me[66] – is disproved by the many cases of moral conflict where I see clearly what moral demands are but see that they clash. In such cases, I precisely must choose what to do knowing that whatever I do will implicate me in some evil. No further attention will reveal that some one thing is required of me and that the alternatives to this one thing are not at all required of me.

Moral conflict as a disproof of moral realism has been made much of in recent moral philosophy.[67] The disproof can be directed at two linked features of realism: its implications for the notion of truth and for a metaphysics of morality. Concerning truth, we note that it is a truism about truth that all genuine truths are compatible with one another. If there are equally compelling moral demands facing us in difficult circumstances this shows deep moral demands cannot partake of the logic of truth.[68] Concerning metaphysics, we associate moral realism with the thought that there is a moral order waiting to be discovered by human beings and which exists independently of any one's perception of it. If moral agents perceive themselves as facing equally compelling but incompatible moral demands, then they cannot be perceiving the moral order aright. How things appear morally cannot be how they are – if there is a moral order to be discovered through moral reflection.[69]

Moral conflicts come in many guises. Some of what critics of moral realism have in mind is the stuff of tragedy (and the theme of many a play and opera): the conflict in given, contingent circumstances between otherwise absolutely compelling obligations (as between: loyalty to friend and loyalty to society). Less dramatic are those many non-tragic circumstances where we face a conflict between values, see clearly that one should prevail but feel inevitable regret that, even while acting rightly, we have done some evil or neglected some good in the process. If moral realism were true, then there would be no irredeemable tragic conflicts between values. If in seeing clearly that we should do this rather than that we were discovering the truth or uncovering the nature of moral reality, regret at moral values we had thereby been unable to realise would be irrational.

The moral interpretation of religion would seem to be committed to moral realism. And it is so because it seeks to preserve one of the features of religion-in-general, namely belief that there is a moral order behind the given world. One of the great contributions of Murdoch to the explication of the moral interpretation of religion is the manner in which she brings out the phenomenology of this common commitment to moral realism. This is one reason why her work can be used by those committed to a traditional theistic metaphysics.[70] So an interim conclusion on the objection from moral dilemmas is that it disproves the moral interpretation only if it also disproves any typical religious outlook.[71] If, for example, the moral order we try to discern, and by reference to which our moral claims are true and false, were constituted by the commands of an omnipotent deity, there would be no conflicts between moral demands that were truly equally compelling. If it appeared otherwise to us, that would be a fact about our limited perceptions.

I cannot here go into the debate about the final weight to be given to the objection to realism from moral dilemmas. I merely want to sketch an answer the moral realist might have.[72] Following Guttenplan, we can distinguish four possible types of moral conflict relevant to the debate. The first is the resolvable. In this type further reflection shows that one of the competing demands is be acknowledged above others and we are able to act on that without regret. The second is the uncertain. We are faced with conflicting values and cannot find a way to resolve the conflict, remaining in a state of uncertainty as what we must do. As Guttenplan notes,[73] these two types of conflict actually reinforce realism. They fit the Murdochian phenomenology of human subjects faced with an overall demand to see the moral world aright when it is all too easy to remain with a clouded vision of the Good. The third type of conflict is that which is resolvable only with a remainder of regret. We discern, we suppose, how to act in the face of competing values, but the values we reject in making our decision remain with a hold over our conscience. We do something which has to be done, but we dirty our hands in the process. The fourth type is the tragic. As the objector presents matters, these are regular occurrences in moral life where we discern that there is no right way of resolving a pressing practical conflict. If we act, we do so with an assurance that we have not done what is right overall, because we see there is no right overall. Hence, we are not merely regretful over evil incurred or good foregone on the way to doing 'the right' thing. We are broken as moral beings.

Conflicts of the third and fourth types present moral realism with problems. The realist must say that the examples of the fourth type are in reality versions of types two and three. We should note that such a response does not at all negate the pain of tragic conflicts of this kind. The realist's view is not the silly 'tragic conflict does not exist'. Type two conflicts will give rise to moral torment. If type three conflicts are compatible with realism, then the problem of 'dirty hands' can be acknowledged as one which frequently gives rise to pain and anguish.

Can moral realism really acknowledge type three moral conflicts? This question bears directly on the nature of moral Platonism. Defenders of the plurality and incommensurability of ultimate values use 'Platonism' as a term of abuse to ridicule a position which says that there is one ultimate value and that good things are good to the extent they manifest this. Individual goods are but occasions for exemplifying the single property that is goodness. This implies a single measure or scale of value, provided by the awareness of the Form of the Good: 'particular values are valuable to the extent to which they partake in the Form of the Good'.[74] There can then be no regret if in choosing an act which most highly manifests the common value, goodness, I reject lesser manifestations of that same value.

How far this kind of moral monism was held by the historical Plato I leave others to determine. We can note that Aristotle took some such doctrine about the uniformity of goodness to be held by believers in the Forms and sought to argue for a more plural account of value.[75] Following the general lines laid down by Aristotle, we can give a rough sketch of how plurality and unity can be maintained together. This should enable us to see how realists can accept type three moral conflicts at face value and thus prevent them standing as refutations of realism.

We can concede to moral pluralists that we are initially aware of different valuable forms of goodness in personal living, such as justice, courage, benevolence and so forth. We are apprised of different sources of obligation and restraint on conduct. We are certainly not first cognisant of the different forms of virtue and obligation as respectworthy because we see them to be merely manifestations of an antecedently grasped monistic value. There is no evidence to suggest that Murdoch's references to the Good are intended to get across this erroneous picture of how we are aware of value in the human world. In this respect, the moral realist, including

Murdoch, is a pluralist about value. However, the realist will want to say that this is not the whole story.

He or she will wish to point (as Murdoch does) to facets of moral experience which appear to call us to integrate our awareness of the plural character traits that are good and the plural demands upon our conduct. One mode of such integration is conveyed in the idea that the various virtues should be capable of being realisable together over a long enough time (given a modest degree of external good fortune) in the good life. Such an idea can be supported by arguments in favour of the good Aristotelian conclusion that the full manifestation of any one of the virtues requires possession of the others. The notion of the good life is the notion of a common form which many concrete styles of life can exemplify. Further integrating ideas about goodness can come from the apparent demand that, when faced with moral perplexity, we should, as Murdoch so cogently calls to mind, search for right vision of our circumstances and the action that is demanded of us by those circumstances. The completion of this task is not given to us and right vision may be hard to discern and achieve. In the course of attaining, if we do, the necessary discernment we may have to set aside values which cannot in the circumstances be realised in pursuit of what is to be done. This is not to say that they are thereby discovered not to be values. Let us put this another way: in a circumstance of value conflict, I will perceive a number of things which ought to be done. Realism supports me in the search for the one that must be done. I may conclude that, overall, I ought to do A. But this verdictive 'ought' does not cancel out the competing deliberative 'oughts' I recognised on the way to this decision. Those 'oughts' registered my perception that there were good reasons for doing other things. Those good reasons remain. Thus I may act with regret at having to decide against those reasons even while I perceive that the greater reason lies with what I think I must do.

The idea that value in human life is plurally manifested and does not present itself as so many instances of a common, invariant property, points not to the unintelligibility of a search for the good life and the right vision of moral reality, but to the human difficulty in such a search. It bears out the Aristotelian point that it takes a peculiar kind of wisdom, borne of practice and emotional development, to distinguish the good from the bad in human affairs. Nobody can be given a measure, a scale, enabling them to make the necessary discriminations. The language of 'incommensurable values' can be used to make this point. Competing values cannot be adjudicated by measuring them one against another, as one measures different pieces of wall-paper against the one tape measure. But that is not to conclude that one should not, and cannot with the right kind of wisdom, make discriminations. Nor is it to conclude that we should not feel compelled to make those discriminations.

In suggesting that moral realism can cope with some of the pluriform character of moral values as these are revealed in moral conflict, I am suggesting that it can depart from aspects of moral Platonism as this is characterised by some defenders of moral pluralism and anti-realism. But it should be noted that I regard nothing of what I have said on this score as incompatible with Iris Murdoch's moral phenomenology. Indeed it chimes in with her continual emphasis on goodness as transcendent. An inextricable part of this transcendence for her is epistemological. What the Good is in any circumstance is frequently not given to us; thus how the Good is manifested is unclear. The Good is not like a ruler each person has in their pocket: 'It is a task to come to see the world as it is'.[76]

CONCLUSION

I have found that Iris Murdoch's moral interpretation of religion ultimately fails. It does so because it does not allow the form and content of morality to support a reference to a religious reality which might exist independently of our perception of it. Her interpretation appears to support such a reference, but once we see that the alleged ontology she postulates behind 'spiritualised morality' is causally inert, this appearance cannot be sustained.

Two points of prime importance do emerge from Murdoch despite my negative verdict overall.

First, there is a renewed sense of the centrality of the belief in moral teleology for the essence of a religious outlook, and hence for a viable moral interpretation of religion that is not reductionist or non-cognitivist. Murdoch's work has the signal merit of raising in its starkest form the question of how far such a belief in moral teleology can avoid the charge of giving way to the desire for consoling fantasy and therefore of being an agent in the corruption of morality.

Second, she opens the possibility of an alternative source of justification for the moral interpretation of religion. In both Chapters 2 and 4 we found that there is no way that either traditional theistic or Kantian thinkers could prove that it was irrational to withhold assent from belief in the moral character of the underlying order behind the given world. At most, they could point to the attractions of such a belief – in its power to bolster moral effort, secure a sense of meaning to the struggle for good and provide an answer to the secular problem of evil. Murdoch points in detail to what other authors delineate in outline, namely that the phenomenology of morals suggests a religious interpretation to reality. She suggests an alternative to the Kantian arguments for the postulates of practical reason. As we have seen, this would be an argument from experience employing the 'best account principle' described and defended by Charles Taylor.[77]

It must be admitted that there are problems in the proposal that we might marry Immanuel Kant and Iris Murdoch. Kantian ethics is, after all, among the targets of her phenomenology of morals. We would have to conceive of a final version of the moral interpretation which accepted the basic thrust of Kant's interpretation of religious language and his response to the problem of evil, while combining these with a Murdochian picture of the dynamics of moral vision.

NOTES

1. 'Vision and Choice in Morality'.
2. 'Spiritualised Morality', p. 78.
3. 'Spiritualised Morality', p. 78.
4. See, for example, Murdoch *Metaphysics as a Guide to Morals*, p. 336.
5. Murdoch *Metaphysics as a Guide to Morals*, p. 426.
6. Cupitt *Taking Leave of God*, p. 98.
7. Murdoch *Metaphysics as a Guide to Morals*, pp. 454–6.
8. Murdoch *Metaphysics as a Guide to Morals*, p. 341.
9. Sprigge 'Refined and Crass Supernaturalism'. What follows draws on pp. 123–4.
10. Murdoch *Metaphysics as a Guide to Morals*, p. 341.
11. Murdoch *Metaphysics as a Guide to Morals*, p. 340.
12. Murdoch *The Sovereignty of Good*, pp. 50–1.
13. Murdoch *The Sovereignty of Good*, p. 52.
14. Murdoch *The Sovereignty of Good*, pp. 17–18.
15. Murdoch *The Sovereignty of Good*, p. 40.
16. As in *The Sovereignty of Good*, p. 74, and *Metaphysics as a Guide to Morals*, p. 301.
17. Lawrence *The Rainbow*, p. 35.
18. See Leavis *D. H. Lawrence*, p. 115; Byrne 'F. R. Leavis and the Religious Dimension in Literature', pp. 119–30, expounds Leavis' ideas on the religious and they bear direct comparison with Taylor *Sources of the Self*, chapters 1–4.
19. Murdoch *The Sovereignty of Good*, p. 64.
20. Murdoch *The Sovereignty of Good*, p. 65.
21. See Murdoch *The Sovereignty of Good*, p. 84.
22. See Falk *Myth, Truth and Literature* for a fuller account of this.
23. Murdoch *The Sovereignty of Good*, p. 55.
24. Murdoch *The Sovereignty of Good*, p. 38.
25. Murdoch *The Sovereignty of Good*, p. 56.
26. Murdoch *The Sovereignty of Good*, pp. 57–8.
27. Murdoch *Metaphysics as a Guide to Morals*, p. 297.
28. Murdoch *The Sovereignty of Good*, p. 75.
29. Taylor *Sources of the Self*, p. 93.
30. Murdoch *Metaphysics as a Guide to Morals*, p. 507.
31. Murdoch *Metaphysics as a Guide to Morals*, p. 406.
32. Murdoch *Metaphysics as a Guide to Morals*, p. 410.
33. *Metaphysics as a Guide to Morals*, p. 430.
34. *Metaphysics as a Guide to Morals*, p. 430.
35. Murdoch *Acastos*, p. 108.
36. Taylor *Sources of the Self*, pp. 57–8.
37. Murdoch *Metaphysics as a Guide to Morals*, p. 413. Our next chapter will describe and adjudicate on interpretations of religion inspired by Wittgenstein.
38. Murdoch *Metaphysics as a Guide to Morals*, p. 412.

39. 'Spiritualised Morality', p. 78.
40. Murdoch *The Sovereignty of Good*, p. 93.
41. See Dunbar 'On Art, Morals and Religion', p. 520.
42. Dunbar 'On Art, Morals and Religion', p. 524.
43 *Metaphysics as a Guide to Morals*, p. 426; my emphasis.
44. Graham 'Spiritualised Morality', p. 81.
45. 'Spiritualised Morality', pp. 81 and 84.
46. For such a case in full see Pailin The *Anthropological Character of Theology*.
47. Murdoch *The Sovereignty of Good*, p. 74.
48. See pp. 268–71.
49. See Rogers 'The Traditional Doctrine of Divine Simplicity' for a full and insightful survey of this tradition.
50. *Summa Theologiae*, 1a. 3. 2. ad 3, p. 27.
51. Murdoch *The Sovereignty of Good*, p. 79.
52. Murdoch *The Sovereignty of Good*, p. 80.
53. Murdoch *The Sovereignty of Good*, p. 59.
54. Murdoch *The Sovereignty of Good*, p. 64.
55. Dunbar 'On Art, Morals and Religion'.
56 'On Art, Morals and Religion', p. 524.
57. *Morality: Religious and Secular*, pp. 86–7.
58. Despland *The Education of Desire*.
59. *The Education of Desire*, p. 67.
60. *The Education of Desire*, p. 145.
61. *The Education of Desire*, pp. 136–7.
62. Murdoch *The Sovereignty of Good*, p. 94.
63. See Mitchell *Morality: Religious and Secular*, pp. 64–72.
64. Sutherland *God, Jesus and Belief*, p. 96.
65. Sutherland *God, Jesus and Belief*, pp. 96–7.
66. Murdoch *The Sovereignty of Good*, pp. 39–40.
67. See, for example, Williams *Moral Luck*, especially chapters 2 and 5.
68. See Guttenplan 'Moral Realism and Moral Dilemmas', p. 61.
69. See Kekes *The Morality of Pluralism*, pp. 64–5.
70. As, for example, Martin Soskice 'Love and Attention' .
71. A fact pointed to by Kekes in *The Morality of Pluralism*, p. 64.
72. This is indebted to Guttenplan 'Moral Realism', pp. 75–6.
73. 'Moral Realism', p. 76.
74. Kekes *The Morality of Pluralism*, pp. 63–4.
75. See Nussbaum *The Fragility of Goodness*, p. 292.
76. Murdoch *The Sovereignty of Good*, p. 91.
77. See Taylor *Sources of the Self*, p. 58.

6

Wittgensteinian Perspectives and the Moral Interpretation of Religion

WITTGENSTEIN, RELIGION AND PRACTICE

The influence of the later philosophy of Wittgenstein has been an important strand in general philosophy taking some contemporary authors in the direction of the moral interpretation of religion. It is noticeable that the moral interpretation has gained followers in post-war English-speaking philosophy as part of the aftermath of debates about the general character of religious language. These flourished in the 1950s, 1960s and 1970s. Their immediate cause was the positivist critique of religious language as meaningless because unverifiable. Wittgensteinian ideas about language were employed by some participants in these debates as a response to positivism. The key idea from Wittgenstein operative in moral interpreters of religious language such as D. Z. Phillips and Stewart Sutherland is contextualism about meaning. Wittgenstein's slogan to the effect that the meaning of a word is its use in the language is taken to imply that to uncover the sense of a term we should find and explore the contexts in which it is used.[1] Meaning is rooted in contexts of employment.

These ideas about meaning carry a message about how to approach the business of philosophical analysis. Where we have language which provokes philosophical puzzlement, we should seek to uncover the practices which underlie use of that language. Consider the following example. Philosophers of mind debate *ad nauseam* whether belief is a disposition to behaviour or a mental act and so on. The Wittgensteinian approach bids us to forget theories while we examine the contexts in which we speak of people's believing things and uncover the practices with which this talk is associated. The aim of Wittgensteinian therapy is to reveal that there is nothing about which we need propose ever more subtle and complex theories (in this example, no one thing, independent of contexts, which is 'belief'). Hence, the impulse to theorise philosophically will be stilled.

Whether or not all philosophical problems can be dissolved in this fashion is a matter we can leave to one side. There appears to be independent merit in the ideas that meaning grows out of contexts of use and that, to get clear about whether or how an area of discourse is intelligible, we should uncover the human practices of which it is part and parcel. Granted that the debates about religious language sparked by positivism show that the precise way in which such language is intelligible is open to debate, Wittgensteinian philosophers have sought to take it back to the human practices and contexts in which it has its home. In so doing they have rejected, as at least the first step, the notion that we should make it intelligible by indulging in metaphysical speculation about its putative object (God) and they have gone to moral practices as the primary background of its meaning.

The reasons why moral practices, or the moral side of more overt religious practices such as prayer, have been chosen in the application of the Wittgensteinian method reminds us of earlier discussions in this study. Moral practices can be seen (whether rightly or wrongly) to be common and open to all, whereas the overtly religious is an area of diversity in which many today can see no point, perhaps because of the prevalence of scepticism about historical and metaphysical routes to religion. Seen in one light the particular application of Wittgensteinian ideas about how to achieve philosophical clarity which has led to writing furthering the moral interpretation to religion is a peculiar descendent of the deists' concern to find a natural religion that would be universal and free of history and mystery – a point noted by Sutherland himself.[2]

There is a general bias among Wittgenstein and his followers against metaphysical speculation as a legitimate means of responding to philosophical problems. Indeed, the philosophical temptation to indulge in metaphysics is seen as the cause and symptom of philosophical perplexity. Both Sutherland and Phillips reject the need to link religion to the postulation of a transcendent ground of being existing in some metaphysical space. Sutherland airs the difficulties in making belief in such an entity sufficiently intelligible.[3] The objections he raises to the God of metaphysics are broadly in the Kantian tradition of questioning how any individual could be delineated for human thought which also enjoyed the radical transcendence claimed for the God of religion (see Chapter 1 above).

Phillips complains that to interpret religious claims as if they were about such a transcendent, metaphysical entity invites a reductionist interpretation of religious belief, one in which the content of typical religious perspectives on reality are lost. The pursuit of a metaphysical referent for 'God' ends by separating talk of God from the practices which give it sense and it leaves the notion of God without any content.[4] Both authors contend that the problem of evil becomes insoluble if 'God' is taken to be the name of a transcendent ground of being who is causally responsible for the evils which beset human beings.[5]

How far these criticisms of traditional philosophical ways of grounding belief in God are just can be set aside for present purposes. The chief issue to be explored in this chapter is the way in which a Wittgensteinian moral interpretation of religion throws up a crucial challenge to the general argument of this book. On the one hand, Sutherland and Phillips offer an interpretation of religious belief (or in Sutherland's case, we should say a 'reconstruction', since he makes no claim to be faithful to what the person in the pew believes)[6] which eschews the idea that religious vocabulary invokes metaphysical referents. On the other hand, both authors reject the claim that their accounts are reductionist or non-cognitivist. They deny that their interpretations of the religious amount to saying that religious language is devoid of cognitive content and merely the vehicle for expressing feelings and attitudes towards reality. They deny that their accounts amount to translating religious discourse into talk about human ideals or the like. Both insist that religious discourse offers a perspective on the real and that it is a means of saying something that cannot be said by using non-religious vocabulary.

We can put the issue of realism versus reductionism and non-cognitivism into context by once more reverting to the typology set out by Sprigge.[7] Wittgensteinian perspectives on religion, practices and morality clearly wish to set aside piecemeal supernaturalism as the appropriate way to interpret or reconstruct religious belief. However, we cannot say that Sutherland and Phillips offer us refined supernaturalism of the sub-type Sprigge designates as 'mystical'. They do not offer a spiritual interpretation of all reality by invoking a general relationship between the world and a metaphysical ground which human experience might mediate. Nor yet would they accept that their views belong to 'scientific' refined supernaturalism of the kind paradigmatically displayed in the writings of Don Cupitt. Religious discourse is not merely a way of giving expression to human ideals and aspirations, leaving the character of reality to be settled wholly by the sciences.

I have tied realism in the interpretation of religion to a minimal referential thesis, which is to be further explicated by linking it to belief in an underlying moral order to reality. Sutherland and Phillips implicitly argue against this understanding of realism, certainly if what is styled 'realism' is what we have left when reductionism and non-cognitivism are set aside in the interpretation of religion. Both Sutherland and Phillips draw inferences from the problem of evil which amount to rejection of belief in a moral order to reality. Both interpret eternal life in such a way that it is not the embodiment of a hope for the future completion of a moral struggle with evil we are now engaged in.[8] Both divorce religious belief (as it is best interpreted or reconstructed) from commitment to a moral teleology behind nature and history. Indeed, as we shall discuss in detail later, Phillips implicitly argues that such a commitment is based on ideas which are morally corrupting.[9]

Discussion of the Wittgensteinian challenge to the moral interpretation of religion as I have outlined that interpretation can begin by looking in detail at the contentions of Sutherland's *God, Jesus and Belief*.

SUTHERLAND AND RELIGION AS A PERSPECTIVE

There are many respects in which Sutherland's approach to the interpretation of religion falls four-square into the neo-Kantianism articulated in these pages.

Sutherland is strongly agnostic about the metaphysics of deity. It is this agnosticism, rather than any dogmatic positivism, which prevents acceptance of the adequacy of traditional philosophical glosses of God-talk. His agnosticism is based on a number of grounds. One is a set of arguments to the effect that we cannot make intelligible the idea that 'God' is the name of an individual who yet transcends space and time.[10] We have aired versions of these arguments in Chapter 1 above. They are parallel to arguments in Kant for the conclusion that the concept of God used in metaphysical theism cannot pick out an intelligible object of knowledge for us.

Sutherland lists a number of criteria philosophers must use if they are to offer an acceptable interpretation of religious belief. One is moral: 'A religious belief which runs counter to our moral beliefs is to that extent unacceptable'.[11] This criterion provides grounds for agnosticism about the God of philosophical theology. Such grounds arise notably in connection with the problem of evil. The defender of the God of traditional philosophy will claim it is certain that a divine person with the attributes of omnipotence, omniscience and omnibenevolence exists. Our awareness of evil is then made to fit the postulation of such a being. We will have to say the omnibenevolent being has morally sufficient reasons for allowing or bringing about all the horrendous evils we are aware of in the history of the world. The character of some of these evils will naturally stretch our credulity as to how they can be backed by morally sufficient purposes. We will, in speculating on these purposes, either directly put our moral convictions under strain by giving God purposes and values we could not admire in a human being, or indirectly test these convictions by appealing to the 'mystery' of the workings of divine goodness. Appeal to mystery in the face of the problem of evil will also produce a major inconsistency in our philosophy of God: we will be sure that there is a God with certain metaphysical attributes, but will suddenly play the agnostic card when faced with giving an account of the nature of that being's values and purposes. Sutherland contends that if we begin religious reflection with the problem of human suffering we must be agnostic about the precise characteristics of whatever, if anything, is referred to by 'God'.[12]

Sutherland's proximity to the Kantian tradition is shown in two further criteria for acceptable philosophical glosses on religious belief and language:

> A revisionary account of religious belief is acceptable to the extent to which it makes and defends a claim to be true.

> A revisionary account of religious belief both commends itself and avoids the dangers of reductionism to the extent to which it gives or preserves insights which are not available elsewhere, into the human condition, or into the world in which we live.[13]

By the first of these criteria, he rejects any attempts to translate religious statements in such a way as to make them devoid of any truth-claims. By the second, he denies that religious statements are dispensable means to the making of claims which could be made by using non-religious vocabulary. By the first criterion for a successful reconstruction of theism, the approach of a Braithwaite is rejected; by the second, Feuerbach's programme is set aside.

Thus far, Sutherland's views seem to involve the application of the Kantian schema we have outlined: the content of the symbol 'God' will be declared to be of use in guiding the religious imagination, but even while it does not pick out any determinate object of knowledge for us, it points to a source of meaning in reality which has vital consequences for our thinking about morality. However, Sutherland is a problematic Kantian just at the point where we come to consider whether 'God' retains any referential force linked to belief in a source of moral order.

Sutherland's positive account of what can be salvaged, philosophically, from the imaginative content of theism is summed up in the pithy phrase 'Theology is the articulation of the possible'.[14] The possibility in question here is that of a set of interlocking kinds of meaning to the moral life: possibilities for 'human fulfilment and human self-knowledge'.[15] These possibilities are created through human beings' ability to interrogate their thoughts and actions from a standpoint *sub specie aeternitatis*. It is the job of religious language and belief to articulate for us this possibility of seeking an eternal perspective upon our lives. To seek such a perspective is in turn to try to view thought and conduct not from the standpoint of our own individual interests, or from the standpoint of our own human community, but rather to view thought and conduct in the light of a postulated transcendent order of values. To endeavour to view our lives in relation to these postulated values is to change the world in which we live, by, for example, making available courses of conduct and reflection which were not otherwise open to us.

Sutherland gives an example to illustrate the above from Robert Bolt's play *A Man for all Seasons*.[16] Thomas More tries to counsel Rich against seeking the fulfilment of his personal, worldly ambitions. He should instead become a teacher and if he is a good one, not only will he and his pupils know it, God will know it too. Sutherland takes the force of 'and God will know it too' in such a context to point to the availability of a significance to contemplated conduct not otherwise revealed. It is a significance quite other than that measured by the fulfilment of the ego's aims and plans. It is a significance which rather arises when we ask how our conduct stands in relation to the enactment of values which we can only regard as transcendent and eternal. A life as a teacher has meaning to it beyond that of succeeding or failing to realise prior personal concerns and the kind of meaning it can have is recognised, through the use of the language of religion, to be available come what may and regardless of worldly success or failure.

Elsewhere, Sutherland points to the way in which:

> some actions do not depend upon future outcome, in so far as they are not subject to trivialisation by changing circumstances. In such cases, whatever happens, the right thing has been done: the demands of justice or integrity or truth have been met.[17]

This contention invokes the kind of thoughts about conduct aired in Chapter 2 where we distinguished between internal and external ends of action. Some acts have their point wholly or largely in their success in fulfilling goals external to them (so: Rich's alternative to being a teacher is advancement in government in order to become wealthy). The point of such acts is doubly contingent. First, their worthwhileness flows from their being in the circumstances the best way to achieve external ends. If other means are better suited to that purpose, they cease to be worthwhile. Second, factors independent of the agent's conduct can prevent the actions being successful. Then, too, they lose their point. To act thus, in pursuit of external ends solely, is to be in the grip of time, in the sense of 'change and chance'. By contrast, Sutherland invokes perspectives on conduct which may give it an eternal, that is timeless, uncontingent, significance. We have seen that some acts appear to be worthwhile just for the sake of the activity involved in doing them. If I can say that, whatever the outcome of my actions, I am witnessing to 'the demands of justice or integrity or truth', then the point of what I am doing is not contingent on my desires (nor on those of any social group I happen to belong to) and that point will not be destroyed if the external end of my action is defeated in its realisation by the contingencies of world beyond my control.

In the light of the above we may speak of the worth of conduct being 'eternal', or of its worth being revealed when viewed from the standpoint of eternity, or of its worth lying in the eye of God. Such language, and the thoughts outlined about human meaning which support it, is obviously related to Iris Murdoch's linkage of religious concerns to the endeavour to fight the claims of the ego and to seek a viewpoint on the world which is ego-transcendent. Evidently, they would also be supported by her leading thought that value, the Good, is an eternal, transcendent object of vision and attainment. The grounding of religious language in moral practice gains strength from the thought that conduct can be worthwhile in enacting values which are somehow eternal, transcendent and uncreated by the human will.[18] If conduct gains a meaning by its relation – of embodiment or enactment – to values, and if those values are somehow thought to have an eternal and transcendent significance, then there is a source of meaning in human life of a distinctively religious kind which falls short of this meaning being derived from the commands or plans of a creator God.

As well as being allied to Murdoch on the religious nature and consequences of the pursuit of moral vision in human life, Sutherland's ideas also share close resemblances with those of Michael Oakeshott in his *On Human Conduct*. He too contends that religion is to be primarily identified as that in human life which is an antidote to finitude and nullity as these are shown in the capture of human conduct by contingency. He too grounds the religious on the nature of morality as a source of human meaning which gives conduct a significance independent of outcome and happenstance.[19]

Yet the exposition of Sutherland so far has omitted a primary element in his account. This is to be found in bringing out the full force of his adoption of the Kantian notion that ideas of the eternal and the divine play a 'regulative' role in human life.[20] For an idea to play such a role is for it to make possible and encourage lines of questioning and reflection in relation to the world or human affairs. Religion as the expression of the possibility of a view on human life *sub specie aeternitatis* enables, then, important questions to be raised about ourselves and plans. It is important for this regulative function that we never think we have attained the eternal perspective on life and conduct. Here Sutherland's thought may be linked to Murdoch's on the transcendence of the Good. This transcendence is in part epistemological: we seek to view things from the standpoint of the Good/the eternal, while yet knowing that any and every attempt to occupy that standpoint by us will be to some greater or lesser degree mistaken. We can always be mistaken and must always be ready to raise the question of whether we are.

That attaining the eternal perspective is a possibility, not a given but a regulative ideal, is important for Sutherland in providing an opening for a vital manifestation of human self-knowledge. This is the self-knowledge which distinguishes the insane fanatic from the genuine saint (that is, moral hero or heroine). Sutherland's argument on this score can be reconstructed as follows.[21]

The notion that conduct may have a worth which is eternal and independent of consequences is a dangerous one. To realise this we have only to think of the many fanatics in power who have ruined the lives of thousands or millions of their fellows in pursuit of some alleged 'higher' value than human welfare. It is a mark of this kind of insane, fanatical pursuit of an alleged value to say to oneself: 'I have got the truth and in the light of that truth everything which flows from it can be justified. My conduct is not subject to the normal standards of criticism in the light of its consequences and so forth'. The notion of having an eternal, extra-human perception on human life has functioned, in this guise, as a buttress to the most absurd and obscene egos in human history. But the moral saint is one who realises the true transcendence of the eternal, divine perspective and can thus always frame the question: 'But have I interpreted the claims of justice and truth aright?'

Sutherland is then drawing attention to the way in which notions of the eternal and transcendent as an anchor for values can (and do) serve to inflate and ground the fat, relentless human ego. For these notions to foster defeat of the ego, we must recognise the true transcendence of the notion of an eternal set of objective values in relation to which human life is to be lived. We need the idea of a perspective provided by a transcendent order of values in order for vital human meanings and possibilities to be available to us. But that need is thwarted once we think we have captured those values in a definitive list. If those values are appropriated in that way, fanaticism results. A true faith corresponding to the search for the eternal must contain the thought that 'even one's most cherished views' on what is mandatory are open to question and may be limited.[22] The relevant kinds of ego-transcendent meaning are only possible given that these important forms of self-questioning are always seen as appropriate.

There is an obvious tension in Sutherland's reasoning thus far. For if human conduct is to gain a meaning through its relation to or enactment of eternal, transcendent values, it must be that agents can be sure on enough occasions that they know what values like truth and justice are and what they demand. But to support Sutherland's points about the necessity of self-questioning, it seems that no such assurance can be guaranteed. The way in which Sutherland could overcome this seeming contradiction would be as follows: the transcendence of values to the human world is relative and not absolute. This implies that the realism involved in this transcendence need not entail a thoroughgoing scepticism about our ability to discover what value is and demands. It implies a critical realism. We can make distinctions between true and false, better and worse, apprehensions of value. But even in making these distinctions we must admit our fallibility and the ever present possibility that we are in touch with the ego's or the herd's promptings. In relation to many of our judgements this possibility will be largely theoretical. But it will always be the mark of the morally sane that they can admit that it is possible for them to be mistaken and that they are ready to listen to any substantive doubts concerning whether they have got it wrong. So, in sum, the Good, though transcendent, can be appropriated to some degree, but never to the extent for anyone warrantably to say, as the fanatic may say, 'I have the God's-eye view of the truth and my judgement is not to be questioned'. That kind of appropriation of the order of values destroys its transcendence.

We can now see in greater detail how far Sutherland's views stand in relation to the moral interpretation of religion. They fall short of anything like traditional theism in key respects. 'God' is not a constitutive concept yielding knowledge of an object causally active upon or in the world. The concept of God invokes the idea of a transcendent order of values. This idea in turn plays a vital regulative function in human, moral life by way of making intelligible the pursuit of an eternal perspective upon our actions and attitudes.

Sutherland's ideas also amount, according to his own presentation of them, to something other than the reduction of religion to the expression of different attitudes towards a world common between both believer and unbeliever. Theology is the articulation of a set of possibilities – possibilities for action, meaning and self-knowledge rooted in the search for the eternal perspective upon the human world. In this unique case it is legitimate to infer from what is possible to what is actual.[23] One who endeavours to appropriate the eternal perspective in the right spirit will see a world which is different from the world of the individual who has no time for this quest. The differences will lie in the possibilities for action, meaning and reflection available to the former but not the latter. The person of faith will find a certain way of living in the world intelligible while one without faith will see no sense in this way of living: 'The possible is here to be understood as the limits of the intelligible – or the rational. The possibility of the life of faith is in this sense the intelligibility of the life of faith'.[24] Believer and unbeliever will describe human conduct differently. They will judge differently of the nature of the lives they see around them. Sutherland goes so far as to say that 'there is an *ontological* difference between a world in which [eternal, moral] fulfilment can be found in human life, and one in which this is not so'.[25] To this idea of the awareness of possibility changing the world for the person of faith we can add Sutherland's repeated affirmations that only the language of religion will do to get across the human possibilities in question. So it is both realist in its thrust and irreplaceable, yet not referential in the fashion outlined in Chapter 3.

We might sum up the central thought behind Sutherland's stance towards the moral interpretation of religion thus: the notion of religious language as the articulation of a *perspective* on human life and conduct provides a means of escaping the choice between postulating a referential object (however vaguely indicated) to correspond to 'God' and making religion consist in the expression of emotions or feelings towards a world which is neutral as between religious and secular outlooks.

Similar points to those above could be made about Phillips on the kind of truth religious language aspires to. He is adamant that the word 'God' does not denote an existent, a thing or an object.[26] Connected with that denial is his claim that 'God' is not a name and does not refer to anything.[27] We have already noted that Phillips wishes to distance his own positive views upon religion from those of a Braithwaite. Like Sutherland he stresses the irreplaceability of religious language: what it says cannot be successfully translated into non-religious discourse.[28] He also affirms that one who is religious lives in a different world from one who is not. Believer and unbeliever do not see the same world. 'Religious language is not an interpretation of how things are, but determines how things are for the believer. The saint and atheist do not interpret the same world in different ways. They see different worlds'.[29] Believer and unbeliever understand the world they face in conduct differently. For example, they measure success and failure in it differently. So the possibilities of action, reflection and meaning are different for believer and unbeliever.

Phillips' fundamental thought on what 'truth' and 'realism' amount to in discussions of religious language comes down to this: the disjunction 'either religious belief posits certain facts about the world (or certain objects) not posited by unbelief, or religion is the mere expression of different attitudes and feelings to the world' is a false one. It is false in the light of a third possibility present in the previous paragraph: believer and unbeliever live in different worlds. The believer comes to live 'in a different world' because religious belief is like a measure or ruler laid against reality: 'The beliefs assess the facts, not the facts the beliefs'.[30] It involves seeing the world in the light of commitment to certain absolute values (that is, values which bind regardless of our own desires, interests and projects, which bid us do so-and-so regardless of our preferences[31]). Taking this ruler to reality changes that reality in so far as it is a sphere for human action. Measuring reality this way rules in and rules out courses of conduct and strands of meaning for us. In this fashion the perspectival view of religious language tells us that while religion posits no new facts in or behind the world, it nonetheless is connected with the facts and with the world. The perspectival view is thus not a rehash of non-cognitivism.

The idea of religion as a perspective upon the world and its facts has a double source in the writings of Wittgenstein. In part it derives from Wittgenstein's conception of ethics and the nature of a commitment to absolute values. In part it can be seen as an application of Wittgenstein's general comments on 'seeing an aspect' in the *Philosophical Investigations*.

In his 'Lecture on Ethics' Wittgenstein stresses the difference between absolute and relative values.[32] The latter are values whose power to compel action and judgement are relative to a subject's prior desires. So we might say to someone: if you want to impress the neighbours, you ought to buy a new car. But we cannot say in the same voice: if you want to be a good person, you ought to stop cheating your friends. Cheating is out for the good person regardless of what he or she might happen to want. It is not open to someone not to want to be morally good. This distinction so far looks like that drawn by Kant between hypothetical and categorical imperatives, or like the one Aristotelian moralists would draw between conduct which is extrinsically good/bad and intrinsically good/bad, that is between conduct which is (un)worthwhile in the light of what it leads to and that which is (un)worthwhile in the light of the activity involved in doing it (see Chapter 2 above). What is distinctive about the Wittgensteinian way of making this familiar distinction in ethics is the manner in which Wittgenstein and his followers stress the extent to which there is no common ground between the one who believes in absolute values and the one who does not and insist that there are no facts about the world which might be used to argue for or against the rationality of a perspective which recognises the existence of absolute values. This stressing of an unbridgeable gulf is linked to remarks Wittgenstein makes in his *Notebooks* and in the *Tractatus* on how the one who is 'happy' or who views the world from an eternal perspective lives in a completely different world from the one who does not.[33]

We have tried to set out the sense of this 'living in a different world' in discussion of Sutherland on the possibilities of meaning, action and self-knowledge created by adoption of what he deems a religious perspective on life. Further sense can be given to the notion of how one's view of the world is changed by turning to Wittgenstein on 'seeing an aspect'.[34]

Wittgenstein's discussion of this topic is centred around the significance of puzzle pictures. There is a sense in which one who sees the famous duck-rabbit picture as a duck sees the same thing as one who sees it only as a rabbit. If asked to draw what they see, they would produce drawings which were isomorphic. If one were shown the other's drawing, he or she could say 'Yes, that is a picture of what I see'. But what they see is also different in each case, in so far as they see different meanings or patterns before them. It was John Wisdom who built on this idea in well-known essays such as 'Gods'.[35] Wisdom teaches us there to avoid the conclusion that theist and atheist differ only in their emotional reaction to the facts if one knows all the facts about the world that the other knows and neither has expectations about the future that the other does not have. They might still have a dispute which is about the real, for one will seem to see a pattern, a meaning, in the world that the other does not. They will connect the facts together in different ways, just as one who sees the duck-rabbit as a duck will connect and interpret the marks on the paper before him or her differently from one who sees it as a rabbit.

What Sutherland and Phillips try to do in their remarks about religious language embodying a unique, untranslatable, eternal perspective on reality can be viewed as giving substance to Wisdom's thought that the dispute between believer and unbeliever is one about the character of the real.[36]

REALISM AND PERSPECTIVES

Whereas I have argued that the moral interpretation of religion must have minimal referential and metaphysical implication to avoid sliding into reductionism or non-cognitivism, Sutherland and Phillips disagree.

Their rejection of any kind of reference on behalf of religious language to metaphysical reality, however meagre and agnostic it may be, is clear. Phillips agues in *Religion without Explanation* that Hume has shown the unintelligibility of the thought that this world might rest upon some transcendent ground.[37] Despite some hints in recent writings allowing that 'God' might have a reference, there seems to be no going back on the idea that it cannot invoke a reality beyond the spatio-temporal on which our world rests. Sutherland might seem to allow the possibility that 'God' has a transcendent reference, since he states that to use the language of God is to invoke the idea of a transcendent order of values. But it is notable that the passages which, superficially, might encourage this idea in fact are clear in linking the view of things *sub specie aeternitatis* to 'the *possibility* of a transcendent order'.[38] He tells us that the notion of a transcendent order of values is not 'descriptive' but purely regulative.[39] It is clear from remarks such as the following that this categorisation means the notion is not referential at all:

> Thus the view of the world *sub specie aeternitatis* is nothing more nor less than a view of the world; it is how the world is seen when it is seen *sub specie aeternitatis*. It is not something other than the world seen and experienced. To postulate such a view is to talk about how it is possible to understand the world and to live in it.[40]

That the view of religion as an eternal perspective on reality evacuates 'God' of referential import can be confirmed by showing that whatever is invoked by 'God' on this view is devoid of causal significance. This point can lead on to questioning its realist credentials.

The lack of any causal implications in the idea of religion as a perspective on things can be seen in Sutherland's and Phillips' treatment of the problem of evil. Both are critics of the way the theological problem of evil is customarily dealt with by philosophers of religion. They reject the popular line of enquiry which seeks to explain why evil suffered by human beings is tolerated in God's creation by uncovering the divine purposes which mean that greater good will come from that evil in the long run. Such accounts place evil within a postulated larger divine teleology in order that God can be seen as having a morally sufficient reason for creating it. Though their discussions contain different emphases, Sutherland and Phillips agree in at least two objections to such theodicies.

In the first place, they unite in placing what might be called a 'deontological stop' in the path of the divine teleology postulated by the theodicies under review. There are evils of certain types and extents such that they could not be allowed or created by a divine planner without irredeemably sullying the goods which might flow from them. It is a mark of moral blindness to toy with the thought that a God worthy of worship could reason in a teleological fashion about such evils.[41]

A second point of agreement on how to tackle the problem of evil is explicit in Phillips and implicit in Sutherland. Both can be interpreted as arguing that traditional theodicy, with its emphasis on finding some redeeming good to flow from evil, actually prevents the realisation of the true religious response to evil. This is a response which enables evil to be overcome in the life of the ethical individual through the defeat and transcending of the ego which facing up to evil from the proper perspective allows. Phillips speaks of the authentic religious response to evil arising out of acceptance of its pointlessness – its coming to one in the absence of any higher planning which would mean that it will serve one's good in the long run. The authentic response takes evil as a reflection of the subject's contingency which further enables an appropriately selfless response to it. This can be linked to Phillips' comments elsewhere about the centrality in the religious vision of dying to one's self, that is of transcending self-centredness.[42] On this account, the language of religion arises out of an awareness of evil, because that language expresses a perspective on life linked to overcoming all that is centred in the ego and its demands and because in turn that perspective is tested and promoted by the apparently pointless sufferings which afflict one.

Such a view endeavours to show how religious talk is anchored in facts such as evil by showing how evil engages with the perspective on self and world which is religion. The substance of Phillips' view is evidently linked to Murdoch's account of how a concern for the Good is connected to the defeat of ego and to her own emphasis on the pointlessness of goodness. Sutherland makes these links to Murdoch in his own account of what the significance of Jesus might amount to on an account of religious discourse such as his own by introducing a notion of ethical transcendence: 'Any account of transcendence in ethical terms will have reference to transcendence of the self, in the sense of the ego'.[43] This notion of transcendence is derived from Bonhoeffer and others as well as from Murdoch and is linked to the idea of dying to the self. Transcendence is manifested in one who is totally invulnerable to what people may do to him or her (and, presumably, what the world, by way of disease or other natural hurt, may do). But Sutherland invokes via reflection on the figure of Jesus the paradox that only one who is totally vulnerable to others can be totally invulnerable.[44] The paradox is intelligible in this way: the one who is ethically invulnerable (transcendent) is the one who's abandonment of self (ego) is total. But such a one is in turn capable of accepting the evil that others (or the world) may visit upon him or her.

For Sutherland, the enduring message of the life and passion of Jesus comes via his manifestation to us in an historical existence of this mode of self-abandonment, of ethical transcendence. The meaning found in such a life is bound up with that life embodying a kind of acceptance of evil and associated weakness and vulnerability. We might then, with one eye on Phillips, read back into Sutherland's criticisms of the teleological approach to evil in traditional theodicies the point that search for a teleology in which evil is embedded is a way of removing the possibility of that acceptance of evil which makes ethical transcendence possible.

In divorcing the religious perspective on reality from any concern with a teleology, Sutherland and Phillips make the notion of God causally inert. By the same token, religion as they reconstruct/interpret it is divorced from that belief in a moral order to reality which I have asserted to be central to religion *per se* and to the moral interpretation of religion.

It follows from all of the above that Sutherland and Phillips make religion out to have no answer to the question 'What may I hope for?' In their view, one who is authentically religious undertakes the struggle for good and against evil with no different expectations about the future from one who has no time for religion. This must mean that the world, understood as an array of substances and processes which generate a series of events in the past, present and future, is handed over to science. Religion has zero implications for our view of the world *in that respect*. It makes a difference merely (of course, Sutherland and Phillips would object to the 'merely') in the way we respond ethically to the world, that is in the possibilities of action and reflection the world allows us.

We might think Sutherland avoids the complaint that the perspectival view of religion is separated from human hope, for he has a chapter defending the idea that the eternal perspective on things is a means of embodying optimism about human life and even of a belief in the possibility of the triumph of good over evil. However, he clearly states that the optimism and triumph he has in mind have nothing to do with the vision of an outcome in the future,[45] so it needs no supporting belief in a moral teleology to the universe. Instead, Sutherland defines optimism in terms of belief in the possibility of human goodness. The optimist is one who answers the question 'Is human goodness a possibility?' in the affirmative.[46] But, again, this goodness does not consist in that human goodness which is fulfilment, the realisation of a satisfied human life in and through perfection in virtue. The human goodness Sutherland speaks of is paradigmatically displayed in the life of Jesus. This goodness is inward. The outward form of the life of the historical Jesus communicates what is essential about goodness 'by pointing away from itself to the inner life'.[47] I take it that the last remark gets its sense from the references we have cited earlier to an admirable life displaying invulnerability, transcendence of the self and acceptance of evil.

Sutherland and Phillips seem to depend crucially on the Socratic conception of evil and human goodness discussed in Chapter 2. The entire weight of their account of how religion can provide us with a response to evil turns out to be a variant on the thought that 'the good man cannot be harmed'. Goodness, virtue of a certain kind, involves acquiring a means of measuring success and failure which is such that the value of the good life and the acts which flow from it is eternal – a value which cannot be threatened by anything that the world and the wicked can throw at that life. Very crudely: Sutherland and Phillips take it that it is precisely the proper job of religious discourse to enable us to express such a vision of goodness. Hence, it is not the proper job of religion to invoke what I have described as belief in a moral order. Hence, religious language need have no referential, metaphysical import. Hence, religion can leave the future of the world and all questions about its fundamental character to the sciences.

It is worth while at this point reminding ourselves of some of the reasons why in Chapter 2 we rejected the Socratic response to evil.

One is that such a conception ignores an important implication of evil for the human subject who might attain a state where he or she could not be harmed. For a human being to reach the state of acting in accordance with the virtues, and therefore of pursuing actions for the sake of the activity involved in performing them, he or she must be able to develop in character and intellect in certain ways. It is a facet of evil that, through natural circumstances and/or the acts of other human beings, many people cannot so develop. Their lives are cut short, or physically or mentally maimed. They cannot then morally develop to the point whereby they become invulnerable, through moral self-transcendence, to evil. The perspectival view of religion appears to have nothing to say about this.

A further problem with the Socratic conception is one aired more than once in this study. It is a fact about those who are morally selfless that the very structure of their selflessness will give them external ends. For example, their selflessness will show itself in deep concern for the welfare of others. They may 'die to the world' in the sense of having a conception of the value of their own conduct which enables them to see worth in what they do regardless of how they fare. But they will have attachments to the well-being of others rooted in the self-same conception of value. So, if they come to see that the good of others is not at all increased by their own and others' efforts, that the evil others suffer is never tangibly mitigated through human conduct, they might (must?) despair of goodness. To preach that the value of goodness in conduct lies in its pointlessness appears to be possible only if that goodness is detached from any deep concern with whether others flourish or suffer.

These two points (and especially the latter) suggest that the eternal perspective and its associated notions of acceptance and renunciation will not do as they stand. A total moral invulnerability to what the world may dish out destroys a viable notion of human good. It is not enough to say that the believer measures success and failure differently.

Another facet of the metaphysical emptiness of the perspectival view can be brought out by further reflection on where it leaves our conception of the moral subject. My point is a simple one: only certain accounts of the nature of the human subject will enable it to be viewed as capable of reaching ethical transcendence; a view which tells that we are nothing but molecules in motion or 'fleshy robots' will not. But to reject such accounts is to question the completeness of a science-based account of reality.[48] That in turn is to get involved in what the facts of this world are and what causal factors influence them.

This is not to argue that we need to base morals on metaphysics, where this involves reasoning first from a metaphysics to a morality. Sutherland and Phillips would be right (in my view) to say that moral experience shows us that certain metaphysical views cannot be right, must be confused. At the least, however, we are committed to saying, Kant-like, that given certain forms of moral experience there are limits to what any scientistic metaphysics might establish about the world. A negative, agnostic metaphysics like this still refuses to leave the question of the ground of the world and its facts wholly to others prepared to chance their arm on what kind of causal powers move the world. The question of the character of the human subject is one where morals inevitably interact with metaphysics.

We can summarise the case mounted so far against Sutherland and Phillips on the score of realism as follows. They give an insufficiently realist account of religious language because they cannot allow 'God' or its cognates a reference to a causally significant reality. Without such a reference, religious language becomes divorced from belief in moral order. Whether or not their own notion of religion providing a way of characterising the facts is sufficient to avoid reductionism or non-cognitivism can be set aside. They do not place the cognitive force of religious language aright.

As a means of reinforcing the above conclusion, let us reconsider a significant aspect of Sutherland's treatment of the topic of theodicy. We noted earlier in this chapter that one of Sutherland's central objections to the monotheistic theologies he wishes to replace is that such theologies bring to the consideration of evil a pre-formed commitment that there must be an omnipotent, omniscient and omnibenevolent God. What we say about evil and its meaning then is made to fit those pre-formed beliefs. It is significant that we commonly find as a consequence the theodicist telling us that, while we may be sure that God is omnipotent and so forth, we must regard his purposes in creating or allowing certain evils as mysterious. From our pre-formed theology, we know all evils must be backed by some morally sufficient reasons, but many evils are so horrendous that we cannot imagine what these might be.

Now, Sutherland asks, why should we be so sure of the pre-formed theology which generates these manœuvres in theodicy, when we are ready to be so agnostic about the moral plans of the God described in the theology?[49] The upshot of the manœuvres is that we suspend judgement on some powerful moral intuitions (for example, those which tell us that some evils are so awful that we cannot decently imagine them as justified by a larger purpose), while in the same breath we accept as certain some highly speculative metaphysical claims. The theodicist asks us to suspend or alter our moral sensibilities, while yet insisting that traditional metaphysical claims stay fixed. Sutherland would have us begin theodicy from the fact of evil and this will involve holding fast to our moral sensibilities but being metaphysically agnostic.[50]

There is much in Sutherland's critique of theodicy with which we can sympathise and which indeed chimes in with the arguments of this study. However, his critique ignores a vital point. Sutherland himself notes that it is possible to argue from evil to the existence of the God of traditional monotheism.[51] If he had reflected on the logic behind that enterprise, he would have recognised a degree of inevitability in the structure of theodicy as traditionally practised. For we know that a central aim in any theodicy is to maintain the conviction that there is a moral order in the world in the face of evil and thus to solve the problem of evil in so far as that problem is one which threatens the meaningfulness of moral endeavour. Theodicy must postulate a something or other in or beyond the given world which is capable of guaranteeing that there is a moral order behind it. Given that the first step is made of seeing the source of moral order as a personal God, there is an inevitability in then giving this God the 'omni' attributes so many philosophers and theologians take for granted. The argument for this conclusion is set out at some length by Kant in the *Critique of Practical Reason* and it turns around the thought of what kind of causality such a personal God must be capable of exercising to be a guarantor of moral order.[52] Any God who is perfectly to adjust virtue to happiness in some future for human beings must have a motive for so acting (hence, omnibenevolence is required), a detailed knowledge of how human beings have acted (hence, omniscience) and power to create the match between our moral state and our external state (hence, omnipotence).

The inevitability of belief in a God with the 'omni' attributes is admittedly severely qualified according to the argument of this study. We must first take the challenge of evil to morality seriously. Morality is possible without a belief in an underlying moral order, though only with a sense of regret and pain. It is possible to conceive of the ground of moral order as other than a personal God. From what comes later in the argument of *God, Jesus and Belief*, it seems that Sutherland regards the traditional theology of an omnipotent, omniscient and omnibenevolent God as open to revision in part because he does not take the challenge of evil to the moral enterprise seriously enough.

EVIL AND THE MORAL ORDER

All the strictures I have offered against Sutherland and Phillips turn around a disagreement with them on how far the moral perspective depends on, or is linked to, a conception of how the world goes. I have argued that the moral perspective is at least helped and supported by the belief that the given world is not all there is and that there is a moral order underlying it. By contrast Phillips on absolute values and Sutherland on the eternal perspective would seem to be united in rejecting the making of any correlations between morals and metaphysics.

The arguments presented in this study point to a number of issues relevant to the debate on whether there is a link between morals and metaphysics. We can close this chapter by noting Phillips' case for saying that any attempt to link the moral perspective to a teleology is doomed to failure, hence, there is no need to link morality to a divinely guaranteed teleology.

Phillips' argument for the hopelessness of linking morality to any teleology is based on the notion that morality is purposeless. Phillips argues that moral considerations characteristically provide a check on the manner in which we act so as to achieve our personal goals. We recognise that we cannot act in certain ways in order to achieve our goals, for that would be to violate the demands of decency, justice, integrity, or what have you. Nor can it be that we check our goal-directed activity in this way because we have yet further, overarching purposes to pursue (such as the goal to live a happy life) which can only be fulfilled if we act decently, justly and with integrity. To reason in that way is to deny the categorical character of moral demands. It is to make their force contingent on our having these overarching purposes. If we did not have these larger purposes the force of moral demands would escape us. So Phillips concludes that moral considerations cannot be accounted for in terms of purposive action but deal with the non-teleological character action may or may not have.[53]

Phillips supports the above argument with the following. Any concern to show that morality must be seen as a component part of a long-term pursuit of a happy satisfied life must be part of a project to recommend morality (by showing it, for example, to be to our advantage). But it is conceptually impossible to recommend morality in this way. For if I look for something outside morality for whose sake I recommend it, what I recommend is not morality itself, but only morality in so far as it serves this purpose. What becomes categorically binding, or of supreme importance, is then the gaining of this purpose (say, my happiness) and not morality itself.[54]

Phillips' endeavour to sever morality from any teleology is a way of spelling out in his own way the Kantian point that moral maxims bind categorically or the Aristotelian point that virtuous activity constitutes its own end and is to be done for the sake of the activity involved in doing it. But we have noted that in both Kantian and Aristotelian thought this point exists alongside a conception of morality as inextricably part of a teleology – a hope for a good life uniting acting well with attaining a satisfied life. The reason why both these styles of moral theory can avoid the force of Phillips' arguments boils down to how the relation of means to ends is considered. Phillips is assuming that if we argue that morality must be seen as an integral part of a teleology of a happy, perfected life, then morality is a contingent or external means to this larger goal. As such, it is at least conceivable that other means might serve the attainment of the goal and morality loses its categorical character or intrinsic worthwhileness as a result. But the kinds of teleology which Phillips needs to confront see morality as a constitutive means to attain a happy, perfected life. This is to say that, in their different ways, both Kantian and Aristotelian thought give an account of the perfected life in which acting well figures as an inescapable way in which such a life is embodied. Acting well in part constitutes the end striven for. It enters into the identification of the end.

The precise sense in which these conceptions of the human good are teleological then needs to be brought out. To speak of acting virtuously as a constitutive means of attaining the supreme human good is to say that the full value of so acting is only realised if it is part of a larger whole. That larger whole consists of the union of acting well and faring well. Acting well is not a contingent part of that whole, since the kind of perfected, satisfied life in view is identified by in part being the life that includes a state of virtuous thought and action. But this does not mean that the whole which is the perfected life consists entirely of a virtuous state. More is needed to constitute the whole and that more connects acting morally with the order in the world.

Artistic analogies are helpful in exposing the fallacy in Phillips' argument. We may conceive a given movement in a truly great symphony, such as the last movement of Mahler's second, as having an intrinsic value. Yet part of its value also consists in the way it contributes to the whole of which it is a part. The full value of the fifth movement of Mahler's 'Resurrection' Symphony would be lost if chance were to remove all knowledge and record of the preceding four movements. But it does not have value solely as a means of completing a musical argument started in previous sections of the work. Only because it has value in and of itself can it make its contribution to the whole. And, as is so in this case, in the truly great work of art any component part will be inextricably bound up with the whole of which it is a part. The components of the great work could not be detached and put in other works without significant loss of value.

In trying to divorce morality from any wider teleology Phillips needs to consider a more sophisticated view than that which says morality is of worth only if it serves these and these purposes. The viewpoint behind the moral interpretation of religion outlined in this study is that the full value of morality depends on its being part of a wider teleology. Morality is not being recommended solely because it is part of a teleology. Rather, the argument is: unless morality is seen as an integral part of a larger, teleological whole some, significant part of its value is lost. In discussing Kantian attempts to link morality to teleology, we have had to enforce the point that the bindingness of moral demands does not rest on a guaranteed teleology of the human good as a necessary condition.

Many of the points made in Chapters 2 and 3 above about morality and the human good are in complete agreement with Phillips' negative point that moral demands are not so many insurance policies for attaining a goal which is extrinsically related to the kind of life prescribed by them. Where his arguments fall down is in the presupposition that only one, crude, way of linking morality to teleology can be in question. The issues are just more complicated than Phillips makes out.

To explore the more complex ways in which morality can be linked to ideas of the perfected, happy life is of course to get at the roots of the absolute opposition in Wittgensteinian thought between the moral (or absolute, or eternal) perspective and a concern for the order to be found in the facts which surround us.

NOTES

1. Wittgenstein *Philosophical Investigations*, §43.
2. Sutherland *God, Jesus and Belief*, p. 3.
3. Sutherland *God, Jesus and Belief*, ch. 4.
4. Phillips 'Great Expectations', p. 203ff.
5. Sutherland *God, Jesus and Belief*, ch. 2, and Phillips 'The Problem of Evil'.
6. Sutherland *God, Jesus and Belief*, p. 6.
7. 'Refined and Crass Supernaturalism', especially pp. 123–4.
8. See Sutherland 'God, Time and Eternity', p. 117ff, and Phillips *Death and Immortality*, p. 42ff.
9. See Phillips *Death and Immortality*, pp. 29–39.
10. See ch. 4 of *God, Jesus and Belief*.
11. *God, Jesus and Belief*, p. 16.
12. *God, Jesus and Belief*, p. 31.
13. *God, Jesus and Belief*, pp. 18 and 17.
14. *God, Jesus and Belief*, p. 73.
15. *God, Jesus and Belief*, p. 85.
16. *God, Jesus and Belief*, pp. 83–6.
17. Sutherland 'God, Time and Eternity', p. 119.
18. Sutherland is happy to ally himself with much, though, as we have noted in Chapter 5, not all, of Murdoch's moral Platonism; see *God, Jesus and Belief*, pp. 105–6.
19. Oakeshott *On Human Conduct*, pp. 81–6 and pp. 69–74.
20. Sutherland *God, Jesus and Belief*, p. 103.
21. *God, Jesus and Belief*, p. 107ff.
22. *God, Jesus and Belief*, p. 110.
23. *God, Jesus and Belief*, p. 79.
24. *God, Jesus and Belief*, p. 80.
25. *God, Jesus and Belief*, p. 86.
26. See Phillips *Faith and Philosophical Enquiry*, pp. 17, 85–6 and 130–1.
27. Phillips *Religion without Explanation*, p. 148; though in his contributions to *Is God Real?* he concedes the claim of his fellow symposiasts that 'God' is to be taken as by intention referential, only then to place his weight on what it might mean for there to be a God: see 'How Real Is Realism?', p. 197.
28. 'Great Expectations', p. 98.
29. *Faith and Philosophical Enquiry*, p. 132.
30. *Faith and Philosophical Enquiry*, p. 166.
31. *Faith and Philosophical Enquiry*, p. 79ff.
32. *Philosophical Review*, vol. 74, 1965, pp. 3–12.
33. See Wittgenstein *Tractatus Logico Philosophicus*, §6.43, and *Notebooks 1914–16*, p. 73.
34. Wittgenstein *Philosophical Investigations*, p. 193ff.
35. Wisdom 'Gods', p. 158ff.
36. Though we should note that Phillips for one objects to much of the detail of Wisdom's writing on religion; see Phillips *Faith and Philosophical Enquiry*, pp. 170–203.
37. *Religion without Explanation*, pp. 18–23.
38. Sutherland *God, Jesus and Belief*, p. 108; my emphasis.

39. *God, Jesus and Belief*, p. 110.
40. *God, Jesus and Belief*, p. 99.
41. See Phillips 'The Problem of Evil', pp. 115–16, and Sutherland *God, Jesus and Belief*, pp. 23–5 for this objection. There are many who see this point as decisive against the teleology in traditional theodicies. For a reply to this critique see McNaughton 'The Problem of Evil'.
42. Phillips *Death and Immortality*, pp. 52–4.
43. Sutherland *God, Jesus and Belief*, p. 121.
44. *God, Jesus and Belief*, p. 124.
45. *God, Jesus and Belief*, pp. 181–2.
46. *God, Jesus and Belief*, p. 183.
47. *God, Jesus and Belief*, p. 192.
48. See Oakeshott *On Human Conduct*, p. 92.
49. *God, Jesus and Belief*, p. 28.
50. *God, Jesus and Belief*, p. 31; a powerful expansion of this theme can be seen in Wetzel 'Can Theodicy Be Avoided?'
51. *God, Jesus and Belief*, p. 23.
52. *Critique of Practical Reason*, pp. 252–3 [5/140–1].
53. *Death and Immortality*, p. 33.
54. *Death and Immortality*, pp. 29–33.

The Moral Interpretation Reviewed

RELIGIOUS FAITH AND THE MORAL INTERPRETATION

The aim of this chapter is to review the nature and status of the moral interpretation of religion. In the course of this review we shall consider some of the main objections to it. We must ask what kind of religious faith the moral interpretation is able to support. This entails considering what kind of God it might justifiably lead to and what kind of certainty it can give to the commitment that such an ultimate is real. These questions turn out to be interconnected. The degree of certainty we can attain in the moral interpretation depends on the kind of transcendent we discover in it. The objections to the moral interpretation to be considered are all in effect ways of pressing the point that the moral interpretation needs to mitigate its agnosticism about the character of the divine in crucial directions to be at all credible.

A vital objection to the moral interpretation arises from the manner in which John Hare questions Kant's invoking of the divine as a means of overcoming the moral gap. One of the needs this invocation must meet is that of explaining how we can sensibly strive for moral perfection when we know that the human moral subject is so defective. The idea of divine aid helps to explain how we can throw off moral evil and thus makes the possibility of attaining the highest good thinkable. But, says Hare, it is essential to Kant's account of autonomous moral agency that we can only improve as moral subjects if we act unaided. Heteronomy is introduced if an external agent is invoked for this purpose. This heteronomy is self-defeating, for nothing could count as moral improvement in me unless my efforts or decisions were responsible for it. This is one of the grounds behind Kant's rejection of a traditional reading of the Christian doctrine of atonement. So Kant is faced with the following dilemma: either human beings are capable of moral improvement through their own efforts or they are not. If they are, there is no need of an external agency, let alone a transcendent one, to explain how this is possible, and, furthermore, Kant's account of human beings as sunk in radical evil loses its force. But if human beings do need external moral agency to save themselves from evil, Kant's objections to traditional religious doctrines on the grounds of the inescapability of moral autonomy are mistaken.[1]

Here we have a clear call for the moral interpretation to specify further the character of its interest in the divine. Hare's objection forces the neo-Kantian thinker to make it clear that, whatever the postulated sacred, transcendent source of meaning might be, it must be something that in part dwells in and works through the human subject. According to the moral interpretation, the problem of evil as it affects morality calls for a belief in a moral teleology upon which faith in the moral struggle can then be grounded. The relevant teleology will be in part external to the human subject, but, since the factors afflicting moral endeavour stem in part from our constitution as moral agents, the teleology will have to flow through us as well. What we are doing in invoking the idea of divine aid is invoking something which is immanent in us as much as it is in the world around us. The whatever it is that words such as 'God' refer to, if they refer to anything at all, must be a ground of our being which can manifest as a force within our lives as persons. This chimes in with a theme present in many forms of religion, particularly in strands of mysticism. It is the theme that the transcendent which underlies the world around us also lies at the deepest levels of the self.[2] Thus, the invoking of the divine to comprehend how the defeat of evil in us may be possible is not the bringing in of a reality external to the human subject. It is more akin to calling upon a deeper level of selfhood which can be brought to life in moral endeavour.

Sharon Anderson Gold has argued that a notion of the divine along the lines described above is in fact present in Kant's *Religion*.[3] In particular, she contends that 'God' functions in the *Religion* as the name for something more akin to the Holy Spirit in Christian thought than a transcendent creator. The divine is a force within human personality released and known only when human beings unite in pursuit of the ethical commonwealth, that is the endeavour to realise the highest good in an earthly society: 'This conception of God is not derived from the function of a world designer . . . It is an activity which cannot be thought of as an external substance'.[4]

Now, if the moral interpreter leaves behind the details of Kant's account in the *Religion*, there is no need to choose between the transcendent as an immanent personal force and as a ground of nature. For, as pointed out above, the history of religions gives ample testimony to the prevalence of the belief that one and the same ultimate reality is both the ground of the world which surrounds us and something which undergirds the deepest level of selfhood. This notion is peculiarly apt in fleshing out a key thought in this study, namely that religion is concerned with overcoming the gap between self and reality through the grounding of values in a transcendent and sacred reality.

Part of Kant's answer to the charge which Hare levels against him consists in appealing to the notion that the self which is enmeshed in evil can be empowered to turn to good through its uniting with other wills. It is a key part of Kant's argument in the *Religion* that the creation of the 'Kingdom of God', which is the society of all people on earth ruled by moral laws alone, is possible only through a 'public form of obligation'.[5] This means that Kant views the highest good as social in two important respects. As the perfection of the moral life, it does not consist simply in the individual becoming fully virtuous, but of that individual taking his or her place in a society which fully manifests the requirements of morality. Moreover the perfection of morality can only be achieved through social means, through a union of people of good will in pursuit of the ethical commonwealth. Kant's underlying thought here – surely a plausible one – is that only in and through co-operative human effort can the full human power to combat evil and pursue the good be realised and enhanced. This will, in part, add to the answer given thus far to Hare's objection that Kant cannot have an ethics of autonomy and one which invokes divine aid. Our own status as individuals who are morally weak and corrupt is not the full story about human agency, for by way of the co-operative effort to attain the good we can transform that agency for the better and release powers which were not available to us as isolated individuals. Membership of a human community united by a public covenant to fight evil and pursue good becomes a necessary condition of the individual's pursuit of moral improvement. A union of imperfect wills is a better means of overcoming evil in human life than the activity of isolated imperfect agents, because through the 'public form of obligation' powers in individuals to fight evil and to consolidate victories over evil can be tapped which are not otherwise available. Kant's thought is, then, that human agency can be significantly transformed through the social, public fight for justice.

Anderson Gold uses the idea of the power released through communal moral effort to define the force of 'God' in the later Kantian account of religion: 'The idea of a moral governor is the correlate of the "we" which the human community requires as the condition of individual moral perfection'.[6] The question arises of whether, in the interpretation of Kant, this is all that the notion of God refers to, namely to those moral powers released by human beings when they unite properly in pursuit of the good and in the defeat of evil. Yovel has argued at length and in detail that this is indeed all that the notion of God comes to when we reach the *Religion*. 'God' has no use in referring to something which may be the ground of nature, which might effect an overarching teleology in it, or which might overcome the gap between the rational human subject under moral law and a world apparently governed by blind, amoral forces.[7] This reading of Kant is supported by the contentions that in the *Religion* the problem of evil has become solely a problem of the human subject and its tendency to subordinate non-moral maxims to moral ones in conditions of social existence; and that in the *Religion* the highest good has become a wholly immanent social and political state on this earth.[8]

If the moral interpretation's invoking of divine aid were no more than a matter of calling in a human power to combat evil created by co-operative pursuit of the good, then it could rightly be accused of having too thin a notion of God to be worth bothering with. The divine would refer to a power for righteousness which is not my own only through its transcending the individual, not the human. It would be a socially created power – a power I could draw on only through participation in a social endeavour – but a power wholly immanent in human beings. It would have no true transcendence. If it were given this reference, the concept of God would not be part of a realist interpretation of religion. In fact, the moral interpretation's account of teleology of human affairs would turn out in substance to be little different from that offered by John Kekes. As noted in Chapter 2, Kekes' response to evil is a form of 'bootstrapping'. He describes mechanisms in the social practice of morality which will enable us to have better hope in fighting evil in the future. The objection levelled against this in Chapter 2 was that it really gives us little hope in facing the future combat against evil, since the relevant mechanisms have been around before and have manifestly not worked to improve the human lot significantly. So these mechanisms by themselves give little ground for faith that moral endeavour will be a means of creating the highest good.

One reason why these readings of the putative reference of 'God' are unsatisfactory in these contexts is that they do not appear to engage with those things in the world external to the human subject which make for evil and defeat the purposes of morality. These readings leave nature to its own purposes. Whatever may be true of the later Kant, there is no reason at all why the moral interpretation of religion should not have its cake and eat it in the matter of what kind of reality 'God' can invoke. It can refer both to a reality which is at the deepest level of selfhood and a reality which is at the deepest level of the world around us. There is much to be said for the moral interpretation accepting the Kantian thought that whatever this transcendent, sacred ground may be in itself, our awareness of it and its power to work for good in our lives are both realised in co-operative moral endeavour. This is not to say that the transcendent is nothing other than a power created in human communities bent on fighting evil and pursuing good. It is rather to insist that the channels to powers for good envisaged in the transcendent in itself are only opened up through such forms of communal effort. There is much in this last thought that echoes Kant's language in the *Religion* and, schematic though my statement of this thought is, I trust it can be seen to chime in with much that is familiar in the beliefs, institutions and practices of the religions.

One very significant benefit for the moral interpretation flows from the idea that both our awareness of, and the power of, the transcendent flow from co-operative moral struggle. It is that morality as a set of practices is seen to be part-creative of the reality it invokes when it appeals to the transcendent as a ground of hope. In a real sense, albeit only in part, the sacred is made real in and through the fight against evil. Moral practice is thus a means of participating in the life of the divine. The sense in which morality creates divinity as just outlined supplements another means of so doing described in Chapter 6 above when we explored via Sutherland the thought that virtuous conduct amounts to a way of sharing in an eternal dimension of meaning. These ideas, showing how morality in part creates the divine, take us back once again to John Hare's complaint about the apparent inconsistency between the call for divine aid and a stress on moral autonomy. Morality, and the individual committed to it, creates and partakes in the reality invoked to rescue it.

I now wish to turn these thoughts about the immanence of the sacred in morality in another direction. For they will be seen to bear on the question of the justification of belief in the sacred according to the moral interpretation of religion. One of the central objections D. Z. Phillips has to any 'realist' interpretation of religion is that it makes faith in the reality of God uncertain through giving that faith a metaphysical object whose existence and character can never be definitively proved. Thus it threatens to separate religious belief from the practices which accompany it and which, according to Phillips, give such belief its sense.[9] The practices we associate with religious belief are only appropriate *to the extent* that there is a God to whom they are directed, but on a realist view whether there is such a God is a matter of chancy speculation. Now it might seem that this complaint gains greater and lethal force when the moral interpretation is in question. For the moral interpretation preaches a radical agnosticism about the character of the whatever it may be that is the transcendent ground of moral teleology. It distances itself from natural theology. Moreover, it argues that the specific conceptions of the sacred in the world's religions are so many humanly, imaginatively useful ways of signifying this underlying reality and contends that none of them can be said to be true as a picture of what it is like in detail. Phillips throws the charge of reductionism back at realists in the philosophy of religion, on the ground that they separate religious belief from the life of religion via their tacit support for a hidden God and it would appear that this charge fits the moral interpretation like a glove.[10]

The moral interpretation's response to these objections will have a number of layers to it. We can note straightway the relevance to these problems of our thoughts about the immanence of the divine in the human moral struggle. They indicate that, if the moral interpretation is true, the divine is not simply an inferred, hypothetical entity. It is rather a reality which can be realised in and through co-operative moral effort. It can be known close at hand, albeit only through moral striving. It can be made available to human beings as reality in the moral life, though not as an object of speculation. Further to this, it is not the case that the practices of the religions are necessarily to be deemed inappropriate or futile because their ultimate focus is unknowable. The moral interpreter of religion can see at least many of these practices as specific forms in which co-operative moral endeavour is channelled, encouraged or initiated. Not only does this give them a point on the moral interpretation of religion, it also indicates how they can be the means of making the divine reality available through human action.[11]

The above reply by no means deflects the full force of the objection that the moral interpretation destroys religious life by making the existence of its focus uncertain. At best it is a gesture in a certain direction. We have to accept the consequences of the fact that the moral interpretation of religion presents no proof from moral experience itself, still less from natural theology, that its form of refined supernaturalism is true. So far we have perhaps two meagre forms of justification for it: an appeal to our need to have something with which to ground moral hope and a vague argument from experience. We can add to these the strength which comes from associating the moral interpretation with the argument of William James's 'The Will to Believe'.[12]

James is famous for arguing that in certain conditions we can be justified in opting for the hypothesis behind religious faith on the basis of what is essential for our practical lives. An hypothesis is an option for faith when it is forced (as opposed to avoidable), living (as opposed to closed or dead for us), momentous (rather than trivial) and when there is insufficient evidence to decide on theoretical grounds whether it is true or false. In such circumstances, James asserts, 'Our passional nature not only lawfully may, but must, decide an option between propositions whenever it is a genuine option that cannot by its nature be decided on intellectual grounds'.[13] Our passional nature is engaged on the positive side of the religious hypothesis according to James, and since the conditions for exercising the will to believe properly are met in this case, we may opt for the truth of the hypothesis.

Large questions are raised by James' argument. If there are theoretical proofs for the religious hypothesis, or successful arguments that it is more probable than not, then the will to believe does not come into play. Nor would it if there were proofs and arguments in the opposite direction. Let us assume for the present that no such successful arguments exist either way.[14] This assumption is indeed an essential underpinning of the moral interpretation of religion. But over and above these large questions, Schlecht reminds us that James's argument has been felt by many commentators to face an overwhelming difficulty.[15] If the religious hypothesis concerns a matter of fact which is independent of the human will, then to decide to adopt it because we should like it to be true is just wishful thinking. To acknowledge that it concerns something independent of us and our doings is to acknowledge that we cannot think it to be true on the basis of our needs. Schlecht offers a defence of James to this charge. It draws on two features of his treatment of these issues. He notes first the extent to which James associates the rightful exercise of the will to believe with those occasions where our adopting and acting upon an hypothesis may create the circumstances in which it is true and thereby the means through which it can be tested. James asserts:

> But in every fact into which there enters an element of personal contribution on my part, as soon as this personal contribution demands a certain degree of subjective energy which, in its turn, calls for a certain amount of faith in the result – so that, after all, the future fact is conditioned by my present faith in it – how terribly asinine would it be for me to deny myself the use of the subjective method, the method of belief based on desire![16]

The obvious examples to illustrate what James has in mind occur in the field of personal goals and relations. The hypothesis that I can be a better parent is capable of being made true, and of thus of being confirmed or disconfirmed, through my acting on the faith that I can be. The hypothesis that so-and-so is offering me friendship is likewise capable of being made true and being confirmed or disconfirmed by acting on the faith that it is true.

The second major step in James's case Schlecht brings to our attention is that of likening the religious hypothesis to one which is made true, or confirmed/disconfirmed, through acting upon it in faith. James portrays religion as claiming that the universe is such that human existence and endeavour have value. The universe is a place where our desire for fulfilment can be achieved. A religious faith is defined as a 'faith in the existence of an unseen order of some kind in which the riddles of the natural order may be explained'.[17] This should strike readers as familiar, for it is similar to the claim we found in Geertz and expounded in Chapter 4 to the effect that religion fundamentally asserts that there is no final gulf between fact and value: what the world is like in its deepest structure coheres with human values. What James adds is the reminder that through the active faith that the religious hypothesis, so construed, is true, we in fact help to make it true. The hypothesis gives impetus to our endeavours to fashion the world into one in which human fulfilment is possible. But, in turn, such endeavour when successful changes the world so that it does have the character religion claims it to have. Just as a faith that someone is offering me friendship may be confirmed in acting upon it, so a faith that the world is morally ordered may be confirmed in acting upon it. In this way, James can avoid the charge that the will to believe involves wishful thinking. Wishing cannot make something so. Hence it is in the normal case wrong to hold a hypothesis on the basis of what would satisfy my practical commitments. But where an active faith in a hypothesis helps create the fact which corresponds to it, the gulf between what I need to be the case and what is the case is no longer an absolute one.

We are now back on familiar territory. For we have already summarised Kant's treatment of the objection that his 'proof' of the postulate of God's existence involves an illegitimate move from 'Our practical reasons tell us that we need to think that reality is morally ordered underneath' to 'Therefore we are entitled to believe that it is'.[18] James on the will to believe and its special applicability to the religious hypothesis can be used to come to Kant's aid. Such aid is strengthened by the evolution in Kant's thought away from conceiving the outcome and reality of moral order as something displayed in a life beyond this. Once, as in the *Religion*, moral order is seen to come to fruition in the creation of a thoroughly morally ordered society on earth, then human effort is more clearly involved in creating the reality we are to have faith in.

In Chapter 3 one means we offered of saving Kant's argument for the postulate from the wishful thinking charge invoked the notion of non-doxastic faith, as derived from Audi.[19] Non-doxastic faith is illustrated in a case such as that of a mother who searches for her lost children with the faith that they are alive and well, but without a belief that they are alive and well. If the idea of faith without belief is accepted, then it aids the general point of our discussion so far: the moral interpretation need not be seen as leaving religious belief uncertain and tentative. A 'faith that p' minus a 'belief that p' may nonetheless pervade someone's life and be associated with an unshakeable conviction and resolve.[20] Moreover, the notion of faith in the absence of belief also supports the thought that the strength of faith, its confirmation, can grow out of the business of acting upon it. In the appropriate circumstances our faith that p may be borne out by the fruitfulness of our active, embodied hope that it is so.

Various strategies have been offered in this section for avoiding the charge that the moral interpretation makes religion out to be founded on a vague and hopelessly uncertain metaphysical speculation. We have argued that the content and certainty of moral faith flows directly from vital, indispensable practical needs we have as moral beings and may be directly confirmed in the business of acting to satisfy those needs. But now we have set up the moral interpretation for the counter-charge that it is no more than a vain exercise in pulling yourself up with your own bootstraps. It seems to be involved in the following kind of circularity. We are told that we need moral faith to engage in the moral struggle with the necessary hope. So we entertain the notion of a transcendent ground of an as yet hidden moral order with which our moral efforts can engage. But we are also told that we can give no content or independent certainty to this conviction of a transcendent ground from historical revelation or from metaphysics. What the conviction gains from sources outside morality is no more that an imaginative, symbolic content which helps indeed to make it graspable by the human mind, but no more than that. If the sole source of the real (as opposed to imaginatively useful) content of the conviction behind moral faith comes from morality, if the sole source of its power to move us comes from the 'confirmation' it gains from acting on it in the moral life, how can it lend support to the moral life? It can only do that if it has some lodgement outside that life. Moral faith is in the same crazy position as I would be if I tried to take the weight off my legs by sitting on a chair which I was holding up.

Let us sharpen the above objection by considering how far the moral interpretation now differs as a response to evil from the position of John Kekes. Kekes, we noted, rejected as 'false hope' any attempt, be it Kantian or theistic, to solve the problem of evil by sending in the transcendental cavalry to defeat the evils afflicting the pursuit of the good. We cannot justifiably both acknowledge how far our world is from one which supports the aims of morality and believe that behind it there lies a moral order hidden from normal perception.[21] But this does not mean that Kekes abandons moral hope. Hope resides in the possibility of developing resources for the defeat of evil out of co-operative moral effort, particularly the resources of what Kekes styles 'character morality'.[22] We have objected that this bootstrapping is flawed, but the moral interpreter is in no better shape. The moral interpretation invokes the idea that there is a something or other guaranteeing a moral order behind appearances. But no transcendent forces are thereby summoned to bring about this order. Because moral faith's supernaturalism is a refined supernaturalism, we can expect nothing from outside to intervene in the human story. Because moral faith is agnostic about non-moral sources for the concept of God, it cannot describe these forces further. And finally, because moral faith is liable to object, on the grounds of the demands of moral autonomy, to the very idea that some agency external to human moral effort could be imported into the moral realm, the notion of transcendent moral forces is useless for the moral interpretation.[23]

I do not know if there is a fully satisfactory answer to this objection. It captures the fundamental charge that the moral interpretation can find no middle ground between abandoning traditional supernaturalism and embracing any one of the non-realist approaches to religion pointed to already. The issues behind the objection, then, are large. In brief, moral faith must say that it has a real role for supernaturalism because it is essential in sustaining moral hope that we think that some transcendent power and ground lies behind the values upon which we draw in the struggle for the good. It matters not to moral faith that we cannot further describe this power and ground, provided that we can give it some imaginative content sufficient for it be a reality in thought and provided that it supports moral hope. The support it gives to moral hope is that of keeping alive the notion that more than the apparent powers of human beings are available in the fight against evil. As we have seen, these powers may both be thought of as transcending the human and as being immanent within it. The moral interpretation's referential commitment above all involves a perspective on the moral life and upon the world in which that life is set which turns around a contrast between how these things appear and what they may be like in themselves. And it is this thought which is the ground of the faith and hope peculiar to the moral interpretation. Here there is a contrast with something Kekes describes as 'moral realism',[24] namely accepting that the moral life and its circumstances are just as they appear to be. In this sense, the moral interpretation embodies a form of 'unrealism', linked to its supernaturalism, faith and hope. Some may, of course, describe this unrealism as monstrous and silly – given that so many traditional props for it have been abandoned.

For the moment, I leave readers to judge of these matters for themselves, though some brief comments on the significance of Feuerbach and Freud at the end of this chapter will bring up these issues again.

MORAL FAITH AND THE COHERENCE OF HUMANISM

A further objection, arising out of that just discussed, is that moral faith is too thin to support the stances essential to it. To support its characteristic commitments it needs to draw upon the specific doctrines of a traditional faith, doctrines which it says are no more than imaginative ways of clothing referential commitments which do not depend on those doctrines. A complaint of this sort is entered by Basil Mitchell against Kant in the first instance. Mitchell goes on to apply it to Iris Murdoch, and it will be seen to apply to any view constructed within the broad paradigm of the moral interpretation of religion.

The substance of Mitchell's case is simple. Moral faith of the kind we find in Kant or Murdoch relies on a principled, deep commitment to the inherent value of human persons. Moralised versions of religion in the style of Murdoch centre around the struggle to pursue the good and defeat egoism. They give such tasks the flavour of religious obligations. Little of such spiritualised moral outlooks makes sense unless we can give a special status to human beings and to our obligation to promote their flourishing. But only within a metaphysics of morals such as that provided by traditional Christian theology can such an assumption of the value of the human be defended. Mitchell notes that many societies, past and present, have regarded many forms of human life (for example, infants, slaves, women) as possessing no inviolable worth, and indeed as quite dispensable. So we need to give some answer to the question 'Why do we set the value of human life so high and rate the obligation to others so severe?' To answer this question we need to offer some metaphysics of the human which will show what it is about human beings that, regardless of their endowments, makes all of them into objects of the deepest respect. The claim, in short, is that spiritualised morality, moralised religion, is committed to a humanism which draws on the capital of traditional theistic metaphysics. It has closed this bank down, leaving nothing to

back the fine-sounding commitments which constitute the moral seriousness it displays.[25]

As a means of enforcing these points, Mitchell devotes considerable
attention to the question of the scope of the moral respect embodied in
spiritualised morality of Murdoch's or Kant's kind.[26] We take human life
to have a kind of sanctity, reflected in our abhorrence of murder, slavery
and the like. But whence do we get the notion that this special respect is due
to all? As Mitchell claims, many human communities have not extended it
to all human beings. Because of its rejection of the literal truth of
traditional metaphysical accounts of the person, one route Kant and
those like him may take is to specify natural, empirically grounded
properties of the person to be the ontological foundation of worth. So
Kant points to the possession of autonomy and reason in human beings as
the foundation of his humanism. But any such set of natural properties will
be found to be possessed by only some human beings. The new-born, the
senile and some of the mentally handicapped will miss out. So this route
leads to the metaphysically agnostic moralist being left with a severely
limited humanist outlook. Another route is that of silence. This is the
route, found surely in Murdoch, of leaving a principle of respect for
persons without a further metaphysical rationale. This can be criticised as
amounting to no more than a blind, unsupported intuitionism.[27]

Mitchell can contrast the weakness of a Kant-Murdoch approach on the
basic principles of humanism with the strength of traditional, Christian
moral theology.[28] All human beings without exception are God's creatures.
All are objects of divine love. All share in the image of God. And all are
subject to the divine command to love one another. It is these beliefs which
constitute the moral capital capable of supporting the humanist outlook of
Kant and Murdoch.

The ramifications of Mitchell's argument can be seen more clearly if we
use some terminology from Charles Taylor's *The Sources of the Self*.
Taylor notes, correctly in my view, that any moral outlook takes shape
only to the extent to which it orientates itself around some strong
evaluations, strong qualitative distinctions.[29] This is connected with their
ability to offer us a picture of 'hyper-goods', things of ultimate transcendent worth which are the object of our deepest allegiances and which call
for a special respect and devotion.[30] Transcendent goods lead us on to the
idea of moral sources. The idea of a moral source is that of a hyper-good
conceived of as 'something the love of which empowers us to do and be
good'.[31]

The moral interpretation adopts as hyper-goods those ideals of respect
for persons and of social and personal fulfilment typical of liberal

humanism. As we have seen in relation to Iris Murdoch and Sutherland, it sees these goods as transcendent moral sources, allegiance to which is capable of adding a dimension of meaning to human life. But it is also bound up in what Taylor styles 'the ethics of inarticulacy' (the title of his third chapter). This stems from the inability of the moral interpretation, one shared with many modern ethical outlooks, to spell out fully the ontology or metaphysics of reality – particularly of the person – which might justify the selection of those particular values treated as hyper-goods and as moral sources by the system. By contrast, traditional Christian ethics is able to be articulate about its hyper-goods and moral sources. The question to be decided is whether such inarticulacy is fatal.

We can note that moral faith is not wholly inarticulate about the metaphysics underlying its selection of hyper-goods. It maintains a minimal form of refined supernaturalism and the corresponding commitment to the postulation of some moral order to reality. So, in one way, it can respond to Mitchell's complaint that it cannot state why human beings, and all human beings, are to be objects of unconditional respect: each and every one of us is part of and is related to the transcendent ground of moral order. This will not satisfy critics of Mitchell's persuasion. It will be seen as irredeemably vague. Moreover, the moral interpretation can only know of this alleged relation of humanity to a transcendent ground of order through morality itself. It offers no independent access to it. So it is involved in bootstrapping. The assurance that liberal humanist views about the worth of persons, about the harm and wrong entailed in destroying or maiming any human life, are reliable comes from moral experience itself. The conception of transcendent hyper-goods comes from within morality. Iris Murdoch's exposition of the ontological argument, laid out in Chapter 5 above, is clear illustration of such bootstrapping.

The debate between the moral interpretation and critics from within traditional moral theologies will be over whether such bootstrapping is sufficient to maintain allegiance to the hyper-goods and moral sources postulated by the moral interpretation. The critic will press for two sources of independent reflection to breach the ethics of inarticulacy. One is some independent warrant, of a metaphysical kind, for the claim that the values of liberal humanism represent true hyper-goods. Another is some spelling out, via a metaphysics independent of the moral outlook concerned, of the ontology of the human and reality which in turn can give substance to the claims about value registered by humanism.

Fortunately for this study, space does not permit us to follow through this debate fully. Mitchell's critique is on the table. What we can do is point to the argumentative resources the moral interpretation can draw on by way of rebuttal. In essence the moral interpretation will draw upon two lines of reply. In the first place it can argue that any response to, for example, a utilitarian claim that only some human beings have moral worth, must come from within morality to be effective. In the second place it can contend that typical attempts to find an external religious grounding or articulation for the values in question are inevitably befuddled.

The first of these responses derives from reflection on what might be lacking in someone who genuinely did not see that the fact that a new-born baby was a human being was a reason for granting it unconditional respect. (I write 'genuinely' here to discount the case of someone who has read a book in 'applied philosophy', or written one, and thereby adopted a position in philosophical debate that only self-conscious, autonomous human beings have a live worth protecting by law and morals.) Any person genuinely doubtful of the respect owing to human infants is suffering from a kind of moral blindness, if they are not just downright wicked. What coming to see the humanity of the new-born baby amounts to is coming to see how the child presents demands upon us and limits to our will.[32] The perception required is through and through a moral one and it cannot be created by way of convincing someone of a putative metaphysical claim about humanity and then getting them to draw a moral conclusion from that. These claims are so far assertions. They turn around the point that genuinely to see a human infant in the way some utilitarian philosophers would have us see it is to lack a mode of perceiving others, rather than to have drawn an unsound conclusion in argument. The contentions offered need further grounding, but they can be given that.[33] Some support for these reflections can be found in facts such as this: though Mitchell and others may claim that Christian beliefs about the metaphysics, or ontology of the human imply humanist attitudes, over many of the Christian centuries practices such as slavery were tolerated, indeed they flourished, in Christian societies. When the idea that enslaving human beings is a gross violation of their humanity took hold of the Western consciousness, it does not appear that the influence of Christian doctrine brought it about; rather, the conviction that Christian teaching about the human really does take us in this direction appears to have resulted from a change (a discovery) in moral sentiment.

So the way in which the moral interpreter would defend the humanist hyper-goods typically adhered to by such as Murdoch from attempts to defeat them would be two-fold. If the critic of humanism has metaphysical views (say, about the human) behind rejection of the granting of uncondi-tional worth to human beings, the proponent of moral faith will endeavour to rebut them. More positively, the moral interpreter will follow the standard path of reason in ethics. Argument of a fruitful kind with the utilitarian, materialist, nihilist, or whatever, is only possible if the parties can find some agreed moral perceptions from which a path of reflection might lead to the resolution of the matter in hand. In this case, those committed to the values of what Mitchell styles 'the traditional conscience'[34]in relation to the treatment of our fellow human beings will endeavour to take utilitarians forward from some shared perception to the recognition of all human beings as constituting 'a limit to our will'.[35] There is of course no guarantee that such a procedure will succeed. Though it is hard to imagine not finding any moral perceptions which are shared between traditional humanism and other outlooks, it is easy to conceive that little progress might be made in getting from them to the removal of the moral blindness in question. But that of itself is no objection to the mode of argument advocated, since no mode of argument can guarantee success in persuading those in error.

The second main response to Mitchell's critique of moral faith was that endeavours to support traditional values befuddle the issues. The sentiment behind this stems from concerns revealed in Euthyphro dilemma. It will be readily apparent that if we say, for example, that all human beings are to be treated by us as supremely valuable because they are in turn loved unconditionally by God, the following dilemma arises: Does God love them because there is some ground of value in them, making them worthy of this love? Or, is it the case that they are valuable simply because they are loved by God? The second horn seems unsatisfactory, since it implies that there is nothing in the human subject which makes us fit objects of divine love prior to that love arising. It also implies that if God had chosen to love bacteria in the same way, they would be objects of unconditional worth and we should treat them as such. If we take the first horn, bringing God into the picture has not advanced the argument, since we are supposing there is something about being a human being which in and of itself, and independently of divine love, makes us fit objects of certain moral attitudes. Mitchell himself is frank with his readers and draws attention to the dilemma of divine love.[36]

If we try variations on the above themes, problems again arise. For example, could we argue that it is because all human beings are creatures of God that they are supremely valuable? But then so are bacteria. Suppose we say it is the fact that all human beings are destined by God for relationship with him that makes them objects of a special respect. But then we can ask as to what it is in human beings which makes God want to save them and whether this thing is present in all of them. Such a question gains force from the fact that many accounts in the Christian tradition of what a perfected relationship to God consists in are highly intellectual, so much so that many human beings (for example, the mentally handicapped) appear excluded by them.

We can create doubts, then, about whether a belief in the sanctity of life gets any clearer by bringing God into the picture. Still less is it evident how the belief that all human beings share in this sanctity is given clear and firm grounding in this manner. Mitchell himself admits the second of these points. He is left making the claim that the moral perceptions of liberal humanism are more 'congruous' with a religious view of the world than a secular one.[37] The attempt to deduce the relevant principles from the details of a theological metaphysics abounds with difficulties.

Moral faith departs from a wholly secular view of reality, but its metaphysical commitments are vague and agnostic. What I have endeavoured to show is how it might answer the charge that these commitments are too vague and agnostic to support its value structure. The basis of its reply can be summed up as follows. Inarticulacy about the ontology or metaphysics of the human is no great problem for ethics: first, because the perceptions we want to maintain to support humanism must be primarily generated from within morality itself; and, second, because attempts to ground or articulate these perceptions via an independent metaphysics run into problems. Though these two points do not provide a final answer to the charge that moral faith rests on moral incoherence, they indicate the direction a reply might come from. The moral interpretation must defend the ethics of the inarticulate as a gain, a virtue in moral argument. Inarticulacy chimes in with its stress on moral autonomy and metaphysical agnosticism.

WISHFUL THINKING?

The moral interpretation of religion as we have presented it has two main manifestations. In one it is a thesis belonging to the science of religion affirming something about religion's definition or essence. In another guise it is a thesis in the philosophy of religion describing what is credible in religious belief and practice in the contemporary world.

Consider it in manifestation number one. At the end of Chapter 4 we endeavoured to bring out the strength of an analysis of all religions as so many symbol-systems serving to unite the human sense of value with the world in which we live by way of postulating a correspondence between our deepest values and an ontology of transcendence. Put another way, religion consists of so many ways of living in the light of the idea that there is a moral order or teleology behind the world as it appears. The moral interpretation of religion does not deny that the symbolic structures of religion have other components than the moral. It merely asserts that what makes these components religious is their relationship to the idea of overcoming the gulf between people's values and the world as it is given to them through the postulation of transcendent grounds of moral order. I contend that there is considerable plausibility in this understanding of the essence of religion, regardless of whether the moral interpretation works as a philosophical account of what is credible in the religious views competing for our allegiance in the present. I have sketched some of the arguments for this conclusion in Chapter 4 and opened up a link between the moral interpretation and contemporary anthropological theorising.[38]

As a philosophical thesis about what is credible in religion, the moral interpretation is also a hermeneutic. It says that, in so far as religious symbols are credible, they are to be interpreted as so many ways of presenting the moral life as rooted in some transcendent source of value or other. The moral interpretation as a thesis in contemporary philosophy and theology is liable to criticism from both of the viewpoints it stands in opposition to: full-blooded theism and naturalism. Traditional theists will see it as having insufficient ground, once historical revelation and metaphysical speculation are jettisoned, to justify or give content to its notion of the transcendent. This chapter has explored such criticisms. Atheists will want to make common cause with such criticism and contend that the only clear road from the agnosticism within the moral interpretation is one which leads to a vision of the world and human life as things without any relationship to a transcendent.

I wish to conclude with a particular criticism of the moral interpretation which might seem tempting to both of the camps described above. It is based on the kind of interpretation of religion offered in Feuerbach's *Lectures on the Essence of Religion* and Freud's *The Future of an Illusion*. Both these writers offer the thought that religion arises out of the relationship between self and the not-self, the latter being represented in other human beings and in nature. Human life is characterised by a cruel dilemma giving rise to deep 'feeling of dependency'.[39] On the one hand the human mind recognises that it faces in nature a world which it cannot wholly control, on the other its desires and needs drive it to seek satisfaction from this same nature, so that nature is at once independent of the self and yet the self is deeply dependent on it. Both these theorists give prominence to theistic forms of religion by suggesting that religion removes (as it thinks) the gap between self and not-self by peopling the world with gods. Their imagined dominance over nature will then ensure that after all it is under the control of something acting to meet our deepest needs and is not therefore opposed to the ego's demands. Feuerbach sums up the process allegedly generating religion in these words: 'a god is nothing other than man's striving for happiness fulfilled in the imagination'.[40]

Freud joins in this general account. Of course, he gives it his own particular slant by linking the self's sense of estrangement-dependence in relation to nature to the memory of an earlier state of estrangement-dependence the infant faces in relation to its parents.[41] After a passage describing the unique way in which the idea of a monotheistic God helps to overcome the dilemma of estrangement-dependence, Freud shows that his account is at heart an attack on what the moral interpretation sees as the essence of all religion:

> And, looking in the other direction, this view announces that the same moral laws which our civilisations have set up govern the whole universe as well, except that they are maintained by a supreme court of justice with incomparably more power and consistency. In the end all good is rewarded and all evil punished . . ..[42]

The credibility of Feuerbach's and Freud's analysis gains force from the fact noted earlier in this chapter that moral faith does not rest on any strict proofs in reason. Instead it is justified by an argument from experience combined with the will to believe. Feuerbach and Freud show that these very factors make possible a debunking of religion so understood.

There is no reason to suppose that, just in showing the similarity between these accounts of religion as an illusion and the moral interpretation, one has refuted the latter. Debate inevitably rages between many viewpoints on whether our experience of moral value is or is not to be taken at face value, can or cannot be explained wholly in natural terms, is or is not revelatory of the structures of reality. But there is no ground for conceding that the case against seeing it as a guide to what is has been proved. The moral interpretation's contention is that, in the absence of such a case, moral seriousness itself bids us take morality as revelatory of reality (see the exposition and discussion of Murdoch in Chapter 5).

The fact that our faith in the reality of something strikingly accords with our wishes is not proof that such faith is merely wishful. In Feuerbach and Freud the characterisation of religion as 'merely wishful' is undoubtedly linked to their prior commitment to some form of materialist/scientist outlook. They think they know independently that morally grounded human needs cannot be a guide to what the world is truly like, because all there is to the world is what natural science can tell us. Freud, for example, plainly shows in *The Future of an Illusion* his commitment to the belief that science fully reflects what is real.[43] Here the value of Kantian agnosticism about our ability to know what the world is like in itself surfaces once more.[44]

The response offered to the powerful threat of a debunking account of religion as wishful thinking is no more than a sketch as to how the argument must go. Let me close on the following point. It might be seen as a strength of the moral interpretation of religion that it leaves the status of religion in human life deeply ambiguous. No one can deny that the kind of 'hermeneutics of suspicion' developed by thinkers such as Freud bites home. Some facets of religion fit Freud's suspicious interpretation of it very well. Religion, on the moral interpretation, does make a grand ontological claim about the match between our deepest moral values and the fundamental structures of reality. It does so from within an argumentative context which excludes offering any proofs from theory or revelation that such a claim is true. It leaves the human experience of living in the light of those values to create a faith in that claim. It is natural and inevitable that the stance of religion, so characterised, can be seen in one of two ways: as a monstrous piece of wishful thinking arising out of a failure to appreciate that the human self is located in a truly independent reality; or as a justified, absolutely necessary commitment to the only hope which can keep human moral endeavour alive.

NOTES

1. See *The Moral Gap*, pp. 60–2.
2. See Otto *The Idea of the Holy*, p. 203ff.
3. See Anderson Gold 'God and Community'.
4. 'God and Community', p. 129.
5. Kant *Religion*, p. 138 [6/105].
6. 'God and Community', p. 129.
7. Yovel *Kant and the Philosophy of History*, pp. 275–6.
8. This reading of Kant's later thoughts on God are also supported by the interpretative arguments of Anderson Gold and linked by her to an interpretation of Kant's *Opus Postumum*; see 'God and Community', p. 129.
9. See, for example, 'How Real Is Realism?', pp. 195–6.
10. Phillips 'On Really Believing', p. 99.
11. Of course, the pattern for this moral interpretation has been set by Kant in Book IV of the *Religion*, 'General Observation'. See also Green *Religious Reason* and *Religion and Moral Reason* for how the moral interpretation can be applied to actual patterns of religious practice in the world's religions.
12. My interpretation of James is deeply indebted to that offered in Schlecht 'Re-Reading "The Will to Believe"'.
13. James 'The Will to Believe' in *The Will to Believe and Other Essays*, p. 11.
14. See Le Poidevin *Arguing for Atheism* and Smart and Haldane *Atheism and Theism* for recent surveys of the debate.
15. 'Re-Reading "The Will to Believe"', p. 217.
16. James 'The Sentiment of Rationality' in *The Will to Believe and Other Essays*, p. 97.

17. James 'Is Life Worth Living?' in *The Will to Believe and Other Essays*, p. 51, and compare Schlecht 'Re-Reading "The Will to Believe"', p. 220.
18. Kant *Critique of Practical Reason*, p. 254 [5/142].
19. Audi 'Faith, Belief and Rationality'.
20. See Audi 'Faith, Belief and Rationality', p. 223ff. for an expansion and defence of this point.
21. Kekes *Facing Evil*, pp. 27–8.
22. See Kekes *Facing Evil*, pp. 223–8.
23. The objection thus put in my own crude terms is pressed in a much more sophisticated way against Kant in Yovel *Kant and the Philosophy of History*, p. 272ff., where it is used to argue for the incoherence of the system of ideas in the *Religion*.
24. Kekes *Moral Wisdom and Good Lives*, pp. 180–1.
25. I have here summarised the contents of chapter 6 of Mitchell *Morality: Religious and Secular*, pp. 79–92. Mitchell has a further line of argument to the effect that the objectivity of moral judgements in general depends on theistic metaphysics. I tried to get to grips with such claims in Chapter 2 above.
26. For what follows see Mitchell *Morality: Religious and Secular*, p. 122ff.
27. Compare Mitchell *Morality: Religious and Secular*, pp. 94–9.
28. *Morality: Religious and Secular*, pp. 123–4 and 127–8.
29. Taylor *Sources of the Self*, p. 27.
30. *Sources of the Self*, p. 64ff.
31. *Sources of the Self*, p. 93.
32. Gaita *Good and Evil*, pp. 77–8.
33. See Gaita *Good and Evil* for an extensive defence of them.
34. Mitchell *Morality: Religious and Secular*, p. 92.
35. Gaita's phrase – *Good and Evil*, p. 5.
36. *Morality: Religious and Secular*, pp. 133–4.
37. *Morality: Religious and Secular*, p. 137.
38. For a fuller defence of the moral interpretation as the means of defining religion see Byrne 'The Definition of Religion: Squaring the Circle'.
39. Feuerbach *Lectures on the Essence of Religion*, p. 31.
40. *Lectures on the Essence of Religion*, p. 230.
41. Freud *The Future of an Illusion*, p. 13.
42. *The Future of an Illusion*, p. 15.
43. *The Future of an Illusion*, pp. 50–2.
44. Kant's thought about the limits of scientific metaphysics can be supported by some powerful contemporary arguments: see Putnam *Realism with a Human Face*, p. 141.

Bibliography

Adams, R. M., A Modified Divine Command Theory of Ethical Wrongness', in P. Helm (ed.) *Divine Commands and Morality* (Oxford University Press, Oxford, 1981) pp. 83–108

Adams, R. M., 'Divine Command Metaethics as Necessary A Posteriori', in P. Helm (ed.) *Divine Commands and Morality* (Oxford University Press, Oxford, 1981) pp. 109–19

Adams, R. M., 'Moral Arguments for Theistic Belief', in Adams *The Virtue of Faith* (Oxford University Press, New York, 1987) pp. 144–63

Allison, H. E., *Kant's Transcendental Idealism* (Yale University Press, New Haven, 1983)

Alston, W. P., 'Some Suggestions for Divine Command Theorists', in Alston *Divine Nature and Human Language* (Cornell University Press, Ithaca, 1989) pp. 253–73

Anderson, Gold, S. 'God and Community: An Enquiry into the Religious Implications of the Highest Good', in P. J. Rossi and M. Wreen (eds) *Kant's Philosophy of Religion Reconsidered* (Indiana University Press, Bloomington and Indianapolis, 1991) pp. 112–31.

Anscombe, G. E. M., 'Authority in Morals', in Anscombe *Ethics, Religion and Politics* (Blackwell, Oxford, 1981) pp. 43–50

Aquinas *Summa Theologiae*, vol. 2, T. McDermott (tr.) (Blackfriars/Eyre and Spottiswoode, London, 1964)

Aquinas *Summa Theologiae*, vol. 3, H. McCabe (tr.) (Blackfriars/Eyre and Spottiswoode, London, 1964)

Aristotle *Nicomachean Ethics*, W. D. Ross (tr.) (Clarendon Press, Oxford, 1925)

Audi, R., 'Faith, Belief and Rationality', in J.E Tomberlin (ed.) *Philosophical Perspectives 5: Philosophy of Religion* (Ridgeview, Atascedero, Calif., 1991) pp. 213–39

Bambrough, R., *Moral Scepticism and Moral Knowledge* (Routledge, London, 1979)

Beck, L. W., *Early German Philosophy* (Belnap Press, Cambridge, Mass., 1969)

Braithwaite, R. B., 'An Empiricist's Account of the Nature of Religious Belief', in I. T.

Ramsey (ed.) *Christian Ethics and Contemporary Philosophy* (SCM Press, London, 1971) pp. 53–73

Byrne, P., 'F. R. Leavis and the Religious Dimension in Literature', *Modern Theology*, vol. 1, 1985, pp. 119–30

Byrne, P., *Natural Religion and the Nature of Religion* (Macmillan, Basingstoke and London, 1989)

Byrne, P., *The Philosophical and Theological Foundations of Ethics* (Macmillan, Basingstoke and London, 1992)

Byrne, P., *Prolegomena to Religious Pluralism* (Macmillan, Basingstoke and London, 1995)

Byrne. P., 'The Definition of Religion: Squaring the Circle', in J. Platvoet (ed.) *The Definition of Religion* (Brill, Leiden, forthcoming)

Cupitt, D., *Taking Leave of God* (SCM Press, London, 1980)

Dent, N. J. H. *The Moral Psychology of the Virtues* (Cambridge University Press, Cambridge, 1984)

Despland, M., *The Education of Desire* (University of Toronto Press, Toronto, 1985)

Devine, P., *Relativism, Nihilism and God* (University of Notre Dame Press, Notre Dame, Ind. 1989)

Dunbar, S., 'On Art, Morals and Religion: Some Reflections on the Work of Iris Murdoch', *Religious Studies*, vol. 14, 1978, pp. 515–24

Falk, C., *Myth, Truth and Literature*, 2nd edn (Cambridge University Press, Cambridge, 1994)

Feuerbach, L., *The Essence of Christianity*, G. Eliot [Mary Anne Evans] (tr.) (Harper & Row, New York, 1957)

Feuerbach, L., *Lectures on the Essence of Religion*, R. Manheim (tr.) (Harper &Row, New York, 1967)

Freud, S., *The Future of an Illusion*, W. D. Robson-Scott (tr.) (Hogarth Press, London, 1978)

Gaita, R., *Good and Evil: An Absolute Conception* (Macmillan, Basingstoke and London, 1991)

Gale, W., *On the Nature and Existence of God* (Cambridge University Press, Cambridge, 1991)

Geertz, C., *The Interpretation of Culture* (Hutchinson, London, 1975)

Gert, B., *The Moral Rules* (Harper & Row, New York, 1973)

Graham, G., 'Spiritualised Morality and Traditional Religion', *Ratio*, vol. 9 NS, 1996, pp. 78–84

Green, R. M., *Religious Reason* (Oxford University Press, New York, 1978)

Green, R. M., *Religion and Moral Reason* (Oxford University Press, New York, 1988)

Guttenplan, S., 'Moral Realism and Moral Dilemmas', *Proceedings of the Aristotelian Society*, vol. 80 NS, 1980, pp. 61–80

Hare, J., *The Moral Gap* (Clarendon Press, Oxford, 1996)

Hare, R. M., 'The Simple Believer', in G. Outka and J. Reeder (eds) *Religion and Morality*, (Anchor, Garden City, New York, 1973) pp. 393–427

Heimbeck, R. S. H., *Theology and Meaning* (Stanford University Press, Stanford, 1969)

Herman, B., *The Practice of Moral Judgement* (Harvard University Press, Cambridge, Mass., 1993)

Hick, J., *Evil and the God of Love* (Collins, Glasgow, 1966)

Hutchinson, D. S., *The Virtues of Aristotle* (Routledge, London, 1986)

James, W., *The Will to Believe and Other Essays in Popular Philosophy* (Dover, New York, 1956)

Kant, I., 'Critique of Teleological Judgement', in *Critique of Judgement*, J. C. Meredith (tr.) (Clarendon Press, Oxford, 1978)

Kant, I., *Critique of Practical Reason*, in Mary J. Gregor (ed. and tr.), *Immanuel Kant: Practical Philosophy*, (Cambridge University Press, Cambridge, 1996) pp. 133–276

Kant, I., *Critique of Pure Reason*, N. K. Smith (tr.) (Macmillan, London, 1929)

Kant, I., *Groundwork of the Metaphysics of Morals*, in M. J. Gregor (ed. tr.), *Immanuel Kant: Practical Philosophy* (Cambridge University Press, Cambridge, 1996) pp. 37–108

Kant, I., *Lectures on Ethics*, L. Infield (tr.) (Methuen, London, 1939)

Kant, *The Metaphysics of Morals*, in M. J. Gregor (ed. tr.), *Immanuel Kant: Practical Philosophy* (Cambridge University Press, Cambridge, 1996) pp. 353–603

Kant, I., *Religion within the Boundaries of Mere Reason*, G. Giovanni (tr.) in A. Wood and G. Giovanni (eds) *Immanuel Kant: Religion and Rational Theology*, (Cambridge University Press, Cambridge, 1996) pp. 39–215

Kekes, J., *Facing Evil* (Princeton University Press, Princeton, 1990)

Kekes, J., *The Morality of Pluralism* (Princeton University Press, Princeton, 1993)

Kekes, J., *Moral Wisdom and Good Lives* (Cornell University Press, Ithaca, 1995)

Lawrence, D. H., *The Rainbow* (Heinemann, London, 1955)

Le Poidevin, R., *Arguing for Atheism* (Routledge, London, 1996)

Leavis, F. R., *D. H. Lawrence: Novelist* (Penguin, Harmondsworth, 1964)

Levine, M., 'Deep Structure and the Comparative Philosophy of Religion', *Religious Studies*, vol. 28, 1992, pp. 387–99

Mackie, J. L., *Ethics: Inventing Right and Wrong* (Penguin, Harmondsworth, 1977)

McNaughton, D., 'The Problem of Evil: A Deontological Perspective' in A. G. Padgett (ed.) *Reason and the Christian Religion* (Clarendon Press, Oxford, 1994) pp. 329–51

Martin Soskice, J., 'Love and Attention', in M. McGhee (ed.) *Philosophy, Religion and the Spiritual Life* (Cambridge University Press, Cambridge, 1992) pp. 59–72

Meynell, H., 'The Euthyphro Dilemma', *Aristotelian Society Supplementary Volume*, vol. 46, 1972, pp. 223–34

Michalson, G. E., *Fallen Freedom* (Cambridge University Press, Cambridge, 1990)

Mitchell, B. G., *Morality: Religious and Secular* (Clarendon Press, Oxford, 1980)

Murdoch, I., *Acastos* (Chatto & Windus, London, 1986)

Murdoch, *Metaphysics as a Guide to Morals* (Penguin, Harmondsworth, 1993)

Murdoch, I., *The Sovereignty of Good* (Routledge, London, 1970)

Murdoch, I., 'Vision and Choice in Morality', in I. T. Ramsey (ed.) *Christian Ethics and Contemporary Philosophy* (SCM Press, London, 1966) pp. 195–218

Nussbaum, M., *The Fragility of Goodness* (Cambridge University Press, Cambridge, 1986)

Oakeshott, M., *On Human Conduct* (Clarendon Press, Oxford, 1975)

O'Leary-Hawthorne J. and D. Howard-Snyder, 'Are Beliefs about God Theoretical Beliefs?: Reflections on Aquinas and Kant', *Religious Studies*, vol. 32, 1996, pp. 233–58.

O'Neil, O., *Constructions of Reason* (Cambridge University Press, Cambridge, 1989)

Otto, R., *The Idea of the Holy*, J. W. Harvey (tr.) (Oxford University Press, New York, 1958)

Pailin, D., *The Anthropological Character of Theology* (Cambridge University Press, Cambridge, 1990)

Phillips, D. Z., *Death and Immortality* (Macmillan, Basingstoke and London, 1970)

Phillips, D. Z., *Faith and Philosophical Enquiry* (Routledge, London, 1970)

Phillips, D. Z., 'Great Expectations: Philosophy, Ontology and Religion', in J. Runzo (ed.) *Is God Real?* (Macmillan, Basingstoke and London, 1993) pp. 203–7

Phillips, D. Z., 'How Real Is Realism?', in J. Runzo (ed.) *Is God Real?* (Macmillan, Basingstoke and London, 1993) pp. 193–8

Phillips, D. Z., 'On Really Believing', in J. Runzo (ed.) *Is God Real?* (Macmillan, Basingstoke and London, 1993) pp. 85–108

Phillips, D. Z., 'The Problem of Evil' in S. C. Brown (ed.) *Reason and Religion* (Cornell University Press, Ithaca, 1977) pp. 103–21.

Phillips, D. Z., *Religion without Explanation* (Blackwell, Oxford, 1976)

Plato *Apology*, in E. Hamilton and H. Cairns (eds) *The Complete Dialogues* (Princeton University Press, Princeton, 1963) pp. 3–26

Pojman, L., 'Faith without Belief', *Faith and Philosophy*, vol. 3, 1986, pp. 156–66

Putnam, H., *Realism with a Human Face* (Harvard University Press, Cambridge, Mass. 1990)

Rachels, J., 'God and Human Attitudes' in P. Helm (ed.) *Divine Commands and Morality* (Oxford University Press, Oxford, 1981) pp. 34–48

Rogers, K., 'The Traditional Doctrine of Divine Simplicity', *Religious Studies*, vol. 32, 1996, pp. 165–86

Sagi, A. and D. Statman, *Religion and Morality* (Rodopi, Amsterdam and Atlanta, 1995)

Schlecht, L. F. 'Re-Reading "The Will to Believe" ', *Religious Studies*, vol. 33, 1997, 217–25

Sherman, N., *The Fabric of Character* (Clarendon Press, Oxford, 1989)

Smart, J. J. C. and J. Haldane, *Atheism and Theism* (Blackwell, Oxford, 1996)

Sorley, W. R., *Moral Values and the Idea of God* (Cambridge University Press, Cambridge, 1918)

Sprigge, T. L. S., 'Refined and Crass Supernaturalism', in M. McGhee (ed.) *Philosophy, Religion and the Spiritual Life* (Cambridge University Press, Cambridge, 1992) pp. 105–25

Strawson, P. F., *The Bounds of Sense* (Methuen, London, 1966)

Sutherland, S. R., *God, Jesus and Belief* (Blackwell, Oxford, 1984)

Sutherland, S. R., 'God, Time and Eternity', *Proceedings of the Aristotelian Society*, vol. 79 NS, 1979, pp. 103–21

Swinburne, R. G., 'Duty and the Will of God' in P. Helm (ed.) *Divine Commands and Morality* (Oxford University Press, Oxford, 1981) pp. 120–34

Tatarkiewicz, W., *The Analysis of Happiness* (Nijhoff, The Hague, 1976)

Taylor, A. E., *Does God Exist?* (Macmillan, London, 1945)

Taylor, C., *Sources of the Self* (Cambridge University Press, Cambridge, 1989)

Ward, K., *The Development of Kant's View of Ethics* (Blackwell, Oxford, 1972)

Wetzel, J., 'Can Theodicy Be Avoided', *Religious Studies*, vol. 25, 1989, pp. 1–13

Williams, B., *Moral Luck* (Cambridge University Press, Cambridge, 1981)

Winch, P., 'Can a Good Man Be Harmed?', in Winch *Ethics and Action* (Routledge, London, 1972) pp. 193–209

Wisdom, J., 'Gods' in Wisdom, *Philosophy and Psychoanalysis* (Blackwell, Oxford, 1953) pp. 149–68.

Wisdom, J., *Paradox and Discovery* (Blackwell, Oxford, 1965)

Wittgenstein, L., 'Lecture on Ethics', *Philosophical Review*, vol. 74, 1965, pp. 3–12

Wittgenstein, L., *Notebooks 1914–16*, G E M. Anscombe (tr.) (Blackwell, Oxford, 1969)

Wittgenstein, L., *Philosophical Investigations*, G E M. Anscombe (tr.) (Blackwell, Oxford, 1963)

Wittgenstein, L., *Tractatus Logico Philosophicus*, B. F. McGuinness (tr.) (Routledge, London, 1961)

Wood, A. W., *Kant's Moral Religion* (Cornell University Press, Ithaca, 1970)

Yovel, Y., *Kant and the Philosophy of History* (Princeton University Press, Princeton, 1980)

Zagzebski, L., 'Does Ethics Need God?', *Faith and Philosophy*, vol. 4, 1987, pp. 294–303

Index